The Gospel and the Modern World

Other Gospel Coalition Titles

Arlo and the Great Big Cover-Up, by Betsy Childs Howard

Confronting Christianity: 12 Hard Questions for the World's Largest Religion, by Rebecca McLaughlin

Does God Care about Gender Identity?, by Samuel D. Ferguson

Finding the Right Hills to Die On: The Case for Theological Triage, by Gavin Ortlund

Growing Together: Taking Mentoring beyond Small Talk and Prayer Requests, by Melissa B. Kruger

Keeping Your Children's Ministry on Mission: Practical Strategies for Discipling the Next Generation, by Jared Kennedy

Mission Affirmed: Recovering the Missionary Motivation of Paul, by Elliot Clark

The New City Catechism: 52 Questions and Answers for Our Hearts and Minds

Rediscover Church: Why the Body of Christ Is Essential, by Collin Hansen and Jonathan Leeman

Remember Death: The Surprising Path to Living Hope, by Matthew McCullough

You're Not Crazy: Gospel Sanity for Weary Churches, by Ray Ortlund and Sam Allberry

To explore all TGC titles, visit TGC.org/books.

The Gospel and the Modern World

A Theological Vision for the Church

D. A. Carson

Brian J. Tabb, Editor

Additional Contributors:
Andrew David Naselli and Collin Hansen

:: CROSSWAY®

WHEATON, ILLINOIS

Library of Congress Cataloging-in-Publication Data

Names: Carson, D. A. (Donald Arthur), 1946– author. | Tabb, Brian J., 1980– editor. | Naselli, Andrew David, 1980– | Hansen, Collin, 1981–

Title: The gospel and the modern world : a theological vision for the Church / D.A. Carson ; [edited by] Brian J. Tabb ; [with additional contributions by] Andrew David Naselli and Collin Hansen.

Other titles: Themelios.

Description: Wheaton, Illinois : Crossway, [2023] | Series: The gospel coalition | Includes bibliographical references and index.

Identifiers: LCCN 2022056294 (print) | LCCN 2022056295 (ebook) | ISBN 9781433590948 (Trade paperback) | ISBN 9781433590955 (PDF) | ISBN 9781433590962 (ePub)

Subjects: LCSH: Evangelicalism. | Theology, Doctrinal.

Classification: LCC BR1640 .C368 2023 (print) | LCC BR1640 (ebook) | DDC 230/.04624–dc23/eng/20230616

LC record available at https://lccn.loc.gov/2022056294

LC ebook record available at https://lccn.loc.gov/2022056295

Contents

Introduction

Brian J. Tabb

DONALD A. CARSON IS WELL-KNOWN for his many academic and popular books, his decades-long tenure at Trinity Evangelical Divinity School where he is now emeritus professor of New Testament, and his influential work as the founding president of the Gospel Coalition (TGC). He has been called "one of the last great Renaissance men in evangelical biblical scholarship."[1] Two collections of essays (*Festschriften*) have been published to commemorate Carson's noteworthy contributions to New Testament studies and to advancing the gospel and strengthening the church.[2] His election as the seventy-third president of the Evangelical Theological Society and the anticipated launch of TGC's Carson Center for Global Christianity reflect his influence as an evangelical scholar and leader.

The present book, *The Gospel and the Modern World*, collects thirty-four short writings by Carson that originally appeared in *Themelios*, "an international, evangelical, peer-reviewed theological journal that expounds and defends the historic Christian faith."[3] Carson began serving as the general editor of *Themelios* in 2008, when TGC assumed responsibility for the theological journal founded in 1962 by the International Fellowship of

---

1 Andreas J. Köstenberger, "D. A. Carson: His Life and Work to Date," in *Understanding the Times: New Testament Studies in the 21st Century*, ed. Andreas J. Köstenberger and Robert W. Yarbrough (Wheaton, IL: Crossway, 2011), 357.

2 Andreas J. Köstenberger and Robert W. Yarbrough, eds., *Understanding the Times: New Testament Studies in the 21st Century: Essays in Honor of D. A. Carson on the Occasion of His 65th Birthday* (Wheaton, IL: Crossway, 2011); Richard M. Cunningham, *Serving the Church, Reaching the World: In Honour of D. A. Carson* (London: Inter-Varsity Press, 2017).

3 *Themelios*, https://www.thegospelcoalition.org/themelios/.

Evangelical Students and operated for many years by the Universities and Colleges Christian Fellowship (UCCF) in the UK. The name *Themelios* derives from the Greek term θεμέλιος ("foundation") in texts such as 1 Corinthians 3:12 and Ephesians 2:20, signaling the journal's commitment to expound and defend the foundational commitments of the historic Christian faith.[4] Carson explained in his first editorial that "the new Themelios aims to serve both theological/religious studies students and pastors" while aspiring to "become increasingly international in representation."[5] TGC's decision to make *Themelios* freely available online has enabled the journal to have a global impact. For example, in 2021 the journal's website had over 1.7 million pageviews from readers in 229 countries.

D. A. Carson wrote the following in one of his early editorial columns:

> Thinking differently from the "world" has been part of the Christian's responsibility and agenda from the beginning. The language Paul uses intimates that this independence of thought will not be easy. The assumption seems to be that the world has its own patterns, its own structured arguments, its own value systems. Because we Christians live in the world, the "default" reality is that we are likely to be shaped by these patterns, structures, and values, unless we consciously discern how and where they stand over against the gospel and all its entailments, and adopt radically different thinking. More: our response must not only be defensive (Rom. 12:2), but offensive, aiming to "demolish arguments and every pretension that sets itself up against the knowledge of God," aiming to "take captive every thought to make it obedient to Christ" (2 Cor. 10:5). . . . If we are to be transformed by the renewing of our mind, then we must be reading the Scriptures perennially, seeking to think God's thoughts after him, focusing on the gospel of God and pondering its implications in every domain of life.[6]

Here we see in brief a number of themes that feature prominently in Carson's writings, including the countercultural nature of the Christian

---

4   For further context, see Brian J. Tabb, "*Themelios* Then and Now: The Journal's Name, History, and Contribution," *Themelios* 44, no. 1 (2019): 1–5.

5   D. A. Carson, "Editorial," *Themelios* 33, no. 1 (2008): 1.

6   D. A. Carson, "Editorial," *Themelios* 33, no. 3 (2008): 1–4; the full essay is included in chap. 16 of this book.

faith, the utter centrality of the gospel, and faithful reading and application of the word of God. Such emphases are contrary to the status quo in the culture and, often, in many churches as well.

This book draws together Carson's most penetrating and robust *Themelios* columns from 2008 to 2022. Carson has written and edited dozens of books on the New Testament, biblical theology, and Christian life and leadership in a pluralistic and sometimes hostile world. The essays collected here offer readers an accessible entrée into Carson's wide-ranging writings that reveal his urgent vision for the evangelical church and exhibit the mature reflections of a scholar, pastor, and public theologian. In addition to thirty-four essays by Carson,[7] this book features two introductory essays by Andy Naselli, Carson's former doctoral student and research assistant, and Collin Hansen, vice president for content and editor in chief of TGC.

The three dozen chapters of *The Gospel and the Modern World* are arranged in six parts. Part 1 examines Carson's theological formation and his vision for the church. The initial chapter by Naselli considers Carson's upbringing in Québec, his education in Canada and the UK, and his influential ministry as a New Testament scholar.[8] Naselli then examines Carson's theological method, drawing deeply on Carson's expansive body of writings and firsthand interviews with him. Chapter 2 by Hansen explores Carson's vision for TGC, focusing on the instrumental three-day gathering of church leaders on the campus of Trinity Evangelical Divinity School in May 2005 that became the council of TGC. In chapters 3 and 4, Carson offers nine reasons why the Reformation still matters for contemporary pastors; then he reflects on the relationship between the local church and parachurch organizations like TGC that calls for reforming our churches in line with New Testament patterns.

Part 2 collects three essays reflecting on the nature and priority of the biblical gospel. In chapter 5, Carson warns that failure to distinguish between the gospel and its various effects tends over time to supplant God's life-changing message with a moralism that is without the power and the glory of the crucified, risen, reigning Christ. Chapter 6 considers the relationship of the "problem" of sin to God's "solution" in Christ's work.

---

7 Each of these have been lightly edited.

8 Chapter 1 revises Naselli's article, "D. A. Carson's Theological Method," *Scottish Bulletin of Evangelical Theology* 29 (2011). Used by permission.

Reflecting on the title of Richard Stearns's 2009 book, Carson contends that the gospel itself is the greatest hold in the contemporary "gospel." Chapter 7 examines the oft-repeated line "x is a gospel issue," which is a truth claim as well as a polemical statement of x's relative importance.[9] Carson explains that such claims are conditioned by how we perceive the dangers and errors of our generation.

Part 3 includes eight essays related to biblical interpretation and biblical theology—signature emphases throughout Carson's teachings and writings.[10] Chapter 8 takes up the theological question "When did the church begin?" Carson stresses the unity and continuity of God's redeemed throughout history while also emphasizing the "newness" associated with the ἐκκλησία after Pentecost: the dawning of the new age, the new birth, the new covenant, and so forth. Chapter 9 commends the beauty of biblical balance, which requires careful thinking, self-examination, ongoing study of the whole counsel of God, humility of mind, and a constant resolve to bring every thought captive to Christ. Chapter 10 examines ten subtle ways to abandon biblical authority in our lives, including appeals to selective evidence, "the art of imperious ignorance,"[11] and failure to tremble before God's Holy Word. Chapter 11 responds to the common refrain "But that's just your interpretation," which manipulatively relativizes all truth claims while feigning humble boldness. Carson urges us to recognize the special character of the Bible and the omniscient God who stands behind it and to read the sacred text with true humility and godly fear. Chapter 12 engages contemporary discussions of the kingdom of God and kingdom ethics. Carson implores readers to be mindful of *all* the great turning points in redemptive history when evaluating proposals about the kingdom to avoid reductionism and to maintain the complexity and balance of biblical priorities. Chapter 13 reviews what the Bible says about education, briefly considers several historical examples, and explores the unique challenges of putting these pieces together in the contemporary Western world. The next essay reflects on changes to the common meaning of the key terms

---

9   D. A. Carson, "What Are Gospel Issues?," *Themelios* 39, no. 2 (2014): 215.

10   See, for example, D. A. Carson and John D. Woodbridge, eds., *Scripture and Truth* (Grand Rapids, MI: Zondervan, 1983); D. A. Carson, ed., *The Enduring Authority of the Christian Scriptures* (Grand Rapids, MI: Eerdmans, 2016).

11   Citing the journal's late columnist, Michael J. Ovey, "The Art of Imperious Ignorance," *Themelios* 41, no. 1 (2016): 5–7.

guilt, shame, conscience, and *tolerance,* which lose a focus on God or an external standard. Carson urges readers to think and speak "worldview-ishly" about such matters. Chapter 15 meditates on the sad account of Hezekiah's pride and selfishness in Isaiah 39, which sharply contrasts with the king's faith and courage earlier in the biblical narrative and prompts a staggering divine rebuke.

Part 4 features eight chapters that discuss Christian engagement with contemporary culture, reflecting themes in Carson's larger body of work, including *The Gagging of God, Christ and Culture Revisited,* and *The Intolerance of Tolerance.*[12] Chapter 16 stresses the Christian obligation to think differently from the world. Rather than being squeezed into the world's mold, pardoned sinners living in the shadow of Christ's cross and empty tomb should pursue holiness and wisdom while awaiting the consummation. Chapter 17, one of Carson's earliest *Themelios* columns, wades into the debate over the place that deeds of mercy should have in Christian witness. Ministers ought to remain focused on the ministry of the word and prayer while teaching the Bible in such a way that they equip God's people with various avenues of service. In the next essay, Carson offers "contrarian reflections on individualism." While contemporary Western authors endlessly condemn individualism, the Scriptures offer a more balanced perspective. Chapter 19 addresses the assumptions and conclusions of postmodernism that are often adopted as cultural "givens" even though those holding to these views may not think of themselves as "postmoderns." Carson stresses that we can responsibly talk of human knowing—about God, the Bible, and other truth claims—even though we as creatures do not know anything omnisciently and are limited and prone to error. Chapter 20 reflects on three examples of "intolerant tolerance" in the United States in which the government or institutions have coercively imposed an agenda related to LGBT issues and abortion. In chapter 21, Carson argues that "the present crisis" in 1 Corinthians 7:26 is not a first-century food shortage or Christ's imminent parousia; rather, the apostle has in view the constraint inherent in the present world that is passing away yet also mysteriously ruled by Christ. Chapter 22 notes that polemical theology is necessary because of

12 D. A. Carson, *The Gagging of God: Christianity Confronts Pluralism* (Grand Rapids, MI: Zondervan, 1996); *Christ and Culture Revisited* (Grand Rapids, MI: Eerdmans, 2008); *The Intolerance of Tolerance* (Grand Rapids, MI: Eerdmans, 2012).

human pride and rebellion against God, yet the best polemicists (like Karl Popper and Tim Keller) compellingly and graciously present opponents' arguments before effectively refuting them. The final chapter in part 4 addresses common objections to Christian missions and urges readers to take up their cross and follow Christ with humility and sacrificial love.

In *The Cross and Christian Ministry*, Carson stresses that "the cross stands as the test and the standard of all vital Christian ministry. The cross not only establishes *what* we are to preach but also *how* we are to preach. It prescribes what Christian leaders must be and how Christians must view Christian leaders."[13] Part 5 consists of seven essays related to this biblical vision for church leadership. Chapter 24 reflects on three terms—pastor, elder, and overseer—that are used for one church office, with particular focus on the need for godly oversight of the church that is not limited to teaching and preaching. The next chapter presents four recommendations to help older and younger church leaders handle generational conflict in ways that honor Christ and advance the gospel. Chapter 26 cautions those who pursue the spotlight against seeking "great things" (Jer. 45:5) for themselves, since our view of a ministry's importance rarely aligns with God's calculations. In chapters 27 and 28, Carson offers five reflections on shortcomings in the young, restless, and Reformed movement and then presents recommendations and warnings for times of genuine revival. Chapter 29 responds to the question from pastors and ministry leaders, "How do I know when it is time to resign?" The last essay in part 5 sets forth eight motivations to appeal to when preaching for conversion; the full range of motivations modeled and sanctioned in the Bible ultimately reflects God's own character and attributes.

Six essays connected in some way to the broad topic of Christian discipleship are gathered together in part 6. Chapter 31 responds to misuses of the principles set forth in Matthew 18. Carson shows that this text properly relates to sins that are serious enough to warrant excommunication in the context of the local church, which can take decisive, meaningful action. In chapter 32, Carson offers ten reflections on what does and does not constitute a theologically disputable matter. Chapter 33 discusses species

---

13   D. A. Carson, *The Cross and Christian Ministry: Leadership Lessons from 1 Corinthians* (Grand Rapids, MI: Baker, 2004), 9.

of perfectionism that spring from over-realized eschatology or intense struggle against sin that is not grounded in God's demonstration of love for us at the cross. In the next chapter, Carson explains that the doctrine of unconditional divine election should instill deep, enduring gratitude in us. Chapter 35 considers popular approaches to spiritual disciplines in light of how Scripture defines spirituality. Carson recommends reserving the term *spiritual disciplines* for biblically prescribed activities that increase our sanctification, our conformity to Christ, and our spiritual maturity. The final chapter reflects on Paul's charge, "Do the work of an evangelist" (2 Tim. 4:5). Carson interprets this as an exhortation to engage in evangel ministry (i.e., gospel ministry), which includes but is not restricted to contemporary understandings of evangelism.

Cumulatively, these essays aptly illustrate TGC's theological vision for discharging Christian ministry and interacting with our culture in biblical and theological faithfulness.[14] Carson responds to contemporary epistemological crises by affirming that truth corresponds to reality, to God, and to God's revelation in Scripture. He commends and models careful biblical theology for the upbuilding of the church while expounding the centrality of the gospel and its implications for life and ministry. And Carson urges Christians to be countercultural while seeking the common good of those around us, appropriately contextualizing the gospel in the modern world while pursuing faithfulness and fruitfulness according to God's standards rather than seeking greatness for ourselves.

14 "Foundation Documents," Gospel Coalition, https://www.thegospelcoalition.org/.

PART 1

A THEOLOGICAL VISION
FOR THE CHURCH

D. A. Carson's Theological Method

Andrew David Naselli

HOW DOES D. A. CARSON do theology? In other words, what is his theological method? That question is challenging to answer for at least two reasons.[1]

First, Carson has authored and edited a lot of publications. Here's how Justin Taylor put it in 2009:

> Dr. Carson's sheer productivity is nothing less than astonishing. One could become tired just working through the latest numbers: he has written 50 books; 235 articles; 112 book reviews; and 46 edited books in the various series he edits. Average it out and it comes to about one book written or edited every four months, with one article and two reviews written every six weeks—for three decades.[2]

Nearly fifteen years later, those numbers are even higher.

1 This chapter was originally published as Andrew David Naselli, "D. A. Carson's Theological Method," *Scottish Bulletin of Evangelical Theology* 29 (2011): 245–74 (used by permission). It was my privilege to complete a PhD under Dr. Carson as my doctoral mentor (2006–2010) and to serve as Dr. Carson's research manager for about nine years (2006–2014), which was like a young lawyer getting to clerk for a supreme court justice. Three notes about this essay: (1) D. A. Carson is the author of all the resources I cite unless I note otherwise; (2) when I list multiple sources, I typically arrange the citations chronologically; (3) italics in quotations are original, not added.

2 Justin Taylor, "D. A. Carson Publications," Gospel Coalition, June 3, 2009, https://www.thegospel coalition.org/. See Carson's comprehensive bibliography at http://www.thegospelcoalition.org. Over 350 of the books, articles, and reviews are available there for free as PDFs.

Second, although Carson has written several works that explain his theological method,[3] he has not written a book or detailed article that systematically presents his theological method.[4] That is what this essay attempts to do.

This essay begins with a biographical sketch of Carson and then focuses on describing (not critiquing) his theological method by answering three questions:

1. What does Carson presuppose for doing theology?
2. What does Carson think the theological disciplines are?
3. How does Carson think the theological disciplines interrelate?

A Biographical Sketch: Carson's Family, Education, and Ministry[5]

If postmodernism has taught theologians anything, it is that humans cannot interpret the Bible with complete objectivity. Theologians bring far too much baggage to the interpretive process, including language, culture, religion, education, upbringing, exposure, ethnicity, and sex. This biographical

---

3   See especially "Unity and Diversity in the New Testament: The Possibility of Systematic Theology," in *Scripture and Truth*, ed. D. A. Carson and John D. Woodbridge (Grand Rapids, MI: Zondervan, 1983), 65–95, 368–75; "The Role of Exegesis in Systematic Theology," in *Doing Theology in Today's World: Essays in Honor of Kenneth S. Kantzer*, ed. John D. Woodbridge and Thomas Edward McComiskey (Grand Rapids, MI: Zondervan, 1991), 39–76; "Approaching the Bible," in *New Bible Commentary: 21st Century Edition*, ed. D. A. Carson et al., 4th ed. (Downers Grove, IL: InterVarsity Press, 1994), 1–19; "Current Issues in Biblical Theology: A New Testament Perspective," *Bulletin for Biblical Research* 5 (1995): 17–41; *The Gagging of God: Christianity Confronts Pluralism* (Grand Rapids, MI: Zondervan, 1996); "New Testament Theology," in *Dictionary of the Later New Testament and Its Developments*, ed. Ralph P. Martin and Peter H. Davids (Downers Grove, IL: InterVarsity Press, 1997), 796–814; "Systematic Theology and Biblical Theology," in *New Dictionary of Biblical Theology*, ed. T. Desmond Alexander and Brian S. Rosner (Downers Grove, IL: InterVarsity Press, 2000), 89–104.

4   The closest is this short article: "The Bible and Theology," in *NIV Biblical Theology Study Bible*, ed. D. A. Carson (Grand Rapids, MI: Zondervan, 2018), 2321–24. I was the managing editor for that study Bible, and for that article I assisted Dr. Carson by initially drafting it, which he then tweaked and expanded; I basically condensed his many writings on theological method, and I based the article's structure on my essay on Carson's theological method (see footnote 1 above).

5   This section is based primarily on Carson's anecdotes in his published works as well as in his sermons and lectures, his curriculum vitae, personal interaction with him, and a tribute by one of his former PhD students: Andreas J. Köstenberger, "D. A. Carson: His Life and Work to Date," in *Understanding the Times: New Testament Studies in the 21st Century; Essays in Honor of D. A. Carson at the Occasion of His 65th Birthday*, ed. Andreas J. Köstenberger and Robert W. Yarbrough (Wheaton, IL: Crossway, 2011), 349–69.

sketch mentions several factors that influence Carson's theological method to some degree. As helpful as it is to mention these factors, it raises a methodological question that I am not sure anyone can answer: How does one objectively measure such influences? Carson raised that question himself when I inquired about influences on his life.[6]

Carson's Family

Carson's father, Thomas Donald McMillan Carson (1911–1992), was born near Belfast, Northern Ireland, and his family immigrated to Ottawa, Canada, in 1913. With the desire to plant churches in Québec, he graduated from Toronto Baptist Seminary in 1937. In 1938, he married Elizabeth Margaret Maybury (1909–1989), and the Lord blessed them with three children. Donald Arthur Carson was their second child, born on December 21, 1946.

Tom Carson faithfully ministered in Drummondville, Québec, from 1948 to 1963, a trying time in which he experienced persecution and little apparent fruit at his church.[7] Don Carson, who entered McGill University in Montreal in 1963, spent his formative years in this environment. His family lived simply, too poor to own a home or pay for his university training. His parents loved him and set a godly example. Carson recalls,

> My life has been blessed by some influential models. I must begin by mentioning my own parents. I remember how, even when we children were quite young, each morning my mother would withdraw from the hurly-burly of life to read her Bible and pray. In the years that I was growing up, my father, a Baptist minister, had his study in our home. Every morning we could hear him praying in that study. My father vocalized when he prayed—loudly enough that we knew he was praying, but not loudly enough that we could hear what he was saying. Every day he prayed, usually for about forty-five minutes. Perhaps there were times when he failed to do so, but I cannot think of one.[8]

---

6 Interview by the author, November 29, 2006.

7 *Memoirs of an Ordinary Pastor: The Life and Reflections of Tom Carson* (Wheaton, IL: Crossway, 2008).

8 *Praying with Paul: A Call to Spiritual Reformation*, 2nd ed. (Grand Rapids, MI: Baker Academic, 2015), 7.

Carson deeply respected his father and was especially close to his mother, who capably led ladies' Bible studies and could use Greek and Hebrew.

Carson, reared in French Canada, is bilingual and remained a Canadian citizen until he became a United States citizen in 2006. While working on his PhD in Cambridge, he met Joy Wheildon, a British schoolteacher, and they married in 1975. They have two children, Tiffany and Nicholas.

Carson's Education

Carson graduated from Drummondville High School (1959–1963) with the highest standing. He earned a BSc in chemistry and mathematics from McGill University (1963–1967), where he took extra courses in classical Greek and psychology. He received various scholarships and awards while earning his MDiv from Central Baptist Seminary in Toronto (1967–1970), and he took four units of New Testament study at Regent College (1970). His PhD is from Emmanuel College, Cambridge University (1972–1975), where he studied under the Rev. Dr. (later Prof.) Barnabas Lindars. His thesis is on God's sovereignty and human responsibility in the Gospel according to John.[9]

Carson's Ministry

Carson, now a world-renowned evangelical New Testament scholar, started as a part-time lecturer in French at Central Baptist Seminary in Toronto (1967–1970) and in mathematics at Richmond College in Toronto (1969–1970). He was an occasional lecturer at Northwest Baptist Theological College in Vancouver (1971–1972) while ministering as the pastor of Richmond Baptist Church in Richmond, British Columbia (1970–1972), where he was ordained under the Fellowship of Evangelical Baptist Churches of Canada in 1972.

After earning his PhD, he served at Northwest Baptist Theological College as the associate professor of New Testament (1975–1978) and academic dean (1976–1978). After hearing Carson present a paper at the Evangelical Theological Society's conference in 1977, Kenneth Kantzer asked him to join the faculty at Trinity Evangelical Divinity School (TEDS), where Carson has served as associate professor of New Testament (1978–1982), professor

---

9   Published as *Divine Sovereignty and Human Responsibility: Biblical Perspectives in Tension*, 2nd ed. (Eugene, OR: Wipf and Stock, 2002).

of New Testament (1982–1991), research professor of New Testament (1991–2018), and emeritus professor of New Testament (2018–present). From 1978 to 1991, he took a sabbatical every third year in England.[10]

He has taught over fifty different graduate courses—many of them multiple times—on various levels: MDiv, MA, ThM, DMin, and PhD. He has served as the book review editor for the *Journal of the Evangelical Theological Society* (1979–1986), the editor of *Trinity Journal* (1980–1986), and the general editor of *Themelios* (2007–2018). In addition to editing dozens of books, he is the general editor of three major series: Pillar Commentaries on the New Testament, New Studies in Biblical Theology, and Studies in Biblical Greek. And with Eric Tully, he is co-editing the Pillar Commentaries on the Old Testament. He is the founding president and theologian-at-large of the Gospel Coalition (TGC).

Carson frequently preaches and teaches internationally at a substantial number of churches, conferences, student groups, colleges, and seminaries, including university missions.[11] He has been familiar with most of the major theological figures in evangelicalism on a first-name basis, and he is an avid critic of culture.[12]

He reads about five hundred books each year (in addition to hundreds of articles), and his reading expands far beyond theology into science, politics, and more. Ever since his days as a PhD student at Cambridge, he has devoted about half a day per week to read and catalog articles in about eighty theological journals, which he enters in a database with tags that enable him to locate and cite articles efficiently. His personal print library consists of about ten thousand choice volumes.

His reputation among the students at TEDS is legendary, and he upholds daunting standards for PhD seminar papers and dissertations. When I was his student, I was daunted to learn that he gives an A grade only if the paper

---

10 Instead of the school years being divided into two semesters, they were divided into three trimesters. The professors could take a sabbatical for one trimester every third year if they could justify it with a specific project. They also had the option of taking off all three trimesters, but the second two were without pay.

11 For example, from 1985 to 2010, Carson made over sixty-five trips to Australia to preach and teach in churches, schools, and conferences (an average of 2.6 times per year).

12 See esp. *Christ and Culture Revisited* (Grand Rapids, MI: Eerdmans, 2007). Cf. "Sin's Contemporary Significance," in *Fallen: A Theology of Sin*, ed. Christopher W. Morgan and Robert A. Peterson, Theology in Community (Wheaton, IL: Crossway, 2013), 21–37.

is publishable in a first-rate journal. On a lighter note, he enjoys woodworking and hiking, and when the weather permits it, he rides a motorcycle.

The most prominent focus of Carson's ministry is the gospel. He writes and speaks about it frequently,[13] and he has said something like the following countless times:

> Recognize that students do not learn everything you teach them. They certainly do not learn everything I teach them! What *do* they learn? They learn what I am excited about; they learn what I emphasize, what I return to again and again; they learn what organizes the rest of my thought. So if I happily *presuppose* the gospel but rarely articulate it and am never excited about it, while effervescing frequently about, say, ecclesiology or textual criticism, my students may conclude that the most important thing to me is ecclesiology or textual criticism. They may pick up my assumption of the gospel; alternatively, they may even distance themselves from the gospel; but what they will almost certainly do is place at the center of their thought ecclesiology or textual criticism, thereby wittingly or unwittingly marginalizing the gospel. Both ecclesiology and textual criticism, not to mention a plethora of other disciplines and sub-disciplines, are worthy of the most sustained study and reflection. Nevertheless, part of my obligation as a scholar-teacher, a scholar-pastor, is to show how my specialism relates to that which is fundamentally central and never to lose my passion for living and thinking and being excited about what must remain at the center. Failure in this matter means I lead my students and parishioners astray. If I am then challenged by a colleague who says to me, "Yes, I appreciate the competence and thoroughness with which you are handling ecclesiology or textual criticism, but how does this relate to the centrality and non-negotiability of the gospel?" I may, regrettably, respond rather defensively, "Why are you picking on me? I believe in the gospel as deeply as you do!" That may be true, but it rather misses the point. As a scholar, ecclesiology or textual criticism may be my specialism; but as a scholar-pastor, I must

---

13 "The Biblical Gospel," in *For Such a Time as This: Perspectives on Evangelicalism, Past, Present and Future* (London: Evangelical Alliance, 1996), 75–85; "Editorial," *Themelios* 34, no. 1 (2009): 1–2; "What Is the Gospel?—Revisited," in *For the Fame of God's Name: Essays in Honor of John Piper* (Wheaton, IL: Crossway, 2010), 147–70; "The Hole in the Gospel," *Themelios* 38, no. 3 (2013): 353–56; "What Are Gospel Issues?," *Themelios* 39, no. 2 (2014): 215–19.

be concerned for what I am passing on to the next generation, its configuration, its balance and focus. I dare never forget that students do not learn everything I try to teach them but primarily what I am excited about.[14]

What Does Carson Presuppose for Doing Theology?

For Carson's theological method, he presupposes particular views about metaphysics, epistemology, and divine revelation.

Carson's Metaphysics: God

Confessions of faith and systematic theology textbooks typically begin with the doctrine of the word of God. But when Carson drafted the confessional statement for TGC,[15] he intentionally began with the triune God, not revelation. He explains why in an essay he coauthored with Tim Keller:

> The Enlightenment was overconfident about human rationality. Some strands of it assumed it was possible to build systems of thought on unassailable foundations that could be absolutely certain to unaided human reason. Despite their frequent vilification of the Enlightenment, many conservative evangelicals have nevertheless been shaped by it. This can be seen in how many evangelical statements of faith start with the Scripture, not with God. They proceed from Scripture to doctrine through rigorous exegesis in order to build (what they consider) an absolutely sure, guaranteed-true-to-Scripture theology. The problem is that this is essentially a foundationalist approach to knowledge. It ignores the degree to which our cultural location affects our interpretation of the Bible, and it assumes a very rigid subject-object distinction. It ignores historical theology, philosophy, and cultural reflection. Starting with the Scripture leads readers to the overconfidence that their exegesis of biblical texts has produced a system of perfect doctrinal truth. This can create pride and rigidity because it may not sufficiently acknowledge the fallenness of human reason. We believe it is best to start with God, to declare (with John

---

14 "The Scholar as Pastor," in *The Pastor as Scholar and the Scholar as Pastor: Reflections on Life and Ministry* (Wheaton, IL: Crossway, 2011), 98–99.

15 See "Foundation Documents," Gospel Coalition, https://www.thegospelcoalition.org/.

Calvin, *Institutes* 1.1) that without knowledge of God we cannot know ourselves, our world, or anything else. If there is no God, we would have no reason to trust our reason.[16]

Carson's Epistemology: Chastened Foundationalism

Carson recognizes both positive and negative elements in the epistemology of premodernism, modernism, and postmodernism. He aligns himself, however, with none of them in its entirety, opting instead for a chastened foundationalism.[17] Here is what Carson thinks of those four types of epistemology.

PREMODERN EPISTEMOLOGY[18]

Positively, this epistemology begins with God rather than one's self. Negatively, it is tied to an open universe as opposed to a closed universe (modern epistemology) or "controlled" universe (Carson's view).

MODERN EPISTEMOLOGY: FOUNDATIONALISM AND THE OLDER HERMENEUTIC[19]

This epistemology begins with one's self rather than God as the foundation on which to build all other knowledge: "I think, therefore, I am."[20] Using a scientific method that is "*methodologically* atheistic," humans can and should reach "epistemological certainty" and discover what is universally true.[21] The older hermeneutic, based on this epistemology, prescribes exegesis with similar methodological rigor and objectively certain results.

---

16 D. A. Carson and Timothy Keller, *Gospel-Centered Ministry*, Gospel Coalition Booklets (Wheaton, IL: Crossway, 2011), 6.

17 *Gagging of God*, 22, 57–137, et al.; "Maintaining Scientific and Christian Truths in a Postmodern World," in *Can We Be Sure about Anything? Science, Faith and Postmodernism* (Leicester: InterVarsity, 2005), 109; "Domesticating the Gospel: A Review of Grenz's *Renewing the Center*," in *Reclaiming the Center: Confronting Evangelical Accommodation in Postmodern Times*, ed. Millard J. Erickson, Paul Kjoss Helseth, and Justin Taylor (Wheaton, IL: Crossway, 2004), 45–46, 54–55; *Becoming Conversant with the Emerging Church: Understanding a Movement and Its Implications* (Grand Rapids, MI: Zondervan, 2005), 88–124.

18 *Becoming Conversant with the Emerging Church*, 88–90.

19 "The Role of Exegesis in Systematic Theology," 48–56; "Approaching the Bible," 10–12; *Gagging of God*, 58–64; "Maintaining Scientific and Christian Truths," 108; *Becoming Conversant with the Emerging Church*, 92–95, 122–24.

20 See René Descartes, *Meditations on First Philosophy* (1641).

21 *Becoming Conversant with the Emerging Church*, 122, 94.

POSTMODERN EPISTEMOLOGY: ANTI-FOUNDATIONALISM AND THE "NEW HERMENEUTIC"[22]

Although this epistemology rejects modernism, it is modernism's "bastard child."[23] It likewise begins with the finite "I," but it rejects foundationalism and universal truth in favor of perspectivalism under the guise of a "tolerance" that is hypocritically intolerant.[24] The orthodox creed of the "new hermeneutic," which is based on this epistemology, is self-contradictory: the only heresy is the view that heresy exists, and the only objective and absolute truth is that objective, absolute truth does not exist.[25] Postmodern epistemology is commendable for emphasizing cultural diversity and human finiteness, especially one's inability to be completely neutral and objective.[26] Its weaknesses, however, outweigh its strengths: it is immoral, absurd, arrogant, and manipulative in its antitheses.[27]

"CHASTENED" FOUNDATIONALISM

Carson includes commendable elements from both the older and new hermeneutic in his approach to Scripture.[28] His "first theology" is God.[29] Both modernism and postmodernism err by making the "I" the starting point and then drawing conclusions (e.g., that God exists). But while God is the

22 "The Role of Exegesis in Systematic Theology," 50–56; *Gagging of God*, 19–72, 195–200; "Maintaining Scientific and Christian Truths," 108–9; *Becoming Conversant with the Emerging Church*, 95–98, 122–24; *Christ and Culture Revisited*, 8, 10–11, 62–63, 67–113, 200, 206–7.

23 *Becoming Conversant with the Emerging Church*, 122.

24 *The Intolerance of Tolerance* (Grand Rapids, MI: Eerdmans, 2012).

25 "Hermeneutics: A Brief Assessment of Some Recent Trends," *Themelios* 5, no. 1 (1980): 14–16; "Christian Witness in an Age of Pluralism," in *God and Culture: Essays in Honor of Carl F. H. Henry* (Grand Rapids, MI: Eerdmans, 1993), 33–42; "Preaching That Understands the World," in *When God's Voice Is Heard: Essays on Preaching Presented to Dick Lucas* (Leicester: Inter-Varsity, 1995), 160; *Gagging of God*, 30–35, 45, 54; "Is the Doctrine of *Claritas Scripturae* Still Relevant Today?" in *Dein Wort ist die Wahrheit: Beiträge zu einer schriftgemäßen Theologie*, ed. Eberhard Hahn, Rolf Hille, and Heinz-Werner Neudorfer (Wuppertal: Brockhaus Verlag, 1997), 105; "An Introduction to Introductions," in *Linguistics and the New Testament: Critical Junctions*, ed. D. A. Carson and Stanley E. Porter, *Journal for the Study of the New Testament Supplement* 168 (Sheffield: Sheffield Academic, 1999), 16; "Systematic Theology and Biblical Theology," 99–100; "Maintaining Scientific and Christian Truths," 112–13.

26 *Gagging of God*, 96–102; "*Claritas Scripturae*," 107–8; *Becoming Conversant with the Emerging Church*, 103–4.

27 *Gagging of God*, 102–37; "*Claritas Scripturae*," 108; "Systematic Theology and Biblical Theology," 100; "Domesticating the Gospel," 46–7; "Maintaining Scientific and Christian Truths," 120–22; *Becoming Conversant with the Emerging Church*, 104–6, 112–15.

28 See his "introductory principles of biblical interpretation" in "Approaching the Bible," 12–19. Cf. *Exegetical Fallacies*, 2nd ed. (Grand Rapids, MI: Baker, 1996), 125–31.

29 Interviews by the author, November 8 and 29, 2006.

foundation of Carson's epistemology, Carson recognizes that humans are finite and sinful—that is, unlike God, humans are limited and are deeply affected by the noetic effects of the fall, not least in their reasoning capacity. This is why Carson prefers to modify his "presuppositions" with the adjective "corrigible" (i.e., correctable, reformable).[30]

This in turn raises further questions regarding the effects of conversion and the Spirit's illumination, but the bottom line is this: humans cannot know anything absolutely (i.e., exhaustively or omnisciently) like God knows it, but they can know some things truly (i.e., substantially or really).[31] I have heard Carson make that point at least one hundred times in various contexts; it is foundational to his epistemology. He often illustrates it in four ways.[32]

THE FUSION OF TWO HORIZONS OF UNDERSTANDING

This model consists of two elements: distanciation and the fusion of two horizons. Distanciation refers to an observer or reader stepping back or distancing himself from an object he is scrutinizing. In the fusion of two horizons, a "horizon" refers to one's worldview, including presuppositions and cultural baggage. The horizon of the author's text and the horizon of theologians are initially separated by a huge gap due to differences such as one's historical and cultural location. Theologians may imperfectly but profitably fuse that horizon (i.e., minimize the gap) by deliberately "self-distancing" themselves from their "own biases and predilections" in order "to understand the other's terminology and points of view and idioms and values."[33]

---

30 Interview by the author, November 29, 2006.
31 "Hermeneutics," 15–16; "Historical Tradition and the Fourth Gospel: After Dodd, What?" in *Studies of History and Tradition in the Four Gospels*, ed. R. T. France and David Wenham, Gospel Perspectives 2 (Sheffield: JSOT, 1981), 100–104; "A Sketch of the Factors Determining Current Hermeneutical Debate in Cross-Cultural Contexts," in *Biblical Interpretation and the Church: Text and Context* (Exeter: Paternoster, 1984), 12–13, 15–17; "Christian Witness in an Age of Pluralism," 60; "Current Issues in Biblical Theology," 34; *Gagging of God*, 349, 544; *Exegetical Fallacies*, 126–28; "New Testament Theology," 809; "*Claritas Scripturae*," 106, 108–9; "An Introduction to Introductions," 16; "Systematic Theology and Biblical Theology," 100; "Domesticating the Gospel," 46–50; "Maintaining Scientific and Christian Truths," 120–22; *Becoming Conversant with the Emerging Church*, 105–6, 114, 116, 216.
32 "A Sketch of the Factors," 13, 15–16; "Recent Developments in the Doctrine of Scripture," in *Hermeneutics, Authority, and Canon* (Grand Rapids, MI: Zondervan, 1986), 38; "The Role of Exegesis in Systematic Theology," 52, 67; "Christian Witness in an Age of Pluralism," 60; "Approaching the Bible," 11; *Gagging of God*, 120–25, 544; *Exegetical Fallacies*, 126–27; "*Claritas Scripturae*," 108; "An Introduction to Introductions," 17; "Domesticating the Gospel," 46, 49–50; "Maintaining Scientific and Christian Truths," 120–22; *Becoming Conversant with the Emerging Church*, 116–21.
33 "The Role of Exegesis in Systematic Theology," 52; cf. 67.

THE HERMENEUTICAL SPIRAL

Rather than a vicious hermeneutical circle in which theologians endlessly go round and round between their own presuppositions, systematic constructions, and encounters with the text, this model illustrates that theologians may "hone in progressively on what is actually there."[34] Consequently, theologians may gradually minimize the radius of the circle as their understanding improves with time.

Thus instead of a straight line from the knower to the text, what really takes place is better schematized as a circle, a hermeneutical circle: I approach the text today, the text makes its impact on me, I (slightly altered) approach the text again tomorrow, and receive its (slightly altered) impact, and so on, and so on, and so on.[35] "We will never know all there is to know about" the Bible or anything else, "but we do spiral in closer than we once were."[36]

THE ASYMPTOTIC APPROACH

"An asymptote is a curved line that gets closer and closer to a straight line without ever touching it" (see figure 1).[37] Similarly, a theologian's knowledge may get closer and closer to God's absolute knowledge without reaching it. "Even fifty billion years into eternity, the asymptote will never touch the line."[38]

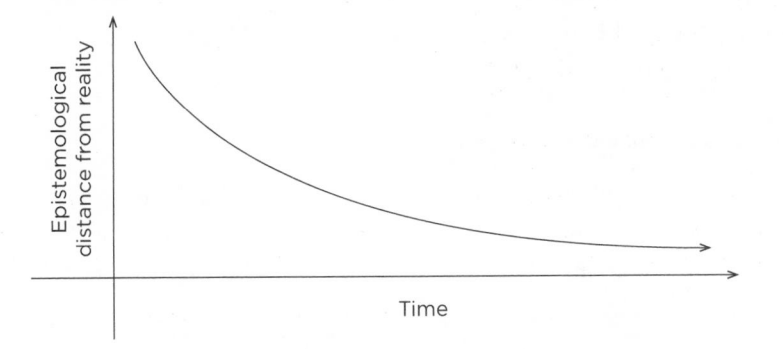

Figure 1: An asymptotic approach to epistemology. Carson has often drawn a figure like this on the board while teaching.

34 "The Role of Exegesis in Systematic Theology," 52.
35 *Gagging of God*, 71.
36 *Becoming Conversant with the Emerging Church*, 119.
37 *Becoming Conversant with the Emerging Church*, 119.
38 *Becoming Conversant with the Emerging Church*, 120. Cf. *Christ and Culture Revisited*, 90–91, 101.

SPEECH ACT THEORY

Building on Paul Ricoeur's insistence "that the text bridges the hermeneutical gulf between reader *and author*,"[39] speech act theory allows "much more interplay than in the past between what a text *means* and what it *does*" while still maintaining "a chastened version of authorial intent."[40] "The Bible's appeal to truth is rich and complex. It cannot be reduced to, but certainly includes, the notion of propositional truth."[41]

Since theologians will never know anything like God knows, their theology is eternally improvable, and it would be most advantageous if theologians recognized that now. "Systematicians with comparable training but from highly diverse backgrounds can come together and check one another *against the standard of the Scripture that all sides agree is authoritative*."[42]

Carson often illustrates this point in lectures by recounting his ten-year experience as the editor of five books sponsored by the World Evangelical Fellowship. Carson would select international evangelical scholars to contribute to a book project and then chair meetings for several days in which they would discuss each other's papers. In these meetings contributors would criticize each other from their vastly different cultural perspectives, and Carson found that despite their many differences they could reach remarkable unity on four conditions: (1) they were well trained, (2) they were willing to be corrected, (3) they affirmed that Scripture is authoritative, and (4) they had sufficient time.

Carson's Bibliology: Sola Scriptura[43]

Methodology is important for Carson,[44] and after God himself, bibliology is most foundational. In an essay on how to approach the Bible, Carson begins by explaining who God is.[45] God is personal, transcendent, and

---

39 *Gagging of God*, 122.

40 *Becoming Conversant with the Emerging Church*, 121. Carson often approvingly cites Kevin J. Vanhoozer's many works on hermeneutics that employ speech act theory.

41 *Gagging of God*, 163; see 163–74, 189–90, 348–53; "Recent Developments in the Doctrine of Scripture," 38; "Systematic Theology and Biblical Theology," 94–95.

42 "The Role of Exegesis in Systematic Theology." Cf. *Gagging of God*, 552–53.

43 For a brief summary of Carson's bibliology, see "Approaching the Bible," 1–10. For a fuller summary, see *Collected Writings on Scripture* (Wheaton, IL: Crossway, 2010).

44 Cf. "Unity and Diversity in the New Testament," 78.

45 "Approaching the Bible," 1–2.

sovereign, and since he created the universe, humans are accountable to him.[46] General revelation is limited; special revelation controls it.[47] God has spoken, and his revelation is authoritative.[48] The Bible is uniquely a subset of both "the word of God" and "the word of human beings."[49] "The locus of God's special revelation is the Bible, the sixty-six canonical books, reliable and truthful as originally given."[50]

Anticipating that some will criticize his view as "hopelessly circular" and "deeply flawed," Carson adds four further reflections:

1. "All human thought . . . is circular in some sense" since humans are finite and must depend on God's revelation by faith.
2. Circularity is not "intrinsically false." Further, Christians should "argue for the utter truthfulness and reliability of Scripture" because Scripture teaches it, "but they will not want to argue for the utter truthfulness and reliability of their doctrine of Scripture."[51]
3. "There are unknowns and difficulties in the formulation of a responsible doctrine of Scripture," but this is not troubling since "the same could be said for almost any biblical doctrine. . . . There will inevitably remain mysteries and areas of hiddenness."[52]

46 "Approaching the Bible," 1. Cf. "Christian Witness in an Age of Pluralism," 46–49; *Gagging of God*, 222–38.

47 "The Role of Exegesis in Systematic Theology," 43–44; cf. "Christian Witness in an Age of Pluralism," 49–54; "Approaching the Bible," 1–2.

48 See *Gagging of God*, 141–91; cf. 547–49; "Approaching the Bible," 5; "Current Issues in Biblical Theology," 27–29; "New Testament Theology," 806–7.

49 "Approaching the Bible," 2–3.

50 "The Role of Exegesis in Systematic Theology," 44. Cf. John D. Woodbridge, *Biblical Authority: A Critique of the Rogers/McKim Proposal* (Grand Rapids, MI: Zondervan, 1982); D. A. Carson, "Three Books on the Bible: A Critical Review," *Journal of the Evangelical Theological Society* 26 (1983): 337–67; D. A. Carson and John D. Woodbridge, eds., *Scripture and Truth* (Grand Rapids, MI: Zondervan, 1983); D. A. Carson and John D. Woodbridge, eds., *Hermeneutics, Authority, and Canon* (Grand Rapids, MI: Zondervan, 1986); Carson, "Approaching the Bible," 7; D. A. Carson and Douglas J. Moo, *An Introduction to the New Testament*, 2nd ed. (Grand Rapids, MI: Zondervan, 2005), 726–43; D. A. Carson, ed., *The Enduring Authority of the Christian Scriptures* (Grand Rapids, MI: Eerdmans, 2016); "Subtle Ways to Abandon the Authority of Scripture in Our Lives," *Themelios* 42, no. 1 (2017): 1–12; "Sola Scriptura Then and Now," Gospel Coalition, October 31, 2017, https://www.thegospelcoalition.org/; "But That's Just Your Interpretation!," *Themelios* 44, no. 3 (2019): 425–32.

51 Cf. "The Role of Exegesis in Systematic Theology," 55.

52 "Approaching the Bible," 9–10.

4. The noetic effects of sin on human thinking are substantial and must not be underestimated. The human desire to control God is idolatry.

What Does Carson Think the Theological Disciplines Are?

While Carson acknowledges that "*theology* can relate to the entire scope of religious studies," he uses "the term more narrowly to refer to the study of what the Scriptures say. This includes exegesis and historical criticism, the requisite analysis of method and epistemology, and the presentation of the biblical data in an orderly fashion."[53] Theology "is disciplined discourse about God,"[54] and the Bible "finally and irrevocably" constrains theology's subject matter.[55]

Carson recognizes that his definitions of the theological disciplines (described below) "do not avoid overlap," but his distinctions "are clear enough and are not novel."[56] So while there is not necessarily anything distinctly "Carsonian" to Carson's theological method itself, it is worth analyzing for at least three reasons: (1) it differs significantly from how many other exegetes and theologians "do" theology, (2) it helps us understand the mechanics of how he does theology in his voluminous publications, and (3) it may help us improve our own theological method.

Exegesis

Exegesis is "careful reading."[57] Exegesis "is the analysis of the final-form of a text, considered as an integral and self-referring literary object."[58] In other words, "Exegesis answers the questions, What does this text actually say? and, What did the author mean by what he said?"[59] "All that exegesis is is reading the text to find out what's there."[60] Exegesis includes but is not limited to parsing, word study, and syntax at various levels (clause,

---

53 "Unity and Diversity in the New Testament," 69.
54 "The Role of Exegesis in Systematic Theology," 40.
55 "The Role of Exegesis in Systematic Theology," 44.
56 "Unity and Diversity in the New Testament," 70.
57 "The Bible and Theology," 2321.
58 "The Role of Exegesis in Systematic Theology," 46.
59 "The Bible and Theology," 2321.
60 "R. C. Sproul Interviews D. A. Carson on Biblical Exegesis," March 10, 2011, https://vimeo .com/.

sentence, discourse, genre) while being sensitive to literary features and the running argument.[61]

> In short, exegesis is open-ended. It is not the sort of thing about which one can say, "I have completed the task; there is no more to do." Of course, in one sense that is exactly what *can* be said if what is meant is that the exegete has come to the end of the text. The exegesis is complete at that level of analysis, when the entire text has been analyzed. But exegesis itself is not a mechanical discipline with a few limited steps that, properly pursued, inevitably churn out the "right answer." On the other hand, progressively sophisticated levels of exegetical analysis may rapidly illustrate the law of diminishing returns! Exegetes with this view are quite happy to speak of discerning the author's intent, provided it is presupposed that the author's intent is expressed in the text. Only in this way can the intentional fallacy be avoided. There is no other access to the author's intent than in the text.[62]

Because Carson locates the text's meaning in the authorial intention as found in the text, he distinguishes between interpretation (i.e., what the text meant) and application (i.e., what the text means).[63] He is well aware that "truth is conveyed in different ways in different literary genres."[64] Carson's dozens of exegetical works demonstrate his proficiency at exegesis.[65]

Biblical Theology

Biblical theology (BT) "is rather difficult to define."[66] For Carson, "BT answers the question, How has God revealed his word historically and

---

61 "The Role of Exegesis in Systematic Theology," 47.
62 "The Role of Exegesis in Systematic Theology," 47–48.
63 "Approaching the Bible," 18.
64 "Approaching the Bible," 14.
65 See "D. A. Carson's Publications," Gospel Coalition, July 24, 2014, http://www.thegospel coalition.org.
66 "Current Issues in Biblical Theology," 17. See pp. 18–26 for a survey of six "competing definitions" of BT. For further reflections on defining BT, see "New Covenant Theology and Biblical Theology," in *God's Glory Revealed in Christ: Essays on Biblical Theology in Honor of Thomas R. Schreiner*, ed. Denny Burk, James M. Hamilton Jr., and Brian Vickers (Nashville: B&H, 2019), 17–31.

organically?"[67] BT may inductively and historically focus on the whole Bible or select biblical corpora.[68] It involves a "salvation-historical study of the biblical texts (*i.e.* the understanding and exposition of the texts along their chronological line of development)."[69] ("Salvation history" is "the history of salvation—i.e., the history of events that focus on the salvation of human beings and issues involving the new heaven and the new earth.[70]) At least five elements are essential:

1. BT reads "the Bible as an historically developing collection of documents."

2. BT presupposes "a coherent and agreed canon."[71]

3. BT presupposes "a profound willingness to work inductively from the text—from individual books and from the canon as a whole." Its task is "to deploy categories and pursue an agenda set by the text itself."

4. BT clarifies "the connections among the corpora"—that is, "it is committed to intertextual study . . . because biblical theology, at its most coherent, is a theology of the Bible."

5. "Ideally," BT will "call men and women to knowledge of the living God"—that is, it does not stop with the Bible's structure, corpus thought, storyline, or synthetic thought; it must "capture" the experiential, "existential element."[72]

BT focuses on the turning points in the Bible's storyline.[73] It recognizes "seeds" in Genesis 1–3 that grow throughout the story,[74] and it makes "theo-

---

67 "The Bible and Theology," 2321.

68 "Current Issues in Biblical Theology," 20, 23. These are definitions two and three in Carson's survey.

69 "Systematic Theology and Biblical Theology," 90. Cf. "Unity and Diversity in the New Testament," 69; "The Role of Exegesis in Systematic Theology," 45; *Gagging of God*, 502; "Systematic Theology and Biblical Theology," 100–101.

70 "A Biblical-Theological Overview of the Bible," in *NIV Biblical Theology Study Bible*, ed. D. A. Carson (Grand Rapids, MI: Zondervan, 2018), 2325.

71 Cf. "Systematic Theology and Biblical Theology," 91–92, 95–97.

72 "Current Issues in Biblical Theology," 27–32.

73 Cf. *Gagging of God*, 193–314; *Christ and Culture Revisited*, xi, 36, 44–61, 67, 81, 202, 226; *The God Who Is There: Finding Your Place in God's Story* (Grand Rapids, MI: Baker, 2010).

74 "Genesis 1–3: Not Maximalist, but Seminal," *Trinity Journal* 39 (2018): 143–63.

logical connections within the entire Bible that the Bible itself authorizes."[75] BT's most "pivotal" concern is tied to the use of the Old Testament in the New Testament.[76] One way to do BT is to "work really carefully with each biblical book or corpus by corpus," and another is to track "themes that run right though the whole Bible."[77] Theologians, not least Old Testament scholars, must read the Old Testament "with Christian eyes."[78] Old Testament and New Testament theology are subsets of BT.[79] BT "forms an organic whole"[80] and serves as "an excellent bridge discipline, building links among the associated disciplines and in certain respects holding them together."[81] The study Bible that Carson edited shows how to do BT: the notes make biblical-theological connections, and the study Bible concludes with twenty-eight essays on biblical theology, most of which trace themes throughout the Bible's storyline.[82]

Historical Theology

Historical theology (HT) answers the questions, How have people in the past understood the Bible? What have Christians thought about exegesis

---

75 "The Bible and Theology," 2321.

76 "Current Issues in Biblical Theology," 39–41. Cf. "New Testament Theology," 811; "Systematic Theology and Biblical Theology," 97–98; G. K. Beale and D. A. Carson, "Introduction," in *Commentary on the New Testament Use of the Old Testament*, ed. G. K. Beale and D. A. Carson (Grand Rapids, MI: Baker, 2007), xxiii–xxviii; "The Hermeneutical Competence of New Testament Commentaries," in *On the Writing of New Testament Commentaries: Festschrift for Grant R. Osborne on the Occasion of His 70th Birthday*, ed. Stanley E. Porter and Eckhard J. Schnabel, Texts and Editions for New Testament Studies 8 (Leiden: Brill, 2013), 166–68. See also G. K. Beale, D. A. Carson, Benjamin L. Gladd, and Andrew David Naselli, eds., *Dictionary of the New Testament Use of the Old Testament* (Grand Rapids, MI: Baker Academic, 2023).

77 "What Is Biblical Theology? And Do We Need It?," *Desiring God*, July 21, 2015, https://www .desiringgod.org/. For examples of tracing a God-designed typological trajectory through the Bible, see "Getting Excited about Melchizedek (Psalm 110)," in *The Scriptures Testify about Me: Jesus and the Gospel in the Old Testament*, ed. D. A. Carson (Wheaton, IL: Crossway, 2013), 145–74; "Why We Must Understand the Temple in God's Plan Today," *Desiring God*, July 22 2015, https://www.desiringgod.org/.

78 "Current Issues in Biblical Theology," 40–41.

79 "New Testament Theology," 796.

80 "Approaching the Bible," 1. Cf. "Unity and Diversity in the New Testament," 83; "A Sketch of the Factors," 26–27.

81 "Systematic Theology and Biblical Theology," 91. On the need for wisely integrating BT, see *Christ and Culture Revisited*, 59–62, 67, 71, 81–85, 87, 94, 121, 127, 143, 172, 207, 227.

82 D. A. Carson, ed., *NIV Biblical Theology Study Bible* (Grand Rapids, MI: Zondervan, 2018). For more information, see Andy Naselli, "NIV Biblical Theology Study Bible," *Andy Naselli* (blog), August 18, 2015, https://andynaselli.com/. See also one of Carson's essays in that volume: "A Biblical-Theological Overview of the Bible," 2325–27.

and theology? and, more specifically, How has Christian doctrine developed over the centuries, especially in response to false teachings? HT is concerned primarily with opinions in periods earlier than our own. But we may also include under this heading the importance of reading the Bible globally—that is, finding out how believers in some other parts of the world read the text. That does not mean that they (or we!) are necessarily right; rather, it means that we recognize that all of us have a great deal to learn.[83]

HT is "the written record of exegetical and theological opinions in periods earlier than our own, a kind of historical parallel to the diversity of exegetical and theological opinions that are actually current."[84] HT is "the diachronic study of theology, *i.e.* the study of the changing face of theology across time."[85]

HT is valuable for at least five reasons: (1) it frees us "from unwitting slavery to our biases," (2) "it induces humility," (3) "it clears our minds of unwarranted assumptions," (4) it "exposes faulty interpretations that others have long since (and rightly) dismissed," and (5) it "reminds us that responsibly interpreting the Bible must never be a solitary task."[86]

Systematic Theology

Systematic theology (ST) "answers the question, What does the whole Bible teach about certain topics? or put another way, What is true about God and his universe?"[87]

> [ST] is Christian theology whose internal structure is systematic; i.e., it is organized on atemporal principles of logic, order, and need, rather than on inductive study of discrete biblical corpora. Thus it can address broader concerns of Christian theology (it is not merely inductive study of the Bible, though it must never lose such controls), but it seeks to be rigorously systematic and is therefore concerned about how various parts of God's gracious self-disclosure cohere. . . . The questions it poses

---

83 "The Bible and Theology," 2321.
84 "The Role of Exegesis in Systematic Theology," 56.
85 "Systematic Theology and Biblical Theology," 91.
86 "The Bible and Theology," 2322.
87 "The Bible and Theology," 2322.

are atemporal . . . the focal concerns are logical and hierarchical, not salvation-historical.[88]

"ST is the most comprehensive of the various theological disciplines."[89] Everyone uses some sort of ST, and it is foolish to denigrate it. The issue is not whether ST is legitimate; the issue, rather, is the quality of one's ST reflected in its foundational data, constructive methods, principles for excluding certain information, appropriately expressive language, and logical, accurate results.[90]

Carson's approach to ST presupposes "that the basic laws of logic" are not human inventions "but discoveries to do with the nature of reality and of communication."[91] The Bible is like part of a massive jigsaw puzzle because it contains only a small fraction of the total number of pieces.[92] More precisely, the Bible is like a massive "multi-dimensional puzzle beyond the third dimension."[93] ST "must be controlled by the biblical data" and must beware of going beyond "how various truths and arguments function in Scripture," not least because "a number of fundamental Christian beliefs involves huge areas of unknown," such as the incarnation, the Trinity, and God's sovereignty and man's responsibility.[94]

The Bible's unity makes ST "not only possible but necessary," and "modern theology at variance with this stance is both methodologically and doctrinally deficient."[95] An approach that recognizes this unity encourages "theological exploration" within the canon:

> [J. I. Packer writes,] "There is . . . a sense in which every New Testament writer communicates to Christians today more than he knew he was communicating, simply because Christians can now read his work as part of the completed New Testament canon." This is not an appeal to *sensus*

88 "The Role of Exegesis in Systematic Theology," 45–46. Cf. "Unity and Diversity in the New Testament," 69–70; "Current Issues in Biblical Theology," 29; "Systematic Theology and Biblical Theology," 101–2.
89 "The Bible and Theology," 2324.
90 "Unity and Diversity in the New Testament," 78; cf. 92.
91 "Unity and Diversity in the New Testament," 80. Cf. *Exegetical Fallacies*, 87–88.
92 "Unity and Diversity in the New Testament," 81–82.
93 "Current Issues in Biblical Theology," 30.
94 "Unity and Diversity in the New Testament," 82, 93–94. Cf. "Approaching the Bible," 17–18.
95 "Unity and Diversity in the New Testament," 95; cf. 90.

plenior, at least not in any traditional sense. Rather, it is an acknowledgment that with greater numbers of pieces of the jigsaw puzzle provided, the individual pieces and clusters of pieces are seen in new relationships not visible before.[96]

Carson's standard for good ST is high. Michael Horton asked Carson, "Do you think there has been a lot of polarization where systematicians aren't always very good exegetes and exegetes aren't very good systematicians?"[97] Carson replied,

The danger springs from a culture of specialization—more and more knowledge about less and less—so that a person who really is on top of the exegetical literature quite frankly just doesn't have time to be right on top of the systematic literature, and vice versa. I've sometimes told students who say they want to do a Ph.D. in systematic theology, that one doctorate won't do—they'll need at least five: one or two in New Testament, at least one in Old Testament, a couple in church history, one in philosophy, and then they can do one in systematics. That's the problem—the nature of the discipline is integrative and synthetic. If instead people do systematics without any grasp of Scripture, they're likely to cut themselves off from what they confess to be their authority base, and so they're not really rigorous.[98]

Examples of how Carson systematically integrates the theological disciplines include his treatments of compatibilism and theodicy,[99] Sabbath

96 "Unity and Diversity in the New Testament," 91. Carson is sympathetic with Douglas J. Moo, "The Problem of *Sensus Plenior*," in *Hermeneutics, Authority, and Canon*, ed. D. A. Carson and John D. Woodbridge (Grand Rapids, MI: Zondervan, 1986), 175–211, 397–405, an article that has recently been updated: Douglas J. Moo and Andrew David Naselli, "The Problem of the New Testament's Use of the Old Testament," in *The Enduring Authority of the Christian Scriptures*, ed. D. A. Carson (Grand Rapids, MI: Eerdmans, 2016), 702–46. Cf. "The Role of Exegesis in Systematic Theology," 56.

97 D. A. Carson and Michael Horton, "Why Can't We Just Read the Bible? An Interview with D. A. Carson," *Modern Reformation* 19, no. 4 (2010): 33.

98 Carson and Horton, "Why Can't We Just Read the Bible?" 33.

99 *Divine Sovereignty and Human Responsibility*; "Divine Sovereignty and Human Responsibility in Philo: Analysis and Method," *Novum Testamentum* 23 (1981): 148–64; *How Long, O Lord? Reflections on Suffering and Evil*, 2nd ed. (Grand Rapids, MI: Baker, 2006); review of *Evil and the Justice of God*, by N. T. Wright, *Review of Biblical Literature* (April 23, 2007); "Biblical-Theological Pillars Needed to Support Faithful Christian Reflection on Suffering and Evil," *Trinity Journal* 38 (2017): 55–77.

and the Lord's Day,[100] spiritual gifts,[101] assurance of salvation,[102] the love and wrath of God,[103] the emerging church,[104] and the Son of God.[105]

Pastoral Theology

Pastoral theology (PT) answers the question, How should humans respond to God's revelation? Sometimes that is spelled out by Scripture itself; other times it builds on inferences of what Scripture says. PT practically applies the other four disciplines—so much so that the other disciplines are in danger of being sterile and even dishonoring to God unless tied in some sense to the responses God rightly demands of us. PT may well address such diverse domains as culture, ethics, evangelism, marriage and family, money, the cure of souls, politics, worship, and much more.[106]

PT applies (i.e., cross-culturally contextualizes) exegesis, BT, HT, and ST to help people glorify God by living wisely with a biblical worldview. Basically, PT answers the question, How then should we live?

How Does Carson Think the Theological Disciplines Interrelate?

ST is like juggling: the balls represent the other theological disciplines, and ST's challenge is to avoid serious consequences by not dropping any

---

100 Carson coordinated and edited the project (what he calls "a unified, cooperative investigation" [18]) that resulted in *From Sabbath to Lord's Day: A Biblical, Historical, and Theological Investigation* (Grand Rapids, MI: Zondervan, 1982); see esp. Carson, "Introduction" (13–19).

101 *Showing the Spirit: A Theological Exposition of 1 Corinthians 12–14* (Grand Rapids, MI: Baker, 1987), 137–88.

102 "Reflections on Assurance," in *Still Sovereign: Contemporary Perspectives on Election, Foreknowledge, and Grace* (Grand Rapids, MI: Baker, 2000), 247–76.

103 *Gagging of God*, 238–42; *The Difficult Doctrine of the Love of God* (Wheaton, IL: Crossway, 2000); "Love," *New Dictionary of Biblical Theology* (Downers Grove, IL: InterVarsity, 2000); "How Can We Reconcile the Love and the Transcendent Sovereignty of God?" in *God Under Fire: Modern Scholarship Reinvents God*, ed. Douglas S. Huffman and Eric L. Johnson (Grand Rapids, MI: Zondervan, 2002), 279–312; *Love in Hard Places* (Wheaton, IL: Crossway, 2002); "The Wrath of God," in *Engaging the Doctrine of God: Contemporary Protestant Perspectives* (Grand Rapids, MI: Baker, 2008), 37–63.

104 *Becoming Conversant with the Emerging Church*. For example, while critiquing their idea of truth, knowledge, and pluralism, Carson uncharacteristically lists Bible verses with very little commentary and notes that the context of each passage supports his theses: fifty-two verses "on what is true" and eighty-eight "on knowing some truths, even with 'certainty'" (188–99).

105 *Jesus the Son of God: A Christological Title Often Overlooked, Sometimes Misunderstood, and Currently Disputed* (Wheaton, IL: Crossway, 2012).

106 "The Bible and Theology," 2322.

balls.[107] Exegesis, BT, HT, and ST should be inseparable for theologians, but this is often not the case, for example, at American Academy of Religion and Society of Biblical Literature conferences, which tend to be high on specialization and low on integration.[108] "We live in an age of increasing specialization (owing in part to the rapid expansion of knowledge), and disciplines that a priori ought to work hand in glove are being driven apart."[109]

Theological Hermeneutics

THE COMPLEX INTERRELATIONSHIP BETWEEN THE THEOLOGICAL DISCIPLINES

Carson explains the interrelationships between the theological disciplines with some diagrams. Some might think it convenient if we could order these disciplines along a straight line: Exegesis → BT → [HT] → ST → PT. (The brackets around HT suggest that HT directly contributes to the development from BT to ST and PT but is not itself a part of that line.) But this neat paradigm is naive because no exegesis is ever done in a vacuum. Before we ever start doing exegesis, we already have an ST framework that influences our exegesis. So are we locked into a hermeneutical circle (see figure 2)?

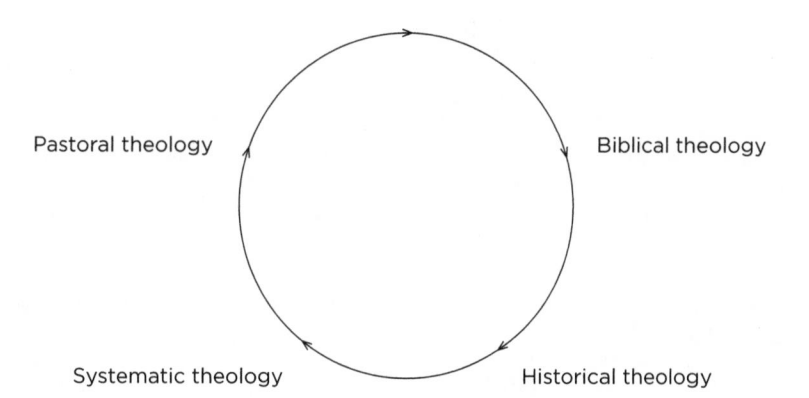

Figure 2. Hermeneutical circle. Carson has often drawn diagrams like these on the board while teaching.

---

107 "The Role of Exegesis in Systematic Theology," 39–40, 72.
108 "The Role of Exegesis in Systematic Theology," 40.
109 "Unity and Diversity in the New Testament," 65.

No; there is a better way. We might diagram it as shown in figure 3:

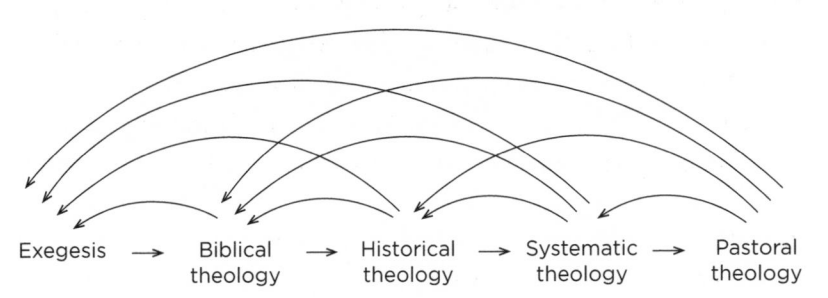

Exegesis → Biblical → Historical → Systematic → Pastoral
theology   theology   theology   theology

Figure 3: From exegesis to theology. Carson has often drawn diagrams like these on the board while teaching.

In other words, there are always feedback loops—information loops that go back and reshape how one does any exegesis or theology. The loops should not take over the final voice, but they shape the process whether one likes it or not. It is absurd to claim that one's ST does not affect one's exegesis. But the line of final control is the straight line from exegesis right through BT and HT to ST and PT. The final authority is the Bible and the Bible alone.

"For this reason," Carson explains, "exegesis, though affected by systematic theology, is not to be shackled by it."[110]

CARSON'S THEOLOGICAL HERMENUTIC: "BREADTH OF VISION"

Carson lists four ways to respond to the fragmented "current state of biblical studies":

1. Ignore or marginalize "all recent developments"—a pious "recipe for obsolescence."
2. Focus "on just one method, preferably the most recent"—a faddish "recipe for reductionism."
3. "Rejoice in the fragmentation," and "insist that such developments are not only inevitable but delightful, even liberating"—a pretentious and absurd postmodern approach.

---

110 "Unity and Diversity in the New Testament," 92.

4. "Try to learn from the most important lessons from the new disciplines—and remain focused on the texts themselves" by emphasizing "the classic disciplines first" while learning from "tools, hermeneutical debates, and epistemological shifts."[111]

Carson takes the fourth approach, insisting, "All truth is God's truth."[112] Carson recognizes that the disciplines are interconnected. If one of the disciplines is a string and one pulls at it, that inevitably affects the other disciplines as well.[113] They are a package, which shows the need for a "thick" interpretation. Probably the loudest note Carson plays is the Christological, salvation-historical unity of the Bible's storyline.

In practice, Carson is a multidisciplinary theologian, perhaps "one of the last great Renaissance men in evangelical biblical scholarship."[114] He is not merely a New Testament scholar. He is also an Old Testament scholar, a biblical theologian, a historical theologian, a systematic theologian, and a practical theologian (e.g., gifted preacher, critic of culture, former pastor, counselor).[115] He also branches out into philosophy, English literature (e.g., poetry), science, math, nature, and other fields. It is no surprise that Kenneth Kantzer, former dean of Trinity Evangelical Divinity School, repeatedly invited Carson to move from the New Testament department to the systematic theology department. Carson explains that he has remained in the New Testament department "partly because while I think it is important to feed biblical stuff into ST . . . it's also important to bring breadth of vision to exegesis."[116] At the 1993 annual meeting of the Institute for Biblical Research, Carson presented this as a formal challenge to BT: "the daunting need for exegetes and theologians who will deploy the full range of weapons in the

---

111 "An Introduction to Introductions," 14–17.

112 Interview by the author, November 29, 2006.

113 Interview by the author, November 29, 2006.

114 Köstenberger, "D. A. Carson," 357.

115 This is evident in D. A. Carson and John D. Woodbridge, *Letters Along the Way: From a Senior Saint to a Junior Saint*, 2nd ed. (Wheaton, IL: Crossway, 2022). My wife and I read this book together during my first year as Carson's teaching assistant and PhD student. We loved it. Reading these fictional letters is almost as personal as if you wrote a challenging theological or practical question to Carson and Woodbridge themselves and then received a thoughtful reply. Now I use this book as a resource for mentoring seminary students.

116 Interview by the author, November 29, 2006.

exegetical arsenal, without succumbing to methodological narrowness or faddishness."[117]

Exegesis and Biblical Theology

BT "mediates the influence of biblical exegesis on systematic theology" because it "forces the theologian to remember that there is before and after, prophecy and fulfillment, type and antitype, development, organic growth, down payment and consummation."[118] The "overlap" between exegesis and BT is the most striking among the theological disciplines: "both are concerned to understand texts," and BT is impossible without exegesis.[119] "Exegesis tends to focus on analysis," and BT "tends towards synthesis."[120] Exegesis controls BT, and BT influences exegesis.[121] BT "more immediately constrains and enriches exegesis than systematic theology can do."[122] In a sense BT is whole-Bible exegesis.

Exegesis and Historical Theology

The historic creeds are valuable, but they are not ultimately authoritative; only Scripture is.[123] The practice of many theologians, however, is to move directly from exegesis to ST with the result that they leave "precious little place for historical theology, except to declare it right or wrong as measured against the system that has developed out of one's own exegesis."[124] "Without historical theology," however, "exegesis is likely to degenerate into arcane atomistic debates far too tightly tethered to the twentieth century. Can there be any responsible exegesis of Scripture that does not honestly wrestle with

117 "Current Issues in Biblical Theology," 34.

118 "The Role of Exegesis in Systematic Theology," 66, 65; cf. 58–66. In this regard the finest example of Carson's combining exegesis and BT is probably this dense 44-page essay: "Mystery and Fulfillment: Toward a More Comprehensive Paradigm of Paul's Understanding of the Old and New," in *The Paradoxes of Paul*, vol. 2 of *Justification and Variegated Nomism*, ed. D. A. Carson, Peter T. O'Brien, and Mark A. Seifrid, Wissenschaftliche Untersuchungen zum Neuen Testament 181 (Grand Rapids, MI: Baker, 2004), 393–436. Cf. "Biblical-Theological Ruminations on Psalm 1," in *Resurrection and Eschatology: Theology in Service of the Church; Essays in Honor of Richard B. Gaffin Jr.* (Phillipsburg, NJ: P&R, 2008), 115–34.

119 "Systematic Theology and Biblical Theology," 91.

120 "Systematic Theology and Biblical Theology," 91.

121 "Systematic Theology and Biblical Theology," 91.

122 "The Role of Exegesis in Systematic Theology," 66.

123 *Gagging of God*, 362–33. Cf. "Domesticating the Gospel," 51.

124 "The Role of Exegesis in Systematic Theology," 51.

what earlier Christian exegesis has taught?"[125] This explains why Carson includes significant sections on historical theology when he edits books that systematically address controversial issues such as the doctrines of justification or Scripture.[126]

HT serves exegesis (and thus ST) in three ways:

1. HT opens up and closes down "options and configurations."
2. HT shows how contemporary theological views are products of "the larger matrix" of contemporary thought.
3. HT contributes to ST's boundaries by showing "remarkable uniformity of belief across quite different paradigms of understanding."[127]

Some may criticize Carson's theological method as "biblicism," but Carson distinguishes between two kinds of biblicism:

> There is a kind of appeal to Scripture, a kind of biblicism—let's call it Biblicism One—that seems to bow to what Scripture says but does not listen to the text very closely and is almost entirely uninformed by how thoughtful Christians have wrestled with these same texts for centuries. There is another kind of biblicism—let's call it Biblicism Two—that understands the final authority in divine revelation to lie in Scripture traceable to the God who has given it, but understands also that accurate understanding of that Scripture is never supported by bad exegesis and always enriched by the work of Christian thinkers who have gone before. . . . To attempt theological interpretation without reference to such developments is part and parcel of Biblicism One; to attempt theological interpretation that is self-consciously aware of such developments and takes them into account is part and parcel of Biblicism Two. We hasten to add that both Biblicism One and Biblicism Two insist that final authority rests with the Bible. All the theological syntheses are in principle revisable. Yet the best of these creeds and confessions have been grounded in such widespread study,

---

125 "The Role of Exegesis in Systematic Theology," 39–40.
126 D. A. Carson, Peter T. O'Brien, and Mark A. Seifrid, eds., *Justification and Variegated Nomism*, 2 vols. (Grand Rapids, MI: Baker, 2001, 2004); Carson, ed., *The Enduring Authority of the Christian Scriptures*.
127 "The Role of Exegesis in Systematic Theology," 56–57; cf. 39–40; "Recent Developments in the Doctrine of Scripture," 18; "Approaching the Bible," 18.

discussion, debate, and testing against Scripture that to ignore them tends to cut oneself off from the entire history of Christian confessionalism. The Bible remains theoretically authoritative (Biblicism One), but in fact it is being manipulated and pummeled by private interpretations cut off from the common heritage of all Christians.[128]

Exegesis and Systematic Theology

Some theologians seem to think that their exegesis neutrally and objectively discovers the text's meaning and that they build their ST on such discoveries, but one's ST "exerts profound influence on" one's exegesis.[129] Without even realizing it, many theologians develop their own "canon within the canon," which to a large degree accounts for conflicting exegesis among Christians.[130] (A "canon within the canon" refers to "favorite passages of the Bible that then become their controlling grid for interpreting the rest of the Bible.")[131]

This problem may develop in at least three ways:

1. "An ecclesiastical tradition may unwittingly overemphasize certain biblical truths at the expense of others, subordinating or even explaining away passages that do not easily 'fit' the slightly distorted structure that results."[132] For example, one's understanding of justification in Galatians may control one's understanding of justification everywhere else in the NT.[133] The solution is "to listen to one another, especially when we least like what we hear," and to employ ST in a way that confronts "the entire spectrum of biblical truth."[134]

2. "An ecclesiastical tradition may self-consciously adopt a certain structure by which to integrate all the books of the canon" with the result that "some passages and themes may automatically be classified and explained in a particular fashion such that other believers find the tradition in question

---

128 "Carson on Jakes and the Elephant Room," Gospel Coalition, February 3, 2012, https://www .thegospelcoalition.org/.

129 "The Role of Exegesis in Systematic Theology," 51. For example, "A person profoundly committed to, say, a pretribulational view of the rapture is unlikely to find anything but verification of this view in 1 Thessalonians 4:13–18, no matter how 'objective' and 'neutral' the exegetical procedures being deployed seem to be" (51).

130 "A Sketch of the Factors," 20.

131 "The Bible and Theology," 2323.

132 "A Sketch of the Factors," 21.

133 Cf. "A Sketch of the Factors," 21.

134 "A Sketch of the Factors," 23; cf. 27.

sub-biblical or too narrow or artificial."[135] Dispensationalism and covenant theology are classic examples, usually employed by earnest theologians who consider their "theological framework" to be "true to Scripture."[136] A more egregious error is a "paradigmatic approach" that uses parts of the Bible "without worrying very much about how the Scriptures fit together."[137] An example of this error is Gustavo Gutiérrez making the exodus narrative a paradigm for the oppressed poor today to revolt.[138]

3. "Many others reject parts of the canon as unworthy, historically inaccurate, mutually contradictory or the like, and adopt only certain parts of the Scripture."[139]

John Calvin is a sterling example of a pastor who responsibly integrates exegesis and ST:

> The Reformation stands out as a movement that sought to integrate exegesis of the biblical books with what we would today call systematic theology. Not all the Reformers did this the same way. Some acted as if they were expounding the biblical texts, but tended in reality to jump from seminal word or phrase to the next seminal word or phrase, stopping at each point to unload theological treatments of the various "loci." Bucer, for example, followed the text more closely but also unloaded his treatment of the "loci" as he went along, making his commentaries extraordinarily long and dense. Calvin strove in his commentaries for what he called "lucid brevity," and he reserved his systematic theology primarily for what grew to become the four volumes of *Institutes of the Christian Religion*. Indeed, Calvin's commentaries are so "bare bones" that not a few scholars have criticized him for not including enough theology in them. But what is striking about all these Reformers, regardless of their successes or failures to bring about appropriate integration, is the way in which they simultaneously attempted to expound the Bible and engage in serious theologizing. By contrast, today few systematicians are excellent exegetes, and few exegetes evince much interest in systematic theology.

---

135 "A Sketch of the Factors," 21.
136 "A Sketch of the Factors," 21, 24.
137 "A Sketch of the Factors," 24.
138 "A Sketch of the Factors," 24–26.
139 "A Sketch of the Factors," 21.

The exceptions merely prove the rule. There are many reasons why the Reformers were models in this regard—but whatever the reasons, we have much to learn from them.[140]

Historical Theology and Systematic Theology

On the one hand, ST can err by undervaluing HT. ST is an attempt "to systematize what is found in the Bible,"[141] and some theologians move from exegesis to ST without sufficiently considering HT.[142] When studying what the Bible teaches about a particular subject (ST), the theologian must integrate HT.[143]

On the other hand, ST can err by overvaluing HT. Consequently, such attempts at ST are not actually systematizing the Bible but instead systematizing what other theologians have said about the Bible: "Countless books that ostensibly belong to the domain of systematic theology are in fact an evaluation and critique of some theologian or of some theological position, based on criteria that are an interesting mix of tradition, Scripture, reason, philosophical structures and internal coherence."[144] "In some measure," ST "deals with" HT's categories, but ST's "priorities and agenda . . . ideally . . . address the contemporary age at the most critical junctures."[145]

Undervaluing and overvaluing HT are dangers that Carson addresses in his article that evaluates the "Theological Interpretation of Scripture" movement.[146] "TIS accords greater credibility to pre-critical exegesis—patristic, medieval, reformational—than to contemporary exegesis, and especially to patristic readings."[147] On the one hand, Carson affirms, "One worries about interpreters who are always striving to find something *new* in Scripture but who rarely take the time to show how their readings are nestled within the massive confessional heritage of historic Christianity."[148] On the other hand, Carson warns,

---

140 "Should Pastors Today Still Care about the Reformation?," *Themelios* 42, no. 3 (2017): 438.

141 "Systematic Theology and Biblical Theology," 102.

142 Cf. "The Role of Exegesis in Systematic Theology," 51.

143 "The Role of Exegesis in Systematic Theology," 46; "Domesticating the Gospel," 33.

144 "Systematic Theology and Biblical Theology," 102. Cf. "The Scholar as Pastor," 100.

145 "Current Issues in Biblical Theology," 29.

146 "Theological Interpretation of Scripture: Yes, But . . ." in *Theological Commentary: Evangelical Perspectives*, ed. R. Michael Allen (London: T&T Clark, 2011), 187–207.

147 "Theological Interpretation of Scripture," 196.

148 "Theological Interpretation of Scripture," 196.

It is not entirely clear why so much emphasis is placed on the patristic period. For many Catholics, the appeal to the magisterial authority expressed through the first seven (ecumenical) councils may be part of the reason; for many others, a similar appeal is made to the Great Tradition. Both parties sometimes write as if either (a) these ecumenical councils share the authority of Scripture, or (b) at very least they are not to be questioned because they were both ecumenical and much closer to Christ and his apostles than we are; and so, further, (c) they constitute all that is necessary to establish a confessional bond of true Christians today—a stance which, of course, marginalizes the Reformation standards. No informed confessional evangelical will agree to (a): there is an ontological gap between the books of the Bible and all other documents. That the early councils were ecumenical—so (b)—is something for which to be grateful, and warrants that Christians everywhere should pay the more careful attention to them, but even council documents and creeds must be tested by Scripture, not the reverse. . . . The fact that the fathers were closer to the events described in the New Testament and to the time of writing of those documents is almost irrelevant. . . . In response to (c), why should we think the Great Tradition is a sufficient ground for a common Christian front? One could make a serious case that it provides a necessary ground, but sufficient? Are we to think that no serious aberrations would or could ever be introduced into the life and thought of the church after the patristic period? . . . If one is looking for excellent models of how the patristic and medieval fathers should be cited and used abundantly if discerningly, one could do a great deal worse than begin with Luther, Calvin, and other Reformers. The links between Calvin and Thomas Aquinas have frequently been probed, and his grasp of patristic sources is wholly admirable. So why the frequent marginalization of Reformational voices in TIS literature?[149]

Biblical Theology and Historical Theology

BT and HT both study "the changing face of the accumulating biblical documents across time," but BT has "abundant interlocking considerations

---

149 "Theological Interpretation of Scripture," 197–98.

(canon, revelation, authority) that demand distinctions."[150] Since theologians are finite, BT functions best when interacting with HT's past ("twenty centuries of Christian witness") and present ("the living church").[151] In other words, "BT focuses on the Bible, while HT focuses on what significant figures have believed about the Bible. BT functions best when interacting with HT."[152]

Biblical Theology and Systematic Theology

Table 1 displays how I compare BT and ST, which repackages what I have learned from Carson.

Table 1. Comparing biblical theology and systematic theology[153]

	Biblical theology	Systematic theology
Final authority	The whole Bible	The whole Bible
Task	Inductively describe what texts say in relation to the whole Bible. Explore how and what each literary genre or canonical unit distinctively communicates.	Deductively describe what the whole Bible teaches (with an objective of engaging and even confronting one's culture). Integrate and synthesize what the Bible's literary genres communicate.
Nature	Historical and literary. Organic. Inductive. Diachronic (traces how salvation history progresses through time). Bridging discipline: a little further from culture and a little closer to the biblical text	Relatively ahistorical. Relatively universal. Relatively deductive. Relatively synchronic (focuses on what is true at a point in time). Culminating and worldview-shaping discipline: a little closer to culture and a little further from the biblical text

---

150 "Systematic Theology and Biblical Theology," 91–92.

151 "Systematic Theology and Biblical Theology," 101. Cf. "New Testament Theology," 811.

152 "The Bible and Theology," 2324.

153 This table is from Andrew David Naselli, "Question 1: What Do We Mean by 'Biblical Theology'?" in Jason S. DeRouchie, Oren R. Martin, and Andrew David Naselli, *40 Questions about Biblical Theology*, 40 Questions (Grand Rapids, MI: Kregel, 2020), 26. Used by permission.

BT is historical and organic; ST is relatively ahistorical and universal.[154] Unlike BT, which "is deeply committed to working inductively from the biblical text" so that "the text itself sets the agenda," ST may be "at a second or third or fourth order of remove from Scripture, as it engages, say, philosophical and scientific questions not directly raised by the biblical texts themselves. These elements constitute part of its legitimate mandate."[155]

On the one hand, exegesis and BT "have an advantage over" ST because "their agenda is set by the text."[156] ST must build on BT's "syntheses of biblical corpora" and "tracing of the Bible's story-line" with the result that "each major strand" of ST will "be woven into the fabric that finds its climax and ultimate significance in the person and work of Jesus Christ."[157] On the other hand, "ST has an advantage over exegesis and BT because it drives hard toward holistic integration."[158]

Literary genre and speech act theory significantly influence the relationship between BT and ST.[159] BT is "a kind of bridge discipline between" exegesis and ST.[160] BT "is admirably suited to build a bridge between" exegesis and ST "because it overlaps with the relevant disciplines," enabling "them to hear one another a little better."[161] BT is "a mediating discipline," but ST is "a culminating discipline" because it attempts to form and transform one's "worldview."[162]

> Systematic theology tends to be a little further removed from the biblical text than does biblical theology, but a little closer to cultural engagement. Biblical theology tends to seek out the rationality and communicative genius of each literary genre; systematic theology tends to integrate the diverse rationalities in its pursuit of a large-scale, worldview-forming synthesis. In this sense, systematic theology tends to be a culminating

---

154 Cf. *Gagging of God*, 502, 542–43; "New Testament Theology," 808; "Systematic Theology and Biblical Theology," 94–95, 101–3.

155 "Current Issues in Biblical Theology," 29.

156 *Gagging of God*, 544.

157 *Gagging of God*, 544–45.

158 "The Bible and Theology," 2324.

159 "Systematic Theology and Biblical Theology," 94–95.

160 "Systematic Theology and Biblical Theology," 94.

161 "Systematic Theology and Biblical Theology," 95.

162 "Systematic Theology and Biblical Theology," 102.

discipline; biblical theology, though it is a worthy end in itself, tends to be a bridge discipline.[163]

"BT is important today because the gospel is virtually incoherent unless people understand the Bible's storyline. ST is important today because, rightly undertaken, it brings clarity and depth to our understanding of what the Bible is about."[164]

Exegesis, Biblical Theology, Historical Theology, Systematic Theology, and Pastoral Theology

Although it is possible to treat pastoral theology as an independent discipline, it is wiser to recognize that the Bible was never given to stir up *merely* or *exclusively* intellectual questions. It was given to transform people's lives; it was given to be practical. The notion of impractical theology—theological study that is unconcerned with repentance, faith, obedience, conformity to Christ, and joy in the Lord—hovers somewhere between the ridiculous and the blasphemous.[165]

Carson is not an ivory tower theologian: "The aim of thoughtful Christians, after all, is not so much to become masters of Scripture, but to be mastered by it, both for God's glory and his people's good."[166] Carson is deeply committed to the purpose for which the theological disciplines exist—namely, "to serve the people of God,"[167] which includes preaching and polemics.

PREACHING AND THE THEOLOGICAL DISCIPLINES

Carson, a former pastor, is a preacher.[168] He explained in 1997,

---

163 "Systematic Theology and Biblical Theology," 103.
164 "The Bible and Theology," 2324.
165 "The Bible and Theology," 2324.
166 "Approaching the Bible," 12.
167 "The Role of Exegesis in Systematic Theology," 71.
168 "The Role of Exegesis in Systematic Theology," 70–72; "Christian Witness in an Age of Pluralism," 31–66; *The Cross and Christian Ministry: Leadership Lessons from 1 Corinthians* (Grand Rapids, MI: Baker, 2004); "The Challenge from Pluralism to the Preaching of the Gospel," *Criswell Theological Review* 7 (1993): 99–117; "The Challenge from the Preaching of the Gospel to Pluralism," *Criswell Theological Review* 7 (1994): 15–39; "Preaching," 145–59; *Gagging of God,* 491–514; "The SBJT Forum: What Do You Consider to Be the Essential Elements of an Expository Sermon?," *Southern Baptist Journal of Theology* 3, no. 2 (1999): 93–96; "Athens Revisited,"

I see myself first and foremost as a pastor, not a professional scholar or writer. The Lord called me to gospel ministry. Three times I have been involved in church planting, and I served a church as pastor before embarking on doctoral studies. If I now teach at a seminary, it is because for the time being I believe the Lord wants me to train other pastors and Christian leaders. But although I may remain here for the rest of my working life, I would certainly not rule out the possibility of a return to pastoring a local church. That is the front line, and there are times when working in a quarter-master's slot (which is where I am) prompts me to examine my own priorities.[169]

Carson has maintained a busy international speaking schedule by regularly preaching and lecturing in a variety of forums with audiences consisting of scholars, pastors, laymen, and university students—both Christians and non-Christians.[170] "There is a sense," Carson explains, "in which the best expository preaching ought also to be the best exemplification of the relationship between biblical exegesis and systematic theology."[171] When expounding a passage, "the first priority is to explain what the text meant when it was written . . . and to apply it, utilizing sound principles . . . to contemporary life."[172] The second priority is to trace how various motifs in that passage develop across the storyline of God's progressive revelation "with some thoughtful reflection and application on the resulting synthesis."[173] Merely to exegete a passage and stop there "would be to fail at the same task" because

---

in *Telling the Truth: Evangelizing Postmoderns* (Grand Rapids, MI: Zondervan, 2000), 384–98; "The Challenges of the Twenty-First-Century Pulpit," in *Preach the Word: Essays on Expository Preaching: In Honor of R. Kent Hughes* (Wheaton, IL: Crossway, 2007), 172–89; "Preaching the Gospels," in *Preaching the New Testament*, ed. Ian Paul and David Wenham (Downers Grove, IL: InterVarsity, 2013), 17–32.

169 "The SBJT Forum: How Does Your Role as a Scholar, Teacher and Writer Fulfill the Great Commission?," *Southern Baptist Journal of Theology* 1, no. 4 (1997): 73. See esp. *Memoirs of an Ordinary Pastor*.

170 Over 550 of Carson's sermons and lectures are available for free as MP3s at www.thegospel coalition.org. For an explanation, see Andy Naselli, "D. A. Carson MP3s Now Hosted by TGC," *Andy Naselli* (blog), http://andynaselli.com/.

171 "The Role of Exegesis in Systematic Theology," 71.

172 "The Role of Exegesis in Systematic Theology," 71.

173 "The Role of Exegesis in Systematic Theology," 71. Cf. "Preaching," 151–54, 160.

the best expository preaching begins with the text at hand but seeks to establish links not only to the immediate context but also to the canonical context, *as determined by the biblico-theological constraints largely governed by the canon itself.* If these lines are sketched out in the course of regular, expository ministry, believers begin to see how their Bibles cohere. With deft strokes, the preacher is able to provide a *systematic* summary of the teaching to be learned, the ethics to be adopted, the conduct to be pursued, *not* by curtailing either exegesis or biblical theology, but by developing these disciplines on the way toward synthesis.[174]

The pressing need in contemporary evangelism to postmoderns is to "start further back and nail down the turning points in redemptive history," give primacy to BT rather than ST, herald "the rudiments of the historic gospel," and "think through what to say" *and* "how to live" (i.e., "contextualization").[175] BT is primary because the gospel "is virtually incoherent unless it is securely set into a biblical worldview."[176] Preaching today should often take a BT approach because modern audiences are largely biblically illiterate and do not understand the Bible's storyline. This is largely what motivated Carson's fourteen-part seminar "The God Who Is There," which simultaneously evangelizes non-Christians and edifies Christians by explaining the Bible's storyline in a nonreductionistic way.[177]

POLEMICS AND THE THEOLOGICAL DISCIPLINES

Carson is committed to contextualizing theology, which occasionally involves engaging in controversial theological debates.[178] He represents his opponents accurately and respectfully and then sheds light on

174 "The Role of Exegesis in Systematic Theology," 71–72.

175 *Gagging of God*, 496–511.

176 *Gagging of God*, 502; cf. 193–345, 496–505, 542–44; "Christian Witness in an Age of Pluralism," 60–64; "Approaching the Bible," 4; "Is the Doctrine of *Claritas Scripturae* Still Relevant Today?," in *Dein Wort ist die Wahrheit: Beiträge zu einer schriftgemäßen Theologie*, ed. Eberhard Hahn, Rolf Hille, and Heinz-Werner Neudorfer (Wuppertal: Brockhaus Verlag, 1997), 109.

177 *The God Who Is There* and *The God Who Is There: Finding Your Place in God's Story* (Grand Rapids, MI: Baker, 2010). MP3s and videos of the fourteen sessions are available for free at https://www.thegospelcoalition.org/.

178 He briefly reflects on polemical theology in "Editorial," *Themelios* 34, no. 2 (2009): 155–57.

sensitive, divisive subjects. Hot topics he addresses include divorce,[179] KJV-onlyism,[180] new hermeneutical trends,[181] church divisions,[182] questionable bibliology,[183] poor exegesis,[184] miraculous spiritual gifts like tongues,[185] complementarianism,[186] the Jesus Seminar,[187] assurance of salvation,[188] Bible translation,[189] imputation,[190] postmodernism and the emerging church,[191] and the changing notion of tolerance.[192]

Carson insists that Christians must adopt a biblical stance "regardless of how unpopular it is likely to be," especially with reference to postmodernism.[193] "Too little reading, especially the reading of older confessional material, not infrequently leads to in an infatuation with current agendas, to intoxication by the over-imbibing of the merely faddish."[194] With reference "to doctrine and cognitive truth," Carson does not shy away from drawing lines "thoughtfully, carefully, humbly, corrigibly" yet boldly.[195]

---

179 "Divorce: A Concise Biblical Analysis," *Northwest Journal of Theology* 4 (1975): 43–59.

180 *The King James Version Debate: A Plea for Realism* (Grand Rapids, MI: Baker, 1978).

181 "Hermeneutics"; *Gagging of God*.

182 "The Doctrinal Causes of Divisions in Our Churches," *Banner of Truth* 218 (November 1981): 7–19.

183 "Gundry on Matthew: A Critical Review," *Trinity Journal* 3 (1982): 71–91; "Three Books on the Bible: A Critical Review"; "Unity and Diversity in the New Testament"; "Recent Developments in the Doctrine of Scripture"; "Three More Books on the Bible: A Critical Review," *Trinity Journal* 27 (2006): 1–62.

184 *Exegetical Fallacies*.

185 *Showing the Spirit*; "The Purpose of Signs and Wonders in the New Testament," in *Power Religion: The Selling Out of the Evangelical Church?* (Chicago: Moody, 1992), 89–118.

186 "'Silent in the Churches': On the Role of Women in 1 Corinthians 14:33b–36," in *Recovering Biblical Manhood and Womanhood: A Response to Evangelical Feminism* (Westchester, IL: Crossway, 1991), 140–53, 487–90.

187 "Five Gospels, No Christ," *Christianity Today* 38, no. 5 (April 1994): 30–33.

188 "Reflections on Assurance," 247–76.

189 *The Inclusive-Language Debate: A Plea for Realism* (Grand Rapids, MI: Baker, 1998).

190 "The Vindication of Imputation: On Fields of Discourse and Semantic Fields," in *Justification: What's at Stake in the Current Debates* (Downers Grove, IL: InterVarsity, 2004), 46–78.

191 *Gagging of God*; "Domesticating the Gospel," 82–97; *Becoming Conversant with the Emerging Church*.

192 *The Intolerance of Tolerance* (Grand Rapids, MI: Eerdmans, 2012); "More Examples of Intolerant Tolerance," *Themelios* 37, no. 3 (2012): 439–41; "The Woman from Kentucky," *Themelios* 41, no. 2 (2016): 209–13.

193 *Gagging of God*, 347; cf. 347–67.

194 "Subtle Ways to Abandon the Authority of Scripture in Our Lives," 9.

195 *Gagging of God*, 365–66; cf. 438–39, 238; "Athens Revisited," 387; *Becoming Conversant with the Emerging Church*, 234.

Spiritual Experience and the Theological Disciplines

Since interpreters are inseparable from the interpretive process, their attitude toward the text is significant. What is the difference between the theological method of a believer and an unbeliever (e.g., an evangelical and an atheist)? Will their assessments differ? The answer is not that believers always interpret the text more accurately.[196]

Unbelieving exegetes and theologians must confront four barriers:[197]

1. The peer pressure that unbelievers experience may affect their approach to the Bible. It takes courage "to break away" from a vast number of unbelieving scholars whose "approach to scriptural exegesis . . . is fundamentally uncommitted."[198]
2. Unbelievers may try to understand "God's gracious self-disclosure . . . on its own terms," but that is insufficient if they do not "respond to God as he has disclosed himself."[199]
3. Unbelievers face more than just intellectual barriers; others include "spiritual experience (or lack of it)" and "moral defection."[200] A theologian's sexual morality likely has a bearing on how he configures what the Bible says about sex: "Spiritual, moral experience may not only shape one's systematic theology but may largely constrain what one actually 'hears' in the exegesis of Scripture."[201]
4. Unbelievers have not embraced the gospel and thus do not approach the text with a worldview that is spiritually discerning (1 Cor. 2:14). They have an entirely different "way of looking at reality."[202] They prefer to master the gospel rather than be "mastered by it."[203]

---

196 "The Role of Exegesis in Systematic Theology," 67.

197 "The Role of Exegesis in Systematic Theology," 67–70.

198 "The Role of Exegesis in Systematic Theology," 67.

199 "The Role of Exegesis in Systematic Theology," 67; cf. 67–69; "Approaching the Bible," 10.

200 "The Role of Exegesis in Systematic Theology," 69. Cf. "Approaching the Bible," 12; *Becoming Conversant with the Emerging Church*, 118.

201 "The Role of Exegesis in Systematic Theology," 69.

202 "The Role of Exegesis in Systematic Theology," 70.

203 "The Role of Exegesis in Systematic Theology," 70. Cf. "Recent Developments in the Doctrine of Scripture," 47; "*Claritas Scripturae*," 109–11.

Regarding Carson's own spiritual experience and theology, he is both scholarly and devotional.[204] He refuses to separate what God has joined together—namely, serious theological study and spirituality.[205] "Scholarship without humility and obedience is arrogant; talk of knowing and loving God without scholarship is ignorant."[206]

"The aim is *never* to become a master of the Word, but to be mastered by it."[207] Carson aims to be academically responsible more than academically respectable, and his scholarship is ultimately about glorifying God by serving Christ's church.[208]

Conclusion

I began this essay by explaining that it focuses on describing—not critiquing—Carson's theological method. You might be thinking, "How would you evaluate Carson's theological method? What do you think of it?" My answer will disappoint those looking for a devastating critique, and I do not mean to sound hagiographic. I think that Carson's theological method is outstanding and that his first-class work is the fruit. Both his method and product are worthy of imitating. That is why in my book on how to interpret and apply the Bible (to which Carson wrote the foreword), I attempt to unpack the theological method I learned from Carson.[209]

Carson's theological method is so rigorous that it is daunting. The way Carson describes a New Testament theologian, for example, is formidable:

204 "The Scholar as Pastor," 71–106.

205 "Approaching the Bible," 18–19. Cf. Köstenberger, "D. A. Carson," 359, 366–67.

206 "The Scholar as Pastor," 77.

207 "The Scholar as Pastor," 91. Cf. "The Trials of Biblical Studies," in *The Trials of Theology: Becoming a "Proven Worker" in a Dangerous Business* (Fearn, Scotland: Christian Focus, 2010), 109–29. For a summary of the chapter, see Andy Naselli, "Carson on the Trials of Biblical Studies," March 25, 2010, Gospel Coalition, https://www.thegospelcoalition.org/.

208 "Is there not an important responsibility to ask, each time I put pen to paper, whether what I write pleases the God of Scripture, the God of all truth, rather than worry about how my academic colleagues will react?" "The Role of Exegesis in Systematic Theology," 68. Cf. Andrew David Naselli, "Three Reflections on Evangelical Academic Publishing," *Themelios* 39, no. 3 (2014): 428–54.

209 Andrew David Naselli, *How to Understand and Apply the New Testament: Twelve Steps from Exegesis to Theology* (Phillipsburg, NJ: P&R Publishing, 2017). See also Jason S. DeRouchie, Oren R. Martin, and Andrew David Naselli, *40 Questions about Biblical Theology*, 40 Questions (Grand Rapids, MI: Kregel, 2020).

Those who write NT theology should ideally become intimately acquainted with the text of the NT, develop a profound grasp of the historical (including social and cultural) frameworks in which the NT books were written, maintain and sharpen the horizon provided by the entire canon, foster literary skills that permit varied genres to speak for themselves, spot literary devices and correctly interpret them, learn to fire imagination and creativity in a disciplined way and acknowledge and seek to accommodate and correct their own cultural and theological biases. All of these elements must be maintained in appropriate balance, nurtured by love for God and fear of God and growing hunger to serve his people.[210]

One wonders if a thorough, relatively comprehensive ST is even possible for a single theologian. It is hard not to come away from studying Carson's theological method with discouraging thoughts such as, "Wow. Who is gifted enough to do all that? Who is able to master exegesis, BT (both Old Testament and New Testament theology), HT, ST, and PT?" Not too far into the exercise, I experience information overload and admit that I cannot master it all. It takes a unique individual to be able to work competently with so much data and to account for Scripture's unity and diversity. It seems impossible to be an expert on both the forest as a whole as well as on all the individual species of trees. Carson recognizes that "the sheer volume of material" is challenging[211] and that "Christians need each other; this is as true in the hermeneutical arena as elsewhere. . . . Responsible interpretation of Scripture must never be a solitary task."[212]

While it is intimidating to do theology as rigorously as Carson describes, it is also hard for us not to come away encouraged for at least three reasons:

1. Carson's example is inspiring. He motivates us to consecrate ourselves to God by employing the theological disciplines "as good stewards of God's varied grace" (1 Pet. 4:10 ESV).
2. God has graced us with gifts to the church like Carson. Instead of feeling jealous or disheartened, we should feel grateful. We should thank God for his kindness to us. One NT scholar who is a close

---

210 "New Testament Theology," 810.
211 "An Introduction to Introductions," 17.
212 "Approaching the Bible," 12, 18; cf. "Current Issues in Biblical Theology," 35.

friend of Carson's shared an insight with me in 2006. He occasionally struggles with feeling inadequate as a New Testament scholar who has not been as prolific as Carson. But he overcomes that feeling by recognizing that God graced him with gifts to the church like Carson. Instead of feeling depressed and inadequate because of scholars like Carson, we should gratefully serve God with the gifts he has given us and not feel inferior for the childish reason that we are not as gifted as someone else. As Paul writes to the Corinthians, "All things are yours, whether Paul or Apollos or Cephas or the world or life or death or the present or the future—all are yours, and you are Christ's, and Christ is God's" (1 Cor. 3:21–23 ESV).

3. Carson continues to build up the church. I thank God that he has preserved Carson's health in his late seventies. If Jesus does not return and if Carson's health continues, Carson plans to continue equipping the church with even more books and articles. Would you pray that God will help Carson be faithful and fruitful to the end?

2

Prophetic from the Center

D. A. Carson's Vision for the Gospel Coalition

Collin Hansen

THE NORTH AMERICAN CHURCH LEADERS who would become the council of the Gospel Coalition (TGC) first met on the campus of Trinity Evangelical Divinity School (TEDS) from May 17 to 19, 2005. Along with his friend Tim Keller, Don Carson issued forty invitations. All forty showed up.[1]

Carson and Keller settled on this plan about ten days before the terrorist attacks of September 11, 2001.[2] They were meeting in New York City to discuss *Worship by the Book*, edited by Carson with Keller as a contributor.[3] They had spoken together in the UK for the Evangelical Ministry Assembly, organized by Proclamation Trust, but they didn't know any similar gathering of North American pastors. What could result from church leaders in the broadly Reformed tradition as they met every year to talk, pray, and learn together? The invitation noted, "It is difficult to think of a regular national gathering or conference or publication or institution that is driven by a rich heritage of biblical theology combined with pastoral commitment to seriously and creatively address the present generation."[4]

1 Don Carson, email message to the author, October 12, 2022.
2 Author's notes from 2005 Pastors' Colloquium, May 17, 2005.
3 D. A. Carson, ed. *Worship by the Book* (Grand Rapids, MI: Zondervan, 2002).
4 Undated draft invitation in the author's possession.

At the time, Carson was better known than Keller, who had not yet published widely. However, Carson explained that Keller, a New York church planter, had demonstrated a helpful knack for explaining sin in postmodern contexts.[5] Three years later Keller released his first two bestselling books, *The Reason for God* and *The Prodigal God*.[6]

The question before this group convened in suburban Chicago was whether they could or even should rally around a new organization. Was someone already fulfilling this purpose? How much theology did they need to hold in common? What would their meetings accomplish? How could they encourage evangelicals still battling liberal theology in mainline denominations? How could they connect evangelicals laboring faithfully in their smaller conservative denominations?[7]

In an exposition of Luke 5:12–13, Keller began the discussion by explaining how Reformed leadership fractured in the aftermath of Jonathan Edwards's death in 1758.[8] As the greatest American theologian to date, Edwards held together theological orthodoxy, experiential revivalism, and cultural apologetics. He critiqued Enlightenment philosophers while writing and preaching in ways that communicated the gospel in an emerging transatlantic culture. After Edwards died, however, his followers splintered into three different groups, Keller explained. The Princeton theologians were strong on confessional theology but not on cultural apologetics. Jonathan Edwards Jr. and the New England theologians advanced cultural apologetics with more vigor than confessional Calvinism. Charles Finney and like-minded revivalists of the Second Great Awakening claimed Edwards as their inspiration but dismissed his cultural apologetics and confessional theology.[9]

Keller saw the same fracturing in 2005 among American evangelicals. Some, especially the Reformed leaders gathered at TEDS, marched under the banner of confessional theology. Other evangelicals eagerly sought to

---

5   Author's notes from 2005 Pastors' Colloquium.

6   Timothy Keller, *The Reason for God: Belief in an Age of Skepticism* (New York: Viking, 2008); Timothy Keller, *The Prodigal God: Recovering the Heart of the Christian Faith* (New York: Viking, 2008).

7   Author's notes from 2005 Pastors' Colloquium, May 18, 2005.

8   Author's notes from 2005 Pastors' Colloquium, May 17, 2005.

9   Mark A. Noll, "Jonathan Edwards and Nineteenth-Century Theology," in *Jonathan Edwards and the American Experience*, ed. Nathan O. Hatch and Harry S. Stout (Oxford: Oxford University Press, 1988), 260–88.

change the perception of Christians through savvy cultural engagement and social justice initiatives. A third group promoted big events filled with evangelistic fervor using the latest technological methods. But who would bring together the best of these three groups? Who would inherit the full mantle of Edwards in the twenty-first century?

Reasons for Hope

In his own address, Carson offered a potted history of Western Christianity from the end of the Second World War to the turn of the century.[10] He observed that between 1880 and 1930, evangelicals lost their hold on nearly every seminary. Yet by the twenty-first century, half of all master of divinity students were evangelical. Carson attributed that change, largely concentrated since 1960, to parachurch ministries that reached evangelicals in mainline denominations. Leaders in the room represented the fruit of those neoevangelical efforts, including Kenneth Kantzer's work to make TEDS a leading global seminary. Keller had attended Gordon-Conwell Theological Seminary, led by Harold John Ockenga. Many of these leaders read and had written for *Christianity Today* magazine, founded by Billy Graham and initially edited by Carl F. H. Henry. *Christianity Today* under Henry had incorporated the wide breadth of evangelicals but still spoke with a "prophetic voice from the center," Carson said.[11]

Even though these leaders might feel like their cause had suffered, due to a secularizing culture and confusion over the meaning of "evangelicalism," Carson found reasons for hope as he surveyed the scene. Compared to fifty years ago, biblical commentaries abounded, especially those written by evangelicals committed to confessional theology. A diverse evangelicalism cried out for biblical and historical definition, rooted in the gospel and in the Reformation tradition. When evangelicals attend church and read their Bibles, Carson said, they stand out from the world as moral exemplars. The ongoing shift toward cultural relativism in North America would reveal itself as morally bankrupt through intolerance. The decline of denominations opened opportunities for new associations as Christians no longer looked for their traditional church when they moved. The rise of peripheral voices

---

10 Author's notes from 2005 Pastors' Colloquium, May 17, 2005.
11 Author's notes from 2005 Pastors' Colloquium.

such as the emerging church would stir hope in the gospel itself. Carson cited theonomy as a trend within the Reformed community that called for renewed attention to core theological confessions. Population decline in Europe suggested to Carson that the future of the church would be urban and multiethnic.

Back in North America, many suggested in the aftermath of President George W. Bush's reelection victory in 2004 that cultural polarization had never been worse. But Carson recalled the Vietnam War and saw an opportunity for the church to speak truth without succumbing to political captivity on either side. And while organized religion was in decline, most Americans still claimed to be spiritual. This meant that even though they understood personal freedom in self-help terms, perhaps Christian formation could guide them toward more noble purposes.

As Carson delivered his talk, the most controversial public matter of personal freedom concerned homosexuality. President Bush's reelection victory had been fueled by so-called values voters. Not for another seven years would same-sex marriage win a popular election. Even California voted down same-sex marriage three years later in 2008 as President Barack Obama replaced Bush. Yet Carson foresaw that homosexuality could become in the twenty-first century what indulgences had been in the sixteenth-century Reformation. Homosexuality could be the "trigger issue" that led to deeper division over biblical authority and ultimately a split across the entire Western church.[12]

Carson turned out to be more prescient than anyone in the room could have imagined at the time. Denominations have indeed split in ways not seen since the American Civil War and even the Reformation. Considering this threat, how could these pastors organize a prophetic movement calling churches back to the center of the gospel? Would they need a confessional statement? A theological vision for ministry? A new publication along the lines of *Christianity Today* that explored contemporary theology and ministry trends and shared creative, hopeful, doctrinally rooted proposals? Regional networks that collaborated on church planting and campus ministry and discipleship resources? A national conference for church leaders that modeled expositional preaching but also shared practical tips

12 Author's notes from 2005 Pastors' Colloquium.

on such concerns as cross-cultural ministry? Could they wield emerging technology through the internet for greater global impact?

Less than five years later, they had already answered every question, "Yes!"

Never Assume

As Carson crafted his initial invite list, he sought pastors who shared commitment to preaching expository sermons, teaching the whole counsel of God, and rooting their churches in theological and historical traditions while maintaining a contemporary feel. Though he knew many of them, they didn't yet know each other. And they didn't have a means of sharing what they learned with the broader church.

In 2007, many of the same pastors from the 2005 meeting reconvened as TGC to finalize their foundation documents and host their first public conference.[13] Carson's inaugural address as president, titled "Prophetic from the Center," exposited the gospel of Jesus Christ from 1 Corinthians 15:1–19.[14]

Carson examined several reasons why churches lose focus on the gospel. Perhaps his most memorable warning came as he explained "the tendency to *assume* the gospel . . . while devoting creative energy and passion to other issues—marriage, happiness, prosperity, evangelism, the poor, wrestling with Islam, wrestling with the pressures of secularization, bioethics, dangers on the left, dangers on the right—the list is endless."[15]

But as every teacher knows, students don't remember everything. They remember what their teacher loves most. "If the gospel is merely assumed, while relatively peripheral issues ignite our passion, we will train a new generation to downplay the gospel and focus zeal on the periphery," Carson said. "It is easy to sound prophetic from the margins; what is urgently needed is to *be* prophetic from the center."[16]

It's not that the peripheral issues don't matter, Carson explained. It's that they only come into focus when we're centered on the gospel. Same-sex marriage, then, deserves the church's attention. But churches should prioritize the gospel so they can develop proper perspective on same-sex marriage.

---

13   "Foundation Documents," Gospel Coalition, https://www.thegospelcoalition.org/.
14   Later published in D. A. Carson, *Prophetic from the Center: The Gospel of Jesus Christ in 1 Corinthians 15:1–19* (Deerfield, IL: Gospel Coalition, 2016).
15   Carson, *Prophetic from the Center*, 3.
16   Carson, *Prophetic from the Center*, 3.

And if they're focusing on the gospel, that means they're devoted to a "nexus of [theological] themes—God, sin, wrath, death, and judgment"—found in 1 Corinthians 15:3.[17] "Whatever else the cross achieves," Carson said, "it must rightly set aside God's sentence, it must rightly satisfy God's wrath, or it achieves nothing."[18] Indeed, these doctrines show us that we're not saved by our thoughts about God. We're saved by Christ himself. That's good news for sinners.

In this vision for TGC, Carson underscored the transformation that this good news brings about for individual Christians and their churches. "Humility, gratitude, dependence on Christ, contrition—these are the characteristic attitudes of the truly converted, the matrix out of which Christians experience joy and love," Carson said. "When the gospel truly does its work, 'proud Christian' is an unthinkable oxymoron."[19]

TGC, Carson explained, wouldn't tout itself as different from everything that had come before. The leaders of TGC would celebrate the inevitable victory of Jesus the king by boldly advancing his gospel under the contested reign of this fallen world. They would trust the gospel to shape the church into a foretaste of heaven in diverse ways. Carson said,

> A Christianity where believers are not patient and kind, a Christianity where believers characteristically envy, are proud and boastful, rude, easily angered, and keep a record of wrongs, is no Christianity at all. What does this say, in concrete terms, about the communion of saints, the urgent need to create a Christian community that is profoundly counter-cultural? What will this say about inter-generational relationships? About race? About how we treat one another in the local church? About how we think of brothers and sisters in highly diverse corners of our heavenly Father's world?[20]

This work would be left for churches affiliated with TGC to figure out in future years. They would be guided by TGC's foundation documents, with Carson as the initial drafter of the confessional statement.

---

17   D. A. Carson, "What is the Gospel?," Gospel Coalition, May 28, 2007, https://www.thegospel coalition.org/.

18   Carson, *Prophetic from the Center*, 14.

19   Carson, *Prophetic from the Center*, 27.

20   Carson, *Prophetic from the Center*, 33.

Reforming to Conform

TGC's theological vision for ministry never claimed to speak for all Christians in all places at all times. It's contextual by definition, occupying the middle space between unchanging doctrine and temporal practice. In the preamble from 2007, the founding council members of TGC identified several threats to keeping the gospel central to church life: personal consumerism, politicized faith, and theological and moral relativism. They lamented how power and affluence had replaced celebration of union with Christ. And they didn't find a viable alternative in monastic retreats into ritual, liturgy, and sacrament. Rather, TGC leaders committed to reforming their ministry practices to conform fully to Scripture. They returned to their Reformation roots, saying, "We have committed ourselves to invigorating churches with new hope and compelling joy based on the promises received by grace alone through faith alone in Christ alone."[21] Since 2007, TGC's confessional statement has been adopted by thousands of individual churches, regional networks across North America, and international coalitions in Europe, Africa, Asia, Australia, and North and South America.

Unlike many other confessions, TGC began with the doctrine of God before moving to revelation. As Carson and Keller later explained, they wanted to avoid a foundationalist approach to knowledge that owed more to the Enlightenment than to the Reformed tradition of John Calvin.[22] Even so, TGC would be distinguished by love and fidelity to God's word: "The Bible is to be believed, as God's instruction, in all that it teaches; obeyed, as God's command, in all that it requires; and trusted, as God's pledge, in all that it promises."[23]

Anyone who heard Carson's inaugural address would recognize the confession's description of the gospel as personal, apostolic, historical, theological, salvific, biblical, and Christological: "the gospel is not proclaimed if Christ is not proclaimed, and the authentic Christ has not been proclaimed if his death and resurrection are not central (the message is: 'Christ died for our sins . . . [and] was raised')."[24]

---

21 "Foundation Documents," Gospel Coalition, https://www.thegospelcoalition.org/.

22 D. A. Carson and Timothy Keller, *Gospel-Centered Ministry*, Gospel Coalition Booklets (Wheaton, IL: Crossway, 2011).

23 "Foundation Documents." Gospel Coalition.

24 "Foundation Documents," Gospel Coalition.

Though Carson worked most of his career as a professor for a parachurch ministry, TGC's confession centered the church in God's plan of redemption. It affirmed,

> The church is the body of Christ, the apple of his eye, graven on his hands, and he has pledged himself to her forever.... The church serves as a sign of God's future new world when its members live for the service of one another and their neighbors, rather than for self-focus. The church is the corporate dwelling place of God's Spirit, and the continuing witness to God in the world.[25]

Through the church, the world catches a glimpse of their true and coming King: "The kingdom of God is an invasive power that plunders Satan's dark kingdom and regenerates and renovates through repentance and faith the lives of individuals rescued from that kingdom."[26]

Carson pushed back against kingdom-oriented narrative theology that undervalues the atoning and justifying work of Christ. But he also criticized systematic theology that fails to trace biblical themes through God's unfolding plan of redemption. Through TGC, Carson pointed Christians toward the "big story of Scripture" so they could see "the God who is there."[27] In his booklet titled *Gospel-Centered Ministry*, written with Keller, Carson explained that biblical theology flows toward Jesus and his gospel, while Christian life and thought flow from Jesus and his gospel.[28] Along with the other council members of TGC, Carson and Keller wanted to encourage Bible reading and preaching that traces the trajectories of Scripture to reveal patterns and promises that take us to Jesus and his gospel. Then, from the gospel, we can align our situation with God's solution. "In short, gospel-centered ministry is biblically mandated," they wrote, "It is the only kind of ministry that simultaneously addresses human need as God sees it, reaches out in unbroken lines to gospel-ministry in other centuries and other cultures, and makes central what Jesus himself establishes as central."[29]

---

25 "Foundation Documents," Gospel Coalition.

26 "Foundation Documents," Gospel Coalition.

27 D. A. Carson, *The God Who Is There: Finding Your Place in God's Story* (Grand Rapids, MI: Baker, 2010).

28 Carson and Keller, *Gospel-Centered Ministry*.

29 D. A. Carson and Timothy Keller, eds., *The Gospel as Center: Renewing Our Faith and Reforming Our Ministry Practices* (Wheaton, IL: Crossway, 2012), 21.

Through TGC, the term "gospel-centered" has become a fixture of the evangelical lexicon. "We wanted to build a community of churches and pastors in which the gospel was the central thing, the exciting thing, what we got out of bed for in the morning," Carson told me.[30] This community, in Carson's vision, would never assume the gospel or drift toward a minimal understanding that overlooks other entailed doctrines. TGC would speak to the broader church but from the Reformed heritage. In keeping with Reformed theology, this gospel would speak to all of life, but in such a way that tied the cross and resurrection to contemporary challenges such as social justice.

The relationship between the organization called TGC and the gospel itself has sometimes confused observers. Carson has explained that TGC never sought to be a boundary-bounded set, meaning a group fixed on who's inside and outside.[31] Instead, he cast a vision for TGC as a center-bounded set, which is less concerned about the periphery than a robust gospel definition at the center. Thus, anyone could read the website or attend the annual conference if they found something useful. But for TGC's institutional leaders, he expected robust allegiance to the gospel core.

I'll never forget when he hired me in the summer of 2010. He was clear that if I ever transgressed the foundation documents, I would lose my job as editorial director. But beyond that core, I was free to feature differences and even debate. And that's how he led as the president. Even when he asked me to publish one particularly controversial article, he never thought it was the only or final word on the subject. He expected that peripheral matters would be treated as peripheral, even as we sought to work out the implications of the gospel for each new day's challenges.

Something Constructive

Carson has often observed that TGC grew more quickly than he anticipated. But more than fifteen years later, TGC looks much like Carson envisioned. An international network developed largely along the lines of Carson's decades of travel, with several friends initiating national TGC organizations in their home countries. His prodigious teaching and publishing built trust

30 D. A. Carson, email message to the author, March 17, 2021.
31 D. A. Carson, "Reflections on Confessionalism, Boundaries, and Discipline," Gospel Coalition, September 11, 2011, https://www.thegospelcoalition.org/.

among pastors who joined councils in French-speaking Europe, Canada, Australia, Italy, and many other regions he visited as TGC's president. Carson's focus on the gospel core allowed international coalitions to develop with close doctrinal affinity to each other and also independence to address the most pressing needs of their context.

The website played a supporting role in Carson's early hopes for TGC. But he took early steps to leverage the unique reach of the internet to promote gospel-centered ministry for the next generation. *Themelios*, a journal for students of theology and religion in Great Britain, ceased publication just as Carson was bringing TGC online. Published by the Universities and Colleges Christian Fellowship (UCCF) in Great Britain, *Themelios* couldn't justify the costs of printing and distributing as they mostly reached pastors instead of their core audience of students. Four groups bid to take over the brand of *Themelios*, which is Greek for "foundation" (see, for example, 1 Corinthians 3:11). In the end, UCCF chose TGC, which has published *Themelios* ever since as a free online journal for pastors as well as theological students. Every issue features columns, articles, and dozens of book reviews overseen by an international team of editors who ascribe to TGC's foundation documents.

Carson anticipated readership would multiply by a factor of 10 once the journal moved online under TGC. His goals were too modest. In 2022, *Themelios* attracted more than 1.9 million pageviews from readers in 235 countries.

Carson envisioned TGC's website as a simple way for friends in ministry to stay connected between conferences. None of us could have foreseen fifteen years ago the pandemic shutdown of March 2020, but as churches closed, in perhaps the greatest disruption to the Western church since the Black Plague in the Middle Ages, pastors looked online for help. In those bleak first two months, the TGC website served more than 11.2 million unique users with nearly 25 million pageviews, including an invitation to fast and pray for God's help. TGC now publishes one of the largest Christian websites in the world.

When Carson and Keller met to conceive what would become TGC, they wanted to help younger church leaders struggling to adjust to the rapidly changing world of the internet age. Just a generation ago, despite the tumult of the 1960s and '70s, even nominal Christians and unbelievers shared many moral assumptions with evangelicals. But that world has largely disappeared. Parents can hardly understand the world their children hold in their hands via smartphones. Secularism has become more unabashedly anti-Christian. Disagreement and indifference to evangelical beliefs have been replaced by anger and incredulity.

In 2011, Carson and Keller wrote,

> The American evangelical world has been breaking apart with wildly different responses to this new cultural situation. To oversimplify, some have simply built the fortress walls higher, merely continuing to do what they have always done, only more defiantly than before. Others have called for a complete doctrinal reengineering of evangelicalism. We think both of these approaches are wrong-headed and, worse, damaging to the cause of the gospel.[32]

Together, Carson and Keller set out to do something constructive. They called for the church to be prophetic from the center. They convened pastors who get out of bed each morning excited about the gospel. They envisioned the gospel spreading to all the world and applying to all of life. Their hopes became TGC, under Don Carson as the founding president.

---

32 Carson and Keller, *Gospel-Centered Ministry*, 8.

3

Should Pastors Today Still Care about the Reformation?

PASTORS DEVOTED TO THEIR MINISTRY have so many things to do. Apart from the careful preparation week by week of fresh sermons and Bible studies, hours set aside for counseling and administration, care in developing excellent relationships, careful and thoughtful (and time-consuming!) evangelism, the mentoring of another generation coming along behind, the incessant demands of administration and oversight—not to mention the nurturing of one's own soul—there is the regular array of family priorities, including care for aging parents, precious grandchildren, an ill spouse (or any number of permutations of such responsibilities), and, for some, energy levels declining in inverse proportion to advancing years. So why should busy pastors set aside valuable hours to read up on the Reformation, usually thought to have kicked off about five hundred years ago? True, the Reformers lived in rapidly changing times, but how many of them gave serious thought to postmodern epistemology, transgenderism, and the new (in)tolerance? If we are to learn from forebears, wouldn't we be wise to choose more recent forebears? I offer nine reasons why the Reformation still matters for today's pastors.[1]

1. A pastor is by definition something akin to a GP (a "general practitioner"). He is not a specialist in, say, divorce and remarriage, mission history, cultural commentary, and particular periods of church history.

---

1 This chapter was originally published as D. A. Carson, "Should Pastors Today Still Care about the Reformation?," *Themelios* 42, no. 3 (2017): 435–39.

Yet most pastors will have to develop competent introductory knowledge in all these areas as part of their application of the word of God to the people around them. Some pastors will feel the need to emphasize one area more than another: for example, a pastor living in a neighborhood with many Muslims will want to devote time and energy to understanding Islam; an Arnold Dallimore will devote forty years' worth of holidays to produce a magisterial two-volume work on George Whitefield. Nevertheless, pastoral ministry is much more akin to the work of a GP than to the work of an ear, nose, and, throat specialist or to that of a surgeon who does nothing but Mohs surgery. And that means he is obligated to devote some time each year to reading in broad areas. One of those areas is historical theology. Well-chosen historical literature exposes us to different cultures and times, expanding our horizons, enabling us to see how Christians in other times and places have thought through what the Bible says and how to apply the gospel to all of life. Keep reading! I was exposed to John Chrysostom and Athanasius of Alexandria when I was a young man; only in recent years have I read much more of them. Reading Reformation sources is one part of this happy privilege and responsibility.

2. More specifically, a growing knowledge of historical theology accomplishes wonders in destroying the illusion that insightful and rigorous exegesis began in the nineteenth or twentieth century. Not everything that was written five hundred years ago, or fifteen hundred years ago, is wholly admirable and worth repeating, any more than everything that is written today is wholly admirable. But such historical reading is the only effective antidote to the tragic attitude of one seminary (name withheld to protect the guilty) that long argued that its students needed to learn only good exegesis and responsible hermeneutics: they didn't need to learn what others think, for with exegesis and hermeneutics under their belt they could turn the crank and deliver faithful theology all by themselves. How naive to think that exegesis and hermeneutics are neutral, value-free disciplines! The reality is that we need to listen to other pastor-theologians, both from our own day and from the past, if we are to grow in richness, nuance, insight, self-correction, and gospel fidelity.

3. But why focus on the Reformation in particular? There are plenty of critics quite happy to write off the Reformation as a period with

merely antiquarian interest. One pundit at an Australian institution recently protested that the Reformation was a great disaster because it "killed missions." Sometimes one doesn't know whether to laugh or cry—but one thing is certain, such negations display no firsthand knowledge of the primary sources. More broadly, any serious exposure to the Reformers' writings makes it hard not to see the sweep and reach of the Reformation. Although it was triggered by the question of indulgences, debate over indulgences soon led, directly or indirectly, to probing debates on authority, the locus of revelation (Should we seize on a deposit ostensibly given to the church embracing both Scripture and tradition, or on *sola Scriptura*?), purgatory, the authority by which sins are forgiven, the treasury of satisfactions, the nature and locus of the church, the nature and authority of priest/presbyters, the nature and function of the Eucharist, saints, justification, sanctification, the nature of the new birth, the enslaving power of sin, and much more. All of these are still central issues in the theological syllabus today. Even the issue of indulgences is still important: both Pope Benedict and Pope Francis have offered plenary special indulgences under certain circumstances (though in a more restrained structure than that adopted by Tetzel). Moreover, the study of the Reformation is especially salutary as a response to those who think the so-called "Great Tradition," as preserved in the earliest ecumenical creeds, is invariably an adequate basis for ecumenical unity—as if there were no heresies invented after the fourth century. On this front, study of the Reformation usefully fosters a little historical realism.

4. In addition to the hermeneutical distinctiveness of the Reformation that sprang from *sola Scriptura*, the Reformers worked hard to develop a rigorous hermeneutic that was clear of the vagaries of the fourfold hermeneutic that crested during the Middle Ages. This does *not* mean they were simplistic literalists, unable to appreciate different literary genres, subtle metaphors, and other symbol-laden figures of speech; it means, rather, that they worked hard to let Scripture speak on its own terms, without allowing external methods to be imposed on the text like an extratextual grid designed to guarantee the "right" answers. In part, this was tied to their understanding of *claritas Scripturae*, the perspicuity of Scripture. Without in any sense reducing the

role of the teacher/preacher of Scripture, let alone the many perplexities of Scripture, they were convinced that Scripture does not need an authoritative interpretation of Scripture provided by the magisterium. Although contemporary discussions of hermeneutics largely focus on slightly different agendas, the parallels are striking. In particular, Calvin's commentaries are so adept at following the line of the text that they are still read appreciatively today.

5. It has been said that if you want good theology grounded in robust exegesis and expository preaching, turn to Reformed theology, but if you want spirituality, turn to Catholicism. In the past I have occasionally addressed that bifurcation.[2] Catholic theory on spirituality commonly distinguishes between the living of ordinary Catholics and the spiritual living of those who are really deeply committed Catholics. It's almost a Catholic version of "higher life" theology. It is said to lead to mystical connection to God and to be characterized by extraordinary spiritual practices and disciplines. But although I have read right through, say, Julian of Norwich, I find a great deal of subjective mysticism and virtually no grounding in Scripture or the gospel. And for the life of me I cannot imagine either Peter or Paul recommending monastic withdrawal in order to attain greater spirituality: it is always a danger when certain ascetic practices become normative paths to spirituality when there is no apostolic support for them. The contemporary generation, tired of merely cerebral approaches to Christianity, is drawn to late patristic and medieval patterns of spirituality. What a relief, then, to turn to the warmest of the writings of the Reformers and discover afresh the pursuit of God and his righteousness well-grounded in Holy Scripture. That is why Luther's letter to his barber remains such a classic: it is full of godly application of the gospel to ordinary Christians, building up a conception of spirituality that is not reserved for the elite of the elect but for all brothers and sisters in Christ. Similarly, the opening chapters of book 3 of Calvin's *Institutes* provide more profound reflection on true spirituality than many much longer contemporary volumes.

6. The Reformation is of central importance for understanding modern Western history. Three large-scale movements set the stage for the

---

2   For example, D. A. Carson, "When Is Spirituality Spiritual? Reflections on Some Problems of Definition," *Journal of the Evangelical Theological Society* 37 (1994): 381–94.

contemporary Western world: the Renaissance, the Reformation, and the Enlightenment. Each of the three is complex, and scholars continue to debate many facets of each. Nevertheless, the raw claim for the pivotal role of these three movements cannot easily be challenged. In addition to the focused clarity on the gospel fostered by the Reformation, many of its ideas—such as the emphasis on Scripture alone as the final authority and increased clarity on the distinguishable differences between giving to God and to Caesar their respective dues (which in turn led to developments in thought, some helpful and some unhelpful, on the relationships between church and state)—led directly or indirectly to Protestant denominations around the world, which in turn contributed, directly or indirectly, to worldwide missionary movements and to several European wars.

7. There are lessons to be learned from the Reformation about the sovereignty of God in movements of revival and reformation. After the fact, it is tempting to trace out what happened and view the sequence of events as almost inevitable—relatively simple arrays of cause and effect. We begin with Luther's Ninety-Five Theses and show the reasons why the Reformation unfolded the way it did. On the other hand, a little historical imagination easily conjures up an alternative world in which the posting of the Ninety-Five Theses proved to be nothing more than a damp squib. After all, there were other reformers and reform movements that showed early promise but largely sputtered out. John Wycliffe (c. 1320–1384) was a theologian, philosopher, churchman, ecclesiastical reformer, and Bible translator, and the work he did anticipated the Reformation, but it could not be said to have precipitated it. Jan Hus (1369–1415) was a Czech priest, reformer, scholar, rector of Charles University in Prague, and architect of a reforming movement, often called "Hussitism," but, of course, he was martyred and his movement, though important in Bohemia, achieved little more in Europe than predecessor status. Why did Luther, Calvin, and Zwingli live on long enough to give direction to a massive Reformation, while Bible translator William Tyndale (1494–1536) was murdered? Historical hindsight offers many reasons why this one lived and that one died, why this reforming action fizzled and that one ignited an irrepressible flame. The historical details are worth understanding, but the eyes of faith will see the hand of God in genuine reformation, and remind us

to offer him our praises for what he has done, and our petitions for what we still beg him to do.

8. The Reformation stands out as a movement that sought to integrate exegesis of the biblical books with what we would today call systematic theology. Not all the Reformers did this the same way. Some acted as if they were expounding the biblical texts, but tended in reality to jump from seminal word or phrase to the next seminal word or phrase, stopping at each point to unload theological treatments of the various "loci." Bucer, for example, followed the text more closely but also unloaded his treatment of the "loci" as he went along, making his commentaries extraordinarily long and dense. Calvin strove in his commentaries for what he called "lucid brevity,"[3] and he reserved his systematic theology primarily for what grew to become the four volumes of *Institutes of the Christian Religion*. Indeed, Calvin's commentaries are so bare bones that not a few scholars have criticized him for not including enough theology in them. But what is striking about all these Reformers, regardless of their successes or failures to bring about appropriate integration, is the way in which they simultaneously attempted to expound the Bible and engage in serious theologizing. By contrast, today few systematicians are excellent exegetes, and few exegetes evince much interest in systematic theology. The exceptions merely prove the rule. There are many reasons why the Reformers were models in this regard—but whatever the reasons, we have much to learn from them.

9. The Reformers read their own times well. While leaning on the "norming norm" of Holy Scripture, they truly understood where the fault lines lay in their own time and place. Some of the same issues prevail today. On the other hand, what we should take away from the Reformers in this regard is not simply the list of topics on which *they* majored, but the importance of understanding *our* times and learning how to engage our times with the truth of Scripture. Doubtless this is the place where it is worth including a few lines on some of the ways in which we should *not* slavishly seek to imitate the Reformers. Their agendas are not always ours, and should not be. Moreover, the mode of discourse they commonly

---

3   John Calvin, *Commentaries on the Epistle of Paul to the Romans*, trans. and ed. John Owen, Christian Classics Ethereal Library, https://ccel.org/.

deployed was far more inflamed then than what is acceptable today—though it is not always clear if the contemporary restraint is a function of increased tolerance and courtesy, or the result of apathy and indifference to truth. After all caveats have been entered, however, the degree of invective in the age of the Reformation, especially (but not exclusively) from the pen of Luther, was not admirable, and his anti-Semitism was utterly without excuse.

There are three wrong approaches to the Reformers and their writings. First, we may ignore them, but that will simply guarantee that we impoverish ourselves. Second, we may idolize them, but like all idolatries this one displeases God and guarantees we will not listen very well to other voices in the history of the church. Third, we may do no more than remind ourselves of their errors, failures, and shortcomings, and in consequence dismiss them with contempt; but if we treat all historical figures this way, consistency demands that we listen to no one, starting with ourselves.

There is so very much that is good in the Reformation heritage, even if I want to distance myself from parts of it. So let me end by mentioning a diversity of sources one may use to get started. The collected works of Luther are available digitally; my copy (given to me by a former student) is much cherished. If you want to warm yourself with Reformation spirituality, start with the wholly admirable book by Calvin: *A Little Book on the Christian Life*.[4] This is a fresh and delightful translation of several of the opening chapters of book 3 of the *Institutes*. I have read it through with the students in my spiritual formation group. Serious readers will want to scan some of Calvin's commentaries and work their way through the *Institutes*. At some juncture, it is important to read good biographies of the main players. For Luther, the standout volume is still that of Roland H. Bainton, *Here I Stand*.[5] I first read it when I was in seminary almost fifty years ago; my wife has also read it and found it no less gripping than I did. I have many biographies of Calvin; I cannot say which one is "best." Stimulating and challenging are the essays in the recent book, *The*

---

4 John Calvin, *A Little Book on the Christian Life*, ed. and trans. Aaron C. Denlinger and Burk Parsons (Sanford, FL: Reformation Trust, 2017).

5 Roland H. Bainton, *Here I Stand: A Life of Martin Luther* (New York: New American Library, 1950).

Reformation Then and Now.[6] For those wanting to immerse themselves in the way Genevan pastors, in the wake of Calvin's teaching and influence, gave themselves to pastoral ministry, one simply cannot do better than read Scott Manetsch, Calvin's *Company of Pastors*[7]—a work both scholarly and lucid, both informative and edifying.

Keep reading!

6   Eric Landry and Michael S. Horton, eds., *The Reformation Then and Now: 25 Years of Modern Reformation Articles Celebrating 500 Years of the Reformation* (Peabody, MA: Hendrickson, 2017).

7   Scott M. Manetsch, *Calvin's Company of Pastors: Pastoral Care and the Emerging Reformed Church, 1536–1609*, Oxford Studies in Historical Theology (New York: Oxford University Press, 2013).

4

Why the Local Church Is More Important Than TGC, White Horse Inn, 9Marks, and Maybe Even ETS

MOST OF US, I'M SURE, have heard the adage, "The church is the only human institution that continues into the new heavens and the new earth." It's the sort of adage with which no Christian can thoughtfully disagree, even though it is spectacularly fuzzy. Does "church" in that old adage refer to the universal church? If so, is the universal church rightly thought of as a "human institution"? It is certainly made up of humans, but it was not designed by humans. Is the universal church usefully thought of as an institution? Organism, company, body, assembly, yes—but institution? We all agree, I imagine, that Christians continue into the new heavens and the new earth, but if that's all we mean, why mention the church? The *body of Christians* continues into the new heavens and the new earth, the *assembly of Christians* continues into the new heavens and the new earth, but is it coherent to assert that the *institution of all Christians* everywhere continues into the new heavens and the new earth?[1]

Suppose, instead, that "church" in the adage, "The church is the only human institution that continues into the new heavens and the new earth"

---

1 This chapter was originally published as D. A. Carson, "Why the Local Church Is More Important than TGC, White Horse Inn, 9Marks, and Maybe Even ETS," *Themelios* 40, no. 1 (2015): 1–9. It was first delivered as a paper at the annual meeting of the Evangelical Theological Society in San Diego, CA (November 2014), alongside presentations from Mark Dever and Michael S. Horton on "The Local Church: Its Message, Marks, and Mission."

refers to the local church. But does the local church continue into the new heavens and the new earth? The answer to that question is going to depend pretty heavily on how we define "local church." Suppose, for argument's sake, that we adopt the three marks of the church defended by much Reformed thought: the church is the assembly where the gospel is faithfully preached, the sacraments are rightly observed, and faithful discipline is carried out. Will such a church continue into the new heaven and the new earth? Will the sacraments—or, if you prefer, the ordinances—then be practiced? If baptism is tied to conversion, surely no one will be eligible for baptism if no one is getting converted. If the Lord's Supper points forward "until he comes," what evidence is there that it will still be celebrated after he has come?

In short, the old adage with which I began this address is so beset with terminological challenges that its sole benefit lies in the domain of senti-mental reassurance rather than in the domain of clearheaded theological reflection. In exactly the same way, the slightly cheeky affirmation advanced by the title of this address easily becomes indefensible unless some termi-nological clarifications are introduced right away.

Terminological Clarifications

The title speaks of the relative importance of the local church, not the universal church: "Why the *local* church is more important than TGC (and all the rest)." No Christian would dispute the importance of the universal church. But two factors weigh against the practical ecclesiastical significance of such an avowal. First, there are surprisingly few references to the universal church in the NT. The overwhelming majority of the occurrences of the word "church" refer to local churches. Second, many Christians think of the universal church as the conglomerate collection of believers drawn from every age who ultimately gather around the throne of God; but, as wonderful as this notion is, such a definition provides little scope to assess the relative importance of the local church and of the Evangelical Theological Society (ETS) since both the local church and ETS, we hope, are made up of such believers. To derive lessons on the importance of the local church from the relatively few passages that refer to the universal church presupposes that one has sorted out the relationships between the two at a deeper level. That is an important subject worth exploring, but, at least at the popular level, it is not one that is well understood.

For instance, although the set of contrasts built into the relevant passage in Hebrews 12 is immensely evocative, precisely how do they help us think through our subject?

> You have not come to a mountain that can be touched and that is burn-ing with fire; to darkness, gloom and storm; to a trumpet blast or to such a voice speaking words that those who heard it begged that no further word be spoken to them, because they could not bear what was com-manded: "If even an animal touches the mountain, it must be stoned to death." The sight was so terrifying that Moses said, "I am trembling with fear." But you have come to Mount Zion, to the city of the living God, the heavenly Jerusalem. You have come to thousands upon thousands of angels in joyful assembly, to the church of the firstborn, whose names are written in heaven. You have come to God, the Judge of all, to the spirits of the righteous made perfect, to Jesus the mediator of a new covenant, and to the sprinkled blood that speaks a better word than the blood of Abel. (Heb. 12:18–24)

The driving contrast in these verses is between, on the one hand, the Mosaic covenant and, more broadly, the approach of the people of God in Old Testament times going all the way back to Abel and, on the other, the privileges of "the church of the firstborn" who gather neither at Sinai nor in the temple in Jerusalem but in the presence of God, in the presence of Jesus the mediator of a new covenant. The identification with him is so strong that the language is reminiscent of Ephesians: just as he is at the right hand of the majesty on high, so those who are in union with him are seated in the heavenlies. The focus, in other words, is on the universal church. There are, I contend, connections between the local church and such passages in Ephesians and Hebrews, but they are not widely recognized, so it is difficult to appeal to them in support of the title of this paper. Perhaps we may return to that in a few moments.

At the other end of the scale lies a different definition of the church that will equally lead us astray in our considerations. Instead of focusing on the universal church, some circles argue that the (local) church is the "assembly" of any Christians gathered together in Jesus's name. For example, two Christian businessmen meet on the platform of the Libertyville Metra station to commute to work in downtown Chicago. On the train they enjoy a quiet Bible study together. Here, surely, is the church. Did not Jesus say that where two or three are gathered together in his name, he himself is present in their midst?

Under such a definition of church, of course, it is impossible to argue that what we refer to as "the local church" is any more important than the assembly of Christians meeting on a university campus under the Cru banner, or the assembly of Christian doctors and nurses at a meeting of the Christian Medical Fellowship, or the assembly of Christians at the 2014 ETS conference. They are all "the church." In practice, this view of the definition of the church, intelligently held by relatively few but unthinkingly adopted by many, serves to reinforce Western individualism. We may rejoice in the presence of Christ when two or more Christians get together for Christian purposes, but it has little bearing on the church, or on the importance of the church as a body, as an institution.

Methodologically, this approach depends on creating a definition of "church" that relies on too narrow a selection of biblical texts, notably passages that speak of the presence of Christ where two or three are gathered together.

Suppose, however, we attempt a definition of church that is far more integrative—that depends on cautious and careful inferences drawn from the wide range of the use of ἐκκλησία in the Greek Bible and from other passages that contribute to the theme of the church even where the word ἐκκλησία is not found. How would our two businessmen on the Metra train look then?

For example, in Matthew 18 Jesus insists that where there is some sort of fault between two of his disciples, the way to deal with it ascends from personal discussion, to the use of others who serve as witnesses, to the final appeal, "tell it to the church" (v. 17). This church then has the authority to excommunicate the guilty party. In the concrete case of discipline portrayed in 1 Corinthians 5, the crucial step is taken "when you are assembled" (v. 4). "Tell it to the church" does not mean "Tell it to two Christian blokes on the Metra train."

Or again, from the pages of the New Testament it is reasonably transparent that there are offices in the church denoted by such labels as elder, pastor, overseer, and deacon. We may disagree on exactly how these offices are configured, but certainly the Pastoral Epistles, to go no further, outline their roles and characteristics in the local church—something that the "assembly" of our two blokes on the Metra train seem to be missing. If someone were to point out that on the first Pauline missionary journey recorded in Acts, the apostle and Barnabas plant churches in a number of cities and get around to appointing elders in those churches only on the return leg through the same cities (Acts 14:23) and therefore infer that one can have churches without the well-known designated officers, it would be a bit like trying to list the characteristics of human beings by referring only to babies. We want to insist that babies are human beings, but we don't think that the characteristics of babies constitute an adequate definition of the characteristics of human beings. In other words, to sustain the thesis in the title of this address, we need to avoid definitions of church that are indefensibly reductionistic.

That leads me, then, to offer four further considerations on the nature of the church.

1. We must say at least a little about what are traditionally called the marks of the church. In the Reformed heritage, borrowed nowadays by many others, there are three: the church is the assembly where the word is rightly taught, where the sacraments (some would say "ordinances") are rightly celebrated, and where discipline is practiced. These three were, of course, shaped in part by the experiences of the Reformers in the sixteenth century. On any "thick" reading of them, however, they presuppose synthetic argumentation. For example, the right teaching of the word of God, for the Reformers, not only questions the magisterial authority of the pope, but presupposes the careful and controlling exegesis of Scripture and the importance of the teaching office in the local church. This does not mean there is no sense in which lay Christians admonish one another, nor does it belittle the ways in which Christians edify one another even in the singing "to one another" (Eph. 5:19) of psalms, hymns, and spiritual songs (all part of what is today called word-based ministry), still less the importance of teaching the word of God, whether by catechism or other means, within the family, but it does recognize a distinctive role for pastors/elders/overseers who have been tested and set aside as those who rule over the church by means of the word.

2. The third mark, the discipline of the church, presupposes the urgency of preserving the church in faithfulness to God in both doctrine and life. One's understanding of how such discipline should be carried out will vary, depending not least on whether one is convinced by what is today called "the believers' church tradition" or by the typically Presbyterian view that holds the local church is made up of the new covenant community that is somewhat larger than the assembly of the elect and regenerate. Regardless of which view you take, discipline is nevertheless needed so that the church is not destroyed by the admission of purely nominal converts, false doctrine, and rampant immorality.

3. Whatever the debates among us, not only over the relative suitability of the words "sacraments" and "ordinances" but also over the precise significance of both baptism and the Lord's Supper, it is very important to our discussion to bring together three things that, in much current evangelical practice, are frequently separated—namely, conversion, baptism, and church membership. A word about each might be helpful. I am using "conversion" not in a purely sociological or phenomenological sense—in which one may convert to, say, Islam or Buddhism or Christianity with exactly the same semantic force—but in a theological sense in which Christian conversion is distinctive and frankly miraculous and works out in allegiance to Jesus Christ. One may convert to Islam by a simple act of will without any pretension of, say, Spirit-enacted regeneration. But in Christian conversion there is a decisive act of God in which an individual is regenerated and justified, and this works out in a change of allegiance and a change of direction. That can take place at any age; it may or may not be experienced as a remembered decisive moment. Nevertheless, we insist that a person either is or is not justified, either is or is not regenerated, even if we cannot always tell when this change occurs. In much evangelical life today, however, this conversion, regardless of when it takes place, is separated from Christian baptism. Ostensible converts declare they are not yet "ready" for baptism. The chronological gap between conversion and baptism may arise out of faulty understanding of both conversion and baptism, but also, as in the case of converts from Islam who live in Islamic cultures, out of the far more portentous and decisive significance of baptism in such cultures. But what is quite clear is that in the New Testament, all believers this side of Pentecost were baptized, and, so far as it was possible for the church to discern, only

believers were baptized. For the sake of simplifying the argument, I shall not here wrestle with the baptism of infants born into new-covenant families, but shall focus on the conversion of those with little or no connection with Christians or the church, for here both credobaptists and paedobaptists alike agree on the connection between conversion and baptism: from the pages of the New Testament it is difficult to warrant a substantial temporal disjunction between the two.

An example I frequently use with my students is drawn from the life of Billy Sunday. Sunday was a foulmouthed but popular baseball player who was soundly converted in the 1880s. Soon he was crisscrossing the country preaching a potent mixture of evangelistic gospel and prohibition (eventually passed in 1919) under the shade of a huge tent. Experience soon taught him that if he pitched his tent on dry ground, when hundreds of people came forward at the end of his meetings, enough dust was kicked up that some people started coughing and sneezing and thereby spoiling the decorum. Alternatively, if he pitched his tent when the ground was wet, the advancing hundreds could churn the walkways to mud, and it was not unknown for some would-be converts to slip and fall. So it became the practice to put sawdust down in all the aisles, making them both dustproof and slip-proof. Out of this expedient arose the expression, "to hit the sawdust trail." If you professed faith at a Billy Sunday meeting, your experience could be labeled "hitting the sawdust trail." So ubiquitous did that expression become that even secular journals sometimes referred to born-again types as those who had hit the sawdust trail. Ask a person when he or she was converted, and they might reply, "I hit the sawdust trail in Cincinnati in 1913"—even though that person had never attended a Billy Sunday meeting. In other words, to hit the sawdust trail stood, by metonymy, for conversion.

Although baptism in the New Testament has far more resonances with conversion than does hitting the sawdust trail in the ministry of Billy Sunday, it can stand by metonymy for conversion. "For all of you who were baptized into Christ have clothed yourselves with Christ" (Gal. 3:27), Paul writes, and this does not speak to the efficacy of baptism but to its closest association with conversion. Ask someone in the first century when they were converted and they might well reply, "Oh, I was baptized in Corinth in 57" (though that would not have been their calendar). Paul can of course *distinguish* preaching the gospel from baptism (1 Cor. 1:17), which shows that in Paul's thought baptism does not have the same logical status as, say, faith. (It is impossible to imagine Paul saying that he did not come to urge faith but to preach the gospel.) Nevertheless, such biblical texts show that baptism and conversion are coextensive in their referents: those who (so far as can be ascertained) are converted are also baptized. Baptism can stand by metonymy for conversion.

I should venture an aside before pressing on with the argument. The close connection between turning to Christ and being baptized in the New Testament does not require that those who make profession of faith be baptized within ten minutes of their profession or upon walking forward at an evangelistic meeting or the like. The close theological connection between conversion and baptism forbids an open-ended delay, and it also forbids a kind of two-step mentality, with baptism associated with a second step in grace or maturity, but it does not forbid a delay until the next baptismal service or until some elementary Bible teaching has taken place as part of the change of life that attends conversion. The point is that baptism in the New Testament is associated with conversion; it is not perceived as an optional extra.

In exactly the same way, this side of Pentecost everyone who is converted also becomes a member of the local church. It is impossible to find anyone saying, in effect,

> Yes, I believe in Christ Jesus, I have been regenerated, and I may decide to get baptized as well, but there is no way I'm going to join a church. I've been burned by previous religious experiences. You should have seen what a fiasco I faced in connection with the temple of Asclepius. This organized religion stuff is not for me. Perhaps someday I'll find a really good church, and then I may join, but for the moment I rather like my independence. Besides, isn't that *extra ecclesiam nulla salus* ["outside the church, no salvation"] stuff the detritus of medieval Catholicism?

One cannot find such voices in the New Testament. In other words, in the pages of the New Testament, to be converted, to be baptized, and to join the local community of believers are all part of the same thing.

If we had more time and space, we could examine afresh the distribution of the singular and plural forms of ἐκκλησία, from which Presbyterians and

Baptists draw slightly different inferences, to say nothing of other groups. In both heritages of interpretation, however, the point of interest to this address is that when first-century folk were converted, they were not joining only the universal church. They were joining the empirical church, the local church. Anything less was simply unthinkable.

4. In what follows, then, the assertion that the local church is more important than TGC, White Horse Inn, 9Marks, and maybe even ETS, depends on a faithful New Testament understanding of what the church is, not what we sometimes assume the church to be, based on some contemporary practices. To put this another way, if the thesis of my title is valid, it becomes a call to reform our churches in line with New Testament patterns.

So Why Is the Church More Important?

The following points are not listed in any order of intrinsic importance.

1. The first answer to the question surely falls out of the terminological discussion in which we have been engaged. The local church is sublimely important because it is the only body made up of all the converted, the only body characterized by certain New Testament-sanctioned identifying "marks" that reflect its essential constitution. Faithful seminaries and ETS may, like churches, undertake commitment to teaching and be made up of Christians, but they do not embrace all the local believers, nor do they typically practice baptism and the Lord's Supper. Both ETS and confessional seminaries have been known to exercise discipline but also to exclude many people who rightly belong to local churches (e.g., those without the requisite theological training). One might reasonably ask the question, "Isn't it as true that members of ETS (and even, dare I say it, of the Gospel Coalition) are as converted as the members of the local church?" Yes, but the exclusions are quite different. In short, our terminological discussion marks out the locus of the local church and implicitly points to its importance.

2. The local church, understood along the lines already laid out, is repeatedly shown to be the fulfillment of many trajectories drawn from antecedent revelation. The church is the community of the Messiah ("I will build my church," Jesus says in Matthew 16:18, not simply, "I will save a lot of individuals"), calling to mind the assembly in the wilderness (cf. Acts 7:38). This church, in the usage of Peter and of the Apocalypse, is the ultimate kingdom of priests, language ultimately drawn from Exodus 19. In its passion to bring

Jews and Gentiles together to constitute one new humanity (Eph. 2)—and, in principle, men and women from every tongue and people and tribe—it is drawing to fulfillment trajectories set by the promise to Eve, by the Abrahamic covenant, by prophetic voices like that in Isaiah 19:23–25 and Psalm 86:9, by surprising patterns of election already established in Old Testament times to be independent of human merit, and much more.

3. When the apostle repeatedly speaks of the diversity of gifts in the body (1 Cor. 12; cf. Rom. 12), the body to which he is referring is the local church (whether in Rome or Corinth), not the universal church. Thus Christians who want to be independent of the local church are (to extend Paul's metaphor) declaring that they are sufficient to themselves, when in fact they are nothing but an eyeball or an ear or a big toe. They know little of how the body works together, as each part does its work. In explaining the difference between Old Testament priests and New Testament pastors, I have often tried to show that the role of the pastor-teacher in the New Testament is not that of a special-class mediator but something akin to the role of a stomach within the body: the stomach takes in a lot of food and distributes it to the rest of the body. I lose all my dignity (and, better, any pomposity) when I am seen not as a priest but as a stomach. And in this light, ETS is made up of a significant collection of stomachs—but that does not make it a church. And that's one of the reasons why the local church is more important than ETS: it is the body of Christ.

In a similar way, we ought to be alarmed when churches set out to be made up of one race or one age demographic or one group of people with an exclusive style of worship or one economic demographic. The challenge of diversity, already experienced in the early chapters of Acts and in such epistles as Galatians and 1 Corinthians, did not lead the apostles to establish a Jewish church and a Gentile church but to oppose such trends tooth and nail with an integrating theology. This is much more difficult than establishing a group of Christians made up of some updated version of the homogeneous unit principle much loved a generation ago, but at the end of the day we have to return to what the church is.

4. So many of our sins are fundamentally relational. To go no farther than the "acts of the flesh" in Galatians 5, the listed sins are grouped: three might be dubbed sexual (sexual immorality, impurity, and debauchery), some are tied to paganism (idolatry and witchcraft), two are tied to excess

(drunkenness and orgies), and all the rest reflect social dysfunction (hatred, discord, jealousy, fits of rage, selfish ambition, dissensions, factions, and envy). Sanctification that mortifies such sins simply cannot take place in splendid isolation, nor even with a group of socially acceptable peers. It takes place in the church, made up of people, some of whom are unlike us and with whom we would have little in common, people who would certainly not be our friends, much less our brothers and sisters, were it not for the grace of God in the gospel.

5. A properly functioning church, precisely because it is concerned for the whole church, is concerned for each member of the church. That includes not only discipline in the ultimate sense, but mutual admonition, the instructions of the church-recognized pastors, the kinds of correction, mutual encouragement, instruction in righteousness, and rebuke that equips the servant of God for every good work. Inevitably, this means more than a sermon a week. It means, to pick up language from Acts, studying and teaching from house to house and examining the Scriptures to see if these things are so.

Indeed, it means a full-orbed teaching ministry, a teaching and living out of the whole counsel of God. Specialist parachurch ministries may have their place—I'll come to that in a moment—but they tend to focus on one or a few areas of biblical truth, sometimes to the exclusion of complementary biblical truths. To take an interesting example, the recent and challenging essay by Andrew Heard, "A Dangerous Passion for Growth," makes a telling point.[2] Our passion to evangelize and grow may become dangerous if it becomes so driven by pragmatics that, in the name of winning more people, we start to trim or domesticate the gospel (after all, we don't want to offend anyone, so we'll stop talking about hell) or prove unconcerned about putting the flesh to death or about sanctification and the building up of the body. But it is the local church that is much more likely to preserve this balance. A parachurch ministry whose goal is outreach is far less likely to perceive the dangers because it does not see itself as responsible for building the entire local church.

6. Perhaps it should be said that this vision of the local church becomes progressively more important as our culture loses whatever Judeo-Christian

---

2 Andrew Heard, "A Dangerous Passion for Growth," *The Briefing*, December 22, 2014, http://matthiasmedia.com/.

moorings it held in the past. It was not that long ago that the Ten Commandments were widely viewed as healthy societal norms. Marriage between one man and one woman, with a vow to preserve it "as long as we both shall live,"[3] was seen as a good thing, and the laws of the state tended to back such ideals. But just as Dorothy is no longer in Kansas, we are no longer in the 1950s. Even then, we needed more biblical teaching than we sometimes thought we did, but now the urgency is even more pressing. We need to build a Christian counterculture, local churches that, however much they preserve lines of civility, courtesy, and communication with the larger world, nevertheless live differently, radically differently. And it takes teaching, lots of it, to shape a faithful, fruitful, gospel-centered, Bible-shaped counterculture. To take but one small example, R. R. Reno has recently written an essay, "A Time to Rend," in which he argues,

> In the past the state recognized marriage, giving it legal forms to reinforce its historic norms. Now the courts have redefined rather than recognized marriage, making it an institution entirely under the state's control. That's why it's now time to stop talking of civil marriage and instead talk about government marriage—calling it what it is.[4]

He then teases out some of the implications. But none of this will prove convincing to millions of ordinary Christians unless the local church builds mental structures that are shaped by what the word says about men and women, marriage, and the like. Many Christians are being sucked into exegetically irresponsible views on many topics—money, the purpose of life, suffering, prosperity, sex, joy, and much more—for lack of teaching. It is the local church that constitutes the body of the counterculture. Or, to put the matter another way, the church is the body that is not only getting ready for the new heavens and the new earth but, owing to the drumbeat of inaugurated eschatology in the Scripture, is the outpost of the new heavens and the new earth. That demands a much more holistic and organic view of Christian life and thought than we have sometimes imagined. But that is the view of the church that courses its way through the New Testament.

---

3   See "The Formal Solemnization of Matrimony," in *The Book of Common Prayer*, https://www.churchofengland.org/.

4   R. R. Reno, "A Time to Rend," *First Things*, November 18, 2014, http://www.firstthings.com/.

7. If we hold that the sacraments/ordinances are a mark of the church, we must stop treating them as optional extras. And similarly, we should avoid treating them as the prerogatives of individuals. A friend of mine likes to tell the story of how a Christian in his purview led someone to Christ on a beach in California. She promptly took her friend out into the sea and baptized her. Her zeal was wholly admirable, but if Philip in Samaria is happy to see the arrival of Peter and John tie together his new converts with the mother church, perhaps we ought to reflect a little more on how sacraments/ordinances function ecclesiologically. Much more needs to be said on that theme, but I rush forward for want of space.

8. The Bible asserts that "Christ loved the church and gave himself up for her" (Eph. 5:25). The context of Ephesians strongly suggests that Paul has both the universal church and the local church in mind—or, better put, the assembly of the local church is a kind of outcropping in history of the assembly of the church of the living God already gathered in solemn assembly before the throne in union with Christ. This is true of several passages that presuppose a porous interface between the universal church and the local church. For example, in Matthew 16:18 Jesus says, "I will build my church, and the gates of Hades will not overcome it," while two chapters later disputants are to tell it to the church, which can scarcely be the universal church. The local church is the historical manifestation, under the new covenant, of this massive, blood-bought assembly. It is characterized by certain marks and order, yet behind it all lies the love of God, the love and sacrifice of the Son, and the life-giving and transforming power of the Spirit. It is important to see the place of individual conversion in the New Testament, and that might be particularly important to emphasize in cultures that think in terms of people movements, tribal movements (as, for example, in northern India). But always, and not least in the individualistic West, it is important to underscore the corporate vision of the church, embodied in the local church, that repeatedly surfaces in the Scriptures.

Concluding Reflections

None of what I have said should be taken as a plea to abolish TGC, 9Marks, White Horse Inn, or even ETS. Were we to do so, we would also have to abolish Westminster Theological Seminary, SIM, Christian schools, Tyndale House, Feed the Children, Crossway, and a host of other parachurch organizations. Arguably, some of these organizations God has raised up to strengthen the church. Many of those who work in such organizations put in more hours each week in these organizations than they do in their local church—as I have in connection with Trinity Evangelical Divinity School and the Gospel Coalition, though I am a member of a local church in the town where I live. But I believe with every fiber of my being that such organizations must serve the church, not the reverse, or they lose their raison d'être. What is especially to be deplored are those specialized, focused parachurch ministries that operate with the arrogance that condescendingly tells the church to follow the lead of the parachurch organization. What is to be pursued is the interest and glory of Christ and his gospel, which is irrefragably tied up with his blood-bought church, the church he is resolved to build until the consummation, when current tensions between the universal church and the local church will be no more.

PART 2

REFLECTIONS ON
THE GOSPEL

5

The Gospel and Its Effects

IN BLOGS, JOURNAL ESSAYS, and books, there has been quite a lot written recently about what "the gospel" is.[1] In the hands of some, the question of what "the gospel" is may be tied to the question of what "evangelicalism" is, since "gospel" = εὐαγγέλιον = evangel, which lies at the heart of evangelicalism. People talk variously of the "simple" gospel or the "robust" gospel or the "pure" gospel—and doubtless a rich array of other adjectives. Some make a distinction between the gospel of the cross and the gospel of the kingdom. Technical New Testament studies in recent years have addressed the question of when "the Gospel according to Matthew" (or Mark or Luke or John) became "the Gospel *of* Matthew" (or Mark or Luke or John), for the former presupposes that there was one gospel with assorted witnesses, while the latter opens the possibility of having a distinct gospel for each community labeled by one of the four canonical gospels—though this latter view, still dominant, has come under severe criticism, not least in the light of Richard Bauckham's edited volume *The Gospels for All Christians*.[2] Ironically, while Bauckham's title nicely captures something true and important—namely, that our four canonical Gospels were not written for hermetically sealed off communities but for the widest circulation among Christians—it uses the plural form of the noun "gospels" in a way that, as far as I know, is frankly anachronistic, for it does not seem to be duplicated anywhere else in the

---

1 This chapter was originally published as D. A. Carson, "Editorial," *Themelios* 34, no. 1 (2009): 1–2.
2 Richard Bauckham, ed., *The Gospels for All Christians: Rethinking Gospel Audiences* (Grand Rapids, MI: Eerdmans, 1998).

first century. A handful of other essays have noted the instance where the gospel is not "good news" for certain people but a promise of terrifying judgment. The writers of these essays argue that εὐαγγέλιον may not mean "good news" but something like "great and important news": whether it is good or bad depends on those who hear it.

A couple of these questions I hope to address shortly elsewhere. For the moment, however, I'd like to underscore another distinction that is still worth making. It was understood better in the past than it is today. It is this: one must distinguish between, on the one hand, the gospel as what God has done and what is the message to be announced and, on the other, what is demanded by God or effected by the gospel in assorted human responses. If the gospel is the (good) news about what God has done in Christ Jesus, there is ample place for including under "the gospel" the ways in which the kingdom has dawned and is coming, for tying this kingdom to Jesus's death and resurrection, for demonstrating that the purpose of what God has done is to reconcile sinners to himself and finally to bring under one head a renovated and transformed new heaven and new earth, for talking about God's gift of the Holy Spirit, consequent upon Christ's resurrection and ascension to the right hand of the majesty on high, and above all for focusing attention on what Paul (and others, though the language I'm using here reflects Paul) sees as the matter "of first importance" (1 Cor. 15:3): Christ crucified. All of this is what God has done; it is what we proclaim; it is the news, the great news, the good news.

By contrast, the first two greatest commands—to love God with heart and soul and mind and strength, and our neighbor as ourselves—do not constitute the gospel, or any part of it. We may well argue that when the gospel is faithfully declared and rightly received, it will result in human beings more closely aligned to these two commands. But they are not the gospel. Similarly, the gospel is not receiving Christ, or believing in him, or being converted, or joining a church; it is not the practice of discipleship. Once again, the gospel faithfully declared and rightly received will result in people receiving Christ, believing in Christ, being converted, and joining a local church; but such steps are not the gospel. The Bible can exhort those who trust the living God to be concerned with issues of social justice (Isa. 2; Amos); it can tell new covenant believers to do good to all human beings, especially to those of the household of faith (Gal. 6); it exhorts us to remember the poor and to ask, not "Who is my neighbor?" but "Who am I serving as neighbor?" We may even argue that some such list of moral commitments is a *necessary* consequence of the gospel. But it is not the gospel. We may preach through the list, reminding people that the Bible is concerned to tell us not only what to believe but how to live. But we may not preach through that list and claim it encapsulates the gospel. The gospel is what *God* has done, supremely in Christ, and especially focused on his cross and resurrection.

Failure to distinguish between the gospel and all the effects of the gospel tends, over the long haul, to replace the good news as to what God has done with a moralism that is finally without the power and the glory of Christ crucified, resurrected, ascended, and reigning.

6

The Hole in the Gospel

JOHN COMPLAINS, "I simply cannot resolve this calculus problem." Sarah offers a solution: "Let's read some Shakespearean sonnets."[1]

"I've got a problem with my car: it won't start. But no problem, I know what to do. I'll go and practice my guitar. That will fix it."

"My cakes always used to fall when I took them out of the oven. But my friend showed me how to fix the problem. He showed me how to adjust the timing on my car engine."

Ridiculous, of course. But this is merely a farcical way of showing that solutions to problems must be closely tied to the problems themselves. You do not have a valid solution unless that solution resolves the problem comprehensively. A shoddy analysis of a problem may result in a solution that is useful for only a small part of the real problem. Equally failing, one can provide an excellent analysis of a problem yet respond with a limited and restricted solution.

So in the Bible, how are the "problem" of sin and the "solution" of the gospel rightly related to each other?

One of the major theses in Cornelius Plantinga's stimulating book is that sin "is culpable vandalism of shalom."[2] That's not bad, provided "shalom" is well-defined. Plantinga holds that shalom resides in a right relation of

---

1 This chapter was originally published as D. A. Carson, "The Hole in the Gospel," *Themelios* 38, no. 3 (2013): 353–56.

2 That was the expression he used in a 2011 address he delivered at Trinity Evangelical Divinity School. For analogous expressions, cf. Cornelius Plantinga Jr., *Not the Way It's Supposed to Be: A Breviary of Sin* (Grand Rapids, MI: Eerdmans, 1994): "sin is culpable shalom-breaking" (14); "sin is culpable disturbance of shalom" (18). Cf. Plantinga, "Sin: Not the Way It's Supposed to

human beings to God, to other human beings, and to the creation. Perhaps the weakness of this approach is that shalom—rather than God—becomes the fundamental defining element in sin. Of course, God is comprehended within Plantinga's definition: sin includes the rupture of the relationship between God and human beings. Yet this does not appear to make God quite as central as the Bible makes him. In Leviticus 19, for example, where God enjoins many laws that constrain and enrich human relationships, the fundamental and frequently repeated motive is "I am the LORD," not "Do not breach shalom." When David repents of his wretched sins of adultery, murder, and betrayal, even though he has damaged others, destroyed lives, betrayed his family, and corrupted the military, he daresay, truthfully, "Against you, you only, have I sinned and done what is evil in your sight" (Ps. 51:4). The majority of the approximately six hundred Old Testament passages that speak of the wrath of God connect it not to the destruction of shalom but to idolatry—the de-godding of God.[3] Human sin in Genesis 3 certainly destroys human relationships and brings a curse on the creation, but treating this comprehensive odium as the vandalism of shalom makes it sound both too slight and too detached from God. After all, the fundamental act was disobeying God, and a central ingredient in the temptation of Eve was the incitement to become as God, knowing good and evil.

To put this another way, the tentacles of sin, the basic "problem" that the Bible's storyline addresses, embrace guilt (genuine moral guilt, not just guilty feelings), shame, succumbing to the devil's enticements, the destruction of shalom (and thus broken relationships with God, other human beings, and the created order), entailments in the enchaining power of evil, death (of several kinds),[4] and hell itself. However many additional descriptors and entailments one might add (e.g., self-deception, transgression of law, folly over against wisdom, all the social ills from exploitation to cruelty to war, and so forth), the heart of the issue is that by our fallen nature, by our choice, and by God's judicial decree, we are alienated from God Almighty.

Be" (paper presented at the Carl F. H. Henry Center for Theological Understanding, Deerfield, IL, 2010), https://henrycenter.tiu.edu/.

3   Cf. D. A. Carson, "The Wrath of God," in *Engaging the Doctrine of God: Contemporary Protestant Perspectives*, ed. Bruce L. McCormack (Grand Rapids, MI: Baker Academic, 2008), 37–63; Carson, "God's Love and God's Wrath," in *The Difficult Doctrine of the Love of God* (Wheaton, IL: Crossway, 2000), 65–84, 88.

4   As Augustine rightly observes in *City of God* 13.12.

For the Bible to be coherent, then, it follows that the gospel must resolve the problem of sin. What is the gospel? In recent years that question has been answered in numerous books, essays, and blogs. Like the word "sin," the word "gospel" can be accurately but rather fuzzily defined in a few words, or it can be unpacked at many levels after one undertakes very careful exegetical study of εὐαγγέλιον[5] and its cognates and adjacent themes.[6] We could begin with a simple formulation such as "The gospel is the great news of what God has done in Jesus Christ." Then one could adopt an obvious improvement: "The gospel is the great news of what God has done in Jesus Christ, especially in his death and resurrection" (cf. 1 Cor. 15). Or we could take several quantum leaps forward, and try again:

> The gospel is the great news of what God has graciously done in Jesus Christ—especially in his atoning death and vindicating resurrection, his ascension, session, and high priestly ministry—to reconcile sinful human beings to himself, justifying them by the penal substitute of his Son, and regenerating and sanctifying them by the powerful work of the Holy Spirit, who is given to them as the down payment of their ultimate inheritance. God will save them if they repent and trust in Jesus.

The proper *response* to this gospel, then, is that people repent, believe, and receive God's grace by faith alone.

The *entailment* of this received gospel, that is, the inevitable result, is that those who believe experience forgiveness of sins, are joined together spiritually in the body of Christ, the church, being so transformed that, in measure as they become more Christlike, they delight to learn obedience to King Jesus and joyfully proclaim the good news that has saved them, and they do good to all men, especially to the household of faith, eager to be good stewards of the grace of God in all the world, in anticipation of the culminating transformation that issues in resurrection existence in the

---

5 E.g., D. A. Carson, "The Biblical Gospel," in *For Such a Time as This: Perspectives on Evangelicalism, Past, Present and Future*, ed. Steve Brady and Harold Rowdon (London: Evangelical Alliance, 1996), 75–85; Carson, "What Is the Gospel?—Revisited," in *For the Fame of God's Name: Essays in Honor of John Piper*, ed. C. Samuel Storms and Justin Taylor (Wheaton, IL: Crossway, 2010), 147–70.

6 E.g., for a brief reflection on what "kingdom" means see chapter 12, "Kingdom, Ethics, and Individual Salvation," originally published in *Themelios* 38, no. 2 (2013): 197–201.

new heaven and the new earth, to the glory of God and the good of his blood-bought people.

Once again, as in our brief treatment of sin, much more could be said to flesh out this potted summary. But observe three things:

1. The gospel is, first and foremost, news—great news, momentous news. That is why it must be announced, proclaimed—that's what one does with news. Silent proclamation of the gospel is an oxymoron. Godly and generous behavior may bear a kind of witness to the transformed life, but if those who observe such a life hear nothing of the substance of the gospel, it may evoke admiration but cannot call forth faith because in the Bible faith demands faith's true object, which remains unknown where there is no proclamation of the news.

2. The gospel is, first and foremost, news about what God has done in Christ. It is not law, an ethical system, or a list of human obligations; it is not a code of conduct telling us what we must do. It is news about what God has done in Christ.

3. On the other hand, the gospel has both purposes and entailments in human conduct. The entailments must be preached. But if you preach the entailments as if they were the gospel itself, pretty soon you lose sight of the reality of the gospel—that it is the good news of what God has done, not a description of what we ought to do in consequence. Pretty soon the gospel descends to mere moralism. One cannot too forcefully insist on the distinction between the gospel and its entailments.

So now I come to the fairly recent and certainly very moving book by Richard Stearns, *The Hole in Our Gospel*.[7] This frank and appealing book surveys worldwide poverty and argues that the American failure to take up God's mandate to address poverty is "the hole in our gospel." Without wanting to diminish the obligation Christians have to help the poor, and with nothing but admiration for Stearns's personal pilgrimage, his argument would have been far more helpful and compelling had he observed three things.

First, "what God expects of us" (Stearns's subtitle) is, by definition, not the gospel. This is not the great news of what God has done for us in Christ Jesus. Had Stearns cast his treatment of poverty as one of the things to

---

7   Richard Stearns, *The Hole in Our Gospel: What Does God Expect of Us* (Nashville: Nelson, 2009).

be addressed by the second greatest commandment, or as one of several entailments of the gospel, I could have recommended his book with much greater confidence. As it is, the book will contribute to declining clarity as to what the gospel is.

Second, even while acknowledging—indeed, insisting on the importance of highlighting—the genuine needs that Stearns depicts in his book, it is disturbing not to hear similar anguish over human alienation from God. The book focuses so narrowly on poverty that the sweep of what the gospel addresses is lost to view. Men and women stand under God's judgment, and this God of love mandates that by the means of heralding the gospel, they will be saved not only in this life but in the life to come. Where is the anguish that contemplates a Christless eternity, that cries, "Repent! Turn away from all your offenses. . . . Why will you die, people of Israel? For I take no pleasure in the death of anyone" (Ezek. 18:30–32). The analysis of the problem is too small, and the gospel is correspondingly reduced.

Third, some studies have shown that Christians spend about five times more mission dollars on issues related to poverty than they do on evangelism and church planting. At one time, "holistic ministry" was an expression intended to move Christians beyond proclamation to include deeds of mercy. Increasingly, however, "holistic ministry" refers to deeds of mercy without any proclamation of the gospel—and that is not holistic. It is not even halfistic, since the deeds of mercy are not the gospel: they are entailments of the gospel. Although I know many Christians who happily combine fidelity to the gospel, evangelism, church planting, and energetic service to the needy, and although I know some who call themselves Christians who formally espouse the gospel but who live out few of its entailments, I also know Christians who, in the name of a "holistic" gospel, focus their full energy on a ministry of presence, wells in the Sahel, fighting disease, and distributing food to the poor, but who never (or only very rarely) articulate the gospel, preach the gospel, announce the gospel to anyone. Judging by the distribution of American mission dollars, the biggest hole in our gospel is the gospel itself.

7

What Are Gospel Issues?

TODAY IT IS VERY COMMON to hear that such and such a topic is "a gospel issue." We must hold to the eternal generation of the Son: it is a gospel issue. We must defend inerrancy: it is a gospel issue. We must espouse complementarianism: it is a gospel issue. We must be Sabbatarians: it is a gospel issue. We must hold to a specific eschatological vision: it is a gospel issue. We must hold to substitutionary penal atonement: it is a gospel issue. Alternatively, the weight of some doctrines may be diminished by our pronouncements if we declare that something or other is *not* a gospel issue. We then hear statements like these: "Inerrancy may be important, but it is not a gospel issue;" "I disagree with your understanding of the role of the nation of Israel in the history of redemption, but that's all right: it's not a gospel issue;" "Why do you make such a fuss over complementarianism? After all, it's not a gospel issue."[1]

Not only do we not agree on what things are gospel issues, I suspect that sometimes we do not agree on what "gospel issue" *means*. The following reflections provide the merest introduction to some of the factors that strike me as relevant.

1. The statement "x is a gospel issue" is simultaneously (a) a truth claim and (b) a polemical assertion attempting to establish relative importance. The latter clearly depends on the former. Both parts bear thinking about. The statement is a truth claim in that it asserts that something either is

---

1 This chapter was originally published as D. A. Carson, "What Are Gospel Issues?," *Themelios* 39, no. 2 (2014): 215–19.

true about x, namely, that it is "a gospel issue." The claim is either valid (if x really is a gospel issue) or invalid (if x is really not a gospel issue). But as used by most people, "x is a gospel issue" is more than a truth claim. If the truth claim is valid, the statement implicitly asserts that x is a more important topic than others that are *not* gospel issues: it is designed to establish the importance of x relative to other topics that are *not* understood to be gospel issues. What is presupposed in the statement, of course, is that the gospel has a very high level of importance, perhaps supreme importance, such that if x is a gospel issue, it too is similarly elevated in importance. It follows, then, that to abandon x, when x is a gospel issue, is somehow to diminish or threaten the gospel.

These initial observations may seem a bit theoretical, but we must see that they carry significant practical consequences. Many people use statements of the sort, "x is a gospel issue" in order to establish the boundaries of Christian fellowship. We may not want to admit Bob to the leadership of our local church or our Christian group because he denies x, and x is a gospel issue. We may decide to admit Rosamund to something or other because although she disbelieves y, in this case y is not a gospel issue, so the topic is not properly used as a criterion of admission or exclusion.

2. What we mean by "gospel issue" needs clarification.

On the one hand, because of the complex entanglements of theology, with a little imagination one might argue that almost any topic is a gospel issue. At one level or another, everything in any theology that is worth the name is tied to everything else, so it is possible to tie everything to the gospel. In that sense, well-nigh everything is a gospel issue.

"In the gospel, Jesus saves us from sin. Sin is comprehensively given clarity by the Ten Commandments. To ignore the Sabbath law is to ignore one of the Ten Commandments. To ignore it or annul it is therefore to break the moral law of God, and such a stance surely demonstrates that one is not seriously confronting sin, the sin from which the gospel saves us. If one claims to be a Christian but does not fight against sin, the ostensible gospel in which we believe is really no gospel at all. So observance of the Sabbath is a gospel issue."

"Our generation is notable for the clever hermeneutical dodges it invents to sidestep what Scripture clearly says. Scripture clearly teaches complementarianism, a conclusion that can be ducked only by the hermeneutical tricks that betray a heart far removed from confessing that Jesus is Lord, which is part of what it means to confess the gospel. To confess Jesus is Lord and not bow to his word is to deny the gospel. Complementarianism is a gospel issue."

"The *filioque* phrase is necessary to preserve the truth that the Spirit proceeds from the Father *and the Son*. Without that confessional point, our understanding of the Trinity is adversely affected, and sooner or later that in turn affects our understanding of the work of the persons of the Godhead in redemption itself. Is it any wonder that Eastern Orthodoxy, which repudiates the *filioque* clause, puts far more weight on Jesus's incarnation and resurrection than on his atoning work on the cross, despite the apostle Paul's insistence that the cross is central? Thus the *filioque* clause is a gospel issue."

I am not arguing that any of these three arguments are necessarily valid. It is easy to imagine how another person might look at the texts and arguments and reach quite different conclusions. For example, someone might hold that Scripture does *not* teach complementarianism and that for some Christians, at least, no hermeneutical tricks are consciously deployed to reach this conclusion. Therefore, the egalitarian may hold that Jesus is Lord with a perfectly clear conscience. If so, then complementarianism is *not* a gospel issue. Once again, at this juncture I am not arguing for the validity or invalidity of either pole. All I am saying is that virtually any topic can be tied to the gospel in some way or another. If that is all we are doing, the argument "x is a gospel issue" is a well-nigh useless argument, because the claim could be advanced for almost any topic, irrespective of that to which x refers. The choice of x will in that case reflect rather more the identity of the individual or group that is making the claim, than the persuasiveness of the argument.

On the other hand, "gospel issue" may continue to be a useful category if it refers not to any biblical or theological topic that can be tied in some way or other to the gospel—for the organic nature of biblical and theological truth demonstrates that just about every topic can be tied to the gospel—but to biblical and theological topics that, if we deny, clearly affect our understanding of the gospel adversely.

3. Clearly "x is a gospel issue" is a useless argument where there is little agreement as to what the gospel is. For example, if by "gospel" we mean

the sort of thing that is often taught in lowest-common-denominator evangelicalism (e.g., "Jesus died on the cross for my sins," without any attempt to establish what is meant by the confession) then in what sense is penal substitutionary atonement a gospel issue? It may be a gospel issue in that in some sense or other it is tied to Jesus's death, but that is not enough to make the statement "Penal substitutionary atonement is a gospel issue" say anything important (my second point, above). More precisely, if "Jesus died on the cross for my sins" is a sufficient definition of the gospel, then it is not clear that failing to believe in penal substitutionary atonement adversely affects or threatens the gospel, for in itself this formulation of the gospel does not specify with any precision what understanding of the atonement the formulation presupposes. By contrast, if by the gospel we specify something a bit more robust (though scarcely comprehensive)—for example, "the gospel is the good news that in Christ, and especially in his death and resurrection, God has taken decisive action to save his people from their sins, such that by Jesus's death sin is cancelled, the judicial wrath of God is averted, believers receive what Christ merited while he receives what we sinners merited, the devil is defeated, and God displays his incalculable love, pouring out his Spirit upon us so as to convict us, regenerate us, and transform us, in anticipation of the consummation still to come" (or something of that order)—then clearly penal substitutionary atonement *is* a gospel issue in a tight sense. It is a gospel issue in the sense that if we deny or disown penal substitutionary atonement, the gospel is adversely affected.

When Christians talk together about what is or what is not a gospel issue, very often they are conversing with fellow believers who share, pretty closely, the same understanding of what the gospel is. For example, when members of the Council of the Gospel Coalition talk about whether x is or is not a gospel issue, at least they share a common mind as to what the gospel is. Such discussion may be useful. But others may conclude that the x in question is *not* a gospel issue precisely because they hold to a different or at least a reduced definition of the gospel.

4. Some issues are very important but are not usefully labeled gospel issues. For example, there are important epistemological issues with which thoughtful Christians must wrestle. Again, some issues—for example, what we mean by "person" and "substance" in discussions on the nature of the Trinity—certainly stretch back into elements of exegesis of the biblical texts,

and can in some sense be tied to the gospel, but might more usefully be thought of as important metaphysical issues. Some topics might be thought of as *both* gospel issues and *other kinds* of issues. For example, Lutherans and Calvinists (to go no further) will defend somewhat differing views on the relationship between law and gospel; doubtless these can be called gospel issues (indeed, they are sometimes so labeled), but it is probably more helpful to think of them as canonical and systematic issues.

This is merely a way of saying that when we decide to talk about the relative importance of topics, we need *more* than the formula "x is a gospel issue." Issues may be hugely important even if they are not gospel issues. Indeed, if our only criterion is whether x is a gospel issue, then if we decide that x is *not* a gospel issue, we may unwittingly generate the impression it is not an important topic. It is always worth asking, Important for what? Important in what domain?

5. We must squarely face the fact that what we judge to be a gospel issue is shaped in part by our location in history, in a particular culture. In other words, the issues are not to be determined by logic alone. Our place in time and space entices us to evaluate whether a particular topic is a gospel issue; believers in another time and place might come to quite different conclusions, even though they share a common understanding of what the gospel is.

Certainly the majority of Christians in America today would happily aver that good race relations are a gospel issue. They might point out that God's saving purpose is to draw to himself, through the cross, men and women from every tongue and tribe and people and nation; that the church is one new humanity, made up of Jew and Gentile; that Paul tells Philemon to treat his slave Onesimus as his brother, as the apostle himself; that this trajectory starts at creation, with all men and women being made in the image of God, and finds its anticipation in the promise to Abraham that in his seed all the nations of the earth will be blessed. Moreover, the salvation secured by Christ in the gospel is more comprehensive than justification alone: it brings repentance, wholeness, love for brothers and sisters in the Christian community.

But the sad fact remains that not all Christians have always viewed race relations within the church as a gospel issue.

More worrying, survey after survey has shown that in America today, even among those with a robust grasp of the gospel, Black Christians and

White Christians do not view these matters exactly the same way. Even where both sides agree, on biblical grounds, that this is a gospel issue, Black Christians are far more likely to see that this is a *crucial* gospel issue, an issue of huge importance, one that is often ignored, while White Christians are more likely to imagine that racial issues have so largely been resolved that it is a distraction to keep bringing them up. In other words, even where both sides agree that we are dealing with a gospel issue (and in that sense, an important issue), they do not agree on the relative importance of this gospel issue. It is impossible not to see that our judgments on these matters are not shaped by Scripture alone in the same sense in which a mathematician may be shaped by Pythagoras's theorem. They are shaped by our relationships, by our race, by our culture, by where we have been brought up, by the income levels we have experienced, by the affronts we have experienced, and much more. In other words, for many topics that we have designated x, whether x is a gospel issue is not a zero-sum game.

For some Christian observers, cessationism is a gospel issue. In their perception, the charismatic movement is characteristically afflicted by one brand or another of health, wealth, and prosperity gospel that distances itself from the gospel of the cross; this makes the matter a gospel issue. Some forms of the charismatic movement so construct a two-stage view of spiritual wholeness, the second stage attested by one or more particular spiritual gifts, that the nature of what Jesus achieved on the cross is in jeopardy. Others, it is argued, adopt a view of revelation that jeopardizes the exclusive, final authority of Scripture, and this threatens the gospel that the Scripture heralds. But other Christian observers, fully aware of these dangers and no less concerned to avoid them, nevertheless remain convinced that at least some charismatics manage to display their gifts without succumbing to any of these errors, while self-consciously holding to the same gospel that the observers hold. In other words, for them the charismatic movement (or, from the obverse direction, cessationism) is not necessarily a gospel issue. They want to avoid building legalistic fences around their positions. Once again, it is difficult not to see that personal experiences and sustained habits of assessment have entered into one's judgments. Determining whether x is a gospel issue is often more than a narrowly exegetical exercise.

To put the same matter another way, another sort of example might be introduced. We have seen how the doctrine of penal substitutionary atonement is usefully considered a gospel issue provided (a) that we have adopted a robust definition of the gospel, such that (b) to disown that facet of the cross-work of Christ necessarily diminishes or threatens the gospel. But I have not heard anyone recently suggest that the exemplary function of the cross is a gospel issue, even though Peter unambiguously insists that Jesus died leaving us an example that we should follow in his steps (1 Pet. 2:21). This is as much a gospel issue as is penal substitutionary atonement, even though it is not treated in that way today, precisely because it is not one of the controverted points. In other words, the things that we debate as to whether they are gospel issues reflect the hot topics, and especially the denials or errors, of our age. That is one of the reasons why I mentioned the *filioque* clause and the eternal generation of the Son at the head of this essay: at one point, they were very much considered gospel issues. The second of these two is currently making something of a comeback—but certainly if we are careless about them, our carelessness suggests how our own theological foci have shifted with time and demonstrates once again that discussions of the sort "x is a gospel issue" commonly address the errors and dangers of a particular age. This is not necessarily a bad thing; it is in any case an inevitable thing. But it should be recognized for what it is.

In sum, to affirm something is or is not a gospel issue is not a transparent expression. It is likely to be clearest among those who share a common confession as to what the gospel is. It is useful only when it means something more stringent than that x can be tied in some way to the gospel: one must show that without this x the gospel itself is seriously threatened. And it is always wise to recognize that some topics are hugely important on grounds other than gospel issues and that our choice of topics is generated in part by our perception of the threats and errors of our own age.

PART 3

REFLECTIONS ON THE BIBLE
AND BIBLICAL THEOLOGY

8

When Did the Church Begin?

WHEN DID THE CHURCH BEGIN? This question is not uncommon, especially among theological students. Sometimes people ask it because they have been exposed to dispensational teaching. In that case, the answer one gives becomes a kind of litmus test to a nest of other questions that dispensationalists pose. People from a dispensational heritage emphasize discontinuity between the covenants and therefore commonly argue that the church begins at Pentecost; people from a covenant-theology heritage emphasize the continuity of the covenant of grace, think in terms of fulfillment of what was promised, and therefore argue that the "assembly" of the people of God is one and that therefore it is a mistake to argue that the church begins at Pentecost. Others ask the question in our title because for them the answer is a way of distinguishing between Reformed Presbyterians and Reformed Baptists. Still others ask the question without a theological agenda, but for no other reason than that it deserves to be asked precisely because the answer seems ambiguous in the biblical texts.[1]

It may be helpful to organize the relevant material in several steps.

1. As for the terminology, although "church" is commonly a New Testament (NT) expression, both the word and the idea surface in the Old Testament (OT) too. For example, a not atypical passage pictures God instructing Moses, "Assemble the people before me to hear my words so that they may learn to revere me as long as they live in the land and may teach them to

---

1 This chapter was originally published as D. A. Carson, "When Did the Church Begin?," *Themelios* 41, no. 1 (2016): 1–4.

their children" (Deut. 4:10): the verb is קהל in Hebrew and ἐκκλησιάζειν (cognate with ἐκκλησία, "church" or "assembly") in the Septuagint. Not less important is the fact that NT writers can refer to the OT people of God as the "church": Stephen speaks of the gathered Israelites in the wilderness as "the assembly [ἐκκλησία] in the wilderness" (Acts 7:38). The writer to the Hebrews uses OT language to depict Jesus saying that he will sing praise to God: "in the assembly [ἐκκλησία] I will sing your praises" (Heb. 2:12, citing Ps. 22:22). When Christians gather together, the language the writer to the Hebrews uses to describe their assembly bursts with fulfilled typological references to the OT: "You have come to Mount Zion, to the city of the living God, the heavenly Jerusalem. You have come to thousands upon thousands of angels in joyful assembly, to the church [ἐκκλησία] of the firstborn . . . to Jesus the mediator of a new covenant, and to the sprinkled blood that speaks a better word than the blood of Abel" (Heb. 12:22–24). The reference to Abel inevitably reminds the reader that Christians are "surrounded by . . . a great cloud of witnesses" (Heb. 12:1)—namely, the faithful heroes from Abel through Enoch, Abraham, Sarah, Gideon, David, and all the rest of the OT figures (Heb. 11). One cannot help but see some kind of profound continuity in the people of God.

2. The issue is broader than merely terminological. When Jesus declares, in a thoroughly Jewish context, that he will build his church (ἐκκλησία, Matt. 16:18), what he has in mind, according to this Gospel, includes Gentiles too (Matt. 28:18–20). His instructions on how to exercise church (ἐκκλησία) discipline (Matt. 18:15–20) show how he is willing to blur distinctions we tend to make: the local church (which must be in view in Matt. 18) is the outcropping of the entire church (Matt. 16), and clearly includes both Jews and Gentiles. They constitute the Messiah's assembly, the Messiah's church. Nowhere is the oneness of Messiah's people, Messiah's church, more powerfully worked out than in Paul's letter to the Ephesians. Jewish believers and Gentile believers have been made "one" by Jesus, who is our peace (Eph. 2:14). At one time the Gentiles were alienated from God, "excluded from citizenship in Israel and foreigners to the covenants of the promise" (Eph. 2:12), but now the two groups constitute "one new human-ity" (Eph. 2:15). Gentiles are "no longer foreigners and strangers, but fellow citizens with God's people and also members of his household" (Eph. 2:19). This is the church (ἐκκλησία) that Christ loved and for which he died (Eph.

5:25). One recalls that in the olive tree metaphor (Rom. 11), there is but one vine, with branches being broken off from that vine or grafted onto it.

3. So what do the two camps—those who think the church began at Pentecost, and those who think the church stretches back in time and ultimately includes all of God's elect—make of such exegetical phenomena? Transparently, different interpretive choices are tied up with each position. The former will observe uses of ἐκκλησία in the Septuagint, or in the NT referring to the OT people of God, and insist that these are not technical uses of the term: they are references to various "assemblies" but not to the NT "church." Those NT passages that speak of the oneness of God's people (e.g., Ephesians) surely establish the difference between that people and the OT assembly, precisely because the OT assembly/church was made up only of Israelites. And thus this first group maintains its position. The latter group will observe the same data and insist that it cannot be wrong to think of the OT assembly of the people of God as the ἐκκλησία when the biblical writers are happy to use that language. To maintain a distinction between "assembly" and "church" when the Greek uses just one word for both is surely no ground for maintaining that the church began at Pentecost, for the church of God is the assembly of God, and it began in OT times. The bringing together of Jews and Gentiles in one olive tree (Rom. 11), in one new humanity (Ephesians), does not mean that the post-Pentecost church is a new body, but that it is the same but expanded body.

4. I have simplified the arguments, of course. The former group has a diversity of stances within its basic position, but it is sometimes in danger of dividing what God has put together, not adequately perceiving the oneness, the wholeness, of God's redemptive purposes. The latter group also has a diversity of stances within its basic position, but it is sometimes in danger of overlooking the "new" things associated with the ἐκκλησία from Pentecost on: new creation, new work of the Holy Spirit, new birth, new age, new covenant, and so on.

5. It begins to appear, then, that both sides of this debate focus attention on slightly different things. If the focus is on the oneness and continuity of the redeemed people of God, all of them secured by the Lord Jesus, surely Scripture demands that we affirm pretty strongly the side of the covenant theologian. The assembly (church) of the firstborn in Hebrews 12:23 seems to include saints from both covenants, including those alive now, who are

"gathered" around the throne of the living God. Add the kind of linguistic evidence I have just briefly surveyed and the case is pretty strong. Nevertheless, some versions of the Reformed construction may be in danger of flattening out the Bible's storyline in such a way there is nothing new in the new covenant except increased information. Under this reading, for example, new birth controls conversion in the days of Abraham as much as in the days of John or Paul, the work of the Holy Spirit is entirely the same under the Mosaic covenant as under the new covenant (even though it is very difficult to read John 14–16 in that way), and many NT writers affirm that with the coming, death, resurrection, and ascension of the Son of God we have entered a new age. All sides acknowledge, of course, that it is rather difficult to nail down precisely what the "newness" consists in, but it is surely a mistake to argue that there is nothing new that is connected with the new covenant—or (as I've indicated) to argue that the only thing that is new is more information now that we live this side of the cross and resurrection of Jesus, but certainly not a new experience. At the very least one must say there is a kind of ratcheting up of various expressions and experiences. For example, expressions such as "I will be their God and they will be my people" (Jer. 31:33) are tied under the Mosaic covenant to God's self-disclosure in the tabernacle, under the new covenant to the mediating work of Christ, and under the final vision of Scripture to the perfections of the new heaven and the new earth.

In short, if one is focusing on God's one redemptive plan, his one ultimate, saving sacrifice, his one assembly before the throne, his one covenant of grace (though there are some problems with that expression), and his one final purpose for the redeemed, the Reformed heritage, in my view, has it right. The church begins when the first human sinner is redeemed and joined with another redeemed human sinner—indeed, in the mind of God the church begins as far back as the death of the Lamb "who was slain from the creation of the world" (Rev. 13:8). If one is focusing on the "new" (ratcheted up?) things connected with the people of God under the new covenant, I can understand why one looks for a term that applies to them and does not apply to OT saints. The problem, of course, is that a claim like "The church begins at Pentecost" might be uttered within the framework of the kind of nuances I've just outlined, but it might be heard to be saying far more things that rightly scandalize Reformed believers; conversely, a claim like "The church is the sum of God's people under both the old covenant and the new" is perfectly defensible along the lines I've outlined here, but it might be heard to be claiming a flattening out of covenantal distinctions that ought to be preserved somehow.

6. Another element to the debate needs to be acknowledged. Presbyterians have an additional reason for preserving the terminology, in this respect, of covenant theology: they hold that, under both the Mosaic covenant and under the new covenant, the locus of the covenant community, the church, is not to be tightly identified with the locus of the elect. (The folk in Moscow, Idaho, prove to be the exception: they would like to do more to obliterate the distinction!) In other words, the structure of their ecclesiology (ἐκκλησία-ology) provides some pressure to emphasize continuity. By contrast, Reformed Baptists think that under the terms of the new covenant, the locus of the covenant community, the church, is ideally to be identified with the locus of the elect—and this is different from the way things work under the old covenant. This difference of opinion is of course tied to their respective understandings of circumcision/baptism. Presbyterians argue that both circumcision and baptism mark entrance into the covenant community, without saying anything decisive about entrance into the empirical community of the redeemed/elect. Reformed Baptists claim that both circumcision and baptism mark entrance into the covenant community, but that under the terms of the new covenant, entrance into the new covenant community also marks entrance into the empirical community of the elect/redeemed: the new covenant, is in this respect different from the Mosaic covenant, and that is part, at least, of what makes it "new." This tying together of the redeemed and the covenant community is admittedly different from the way things work under the old covenant. So at this juncture their ecclesiology exercises a subtle pressure toward a measure of discontinuity.

7. In any case, some parallels can be drawn between two formally similar questions, namely, "When did the church begin?" and "When did the messianic kingdom dawn?" This is not the place to tease out the answers to the latter question in any detail. Yet students of Scripture often point out that in one sense the kingdom dawned when he ascended to his Father's right hand, where he must reign until he has vanquished the last enemy. Yet the passion narratives make much of Jesus reigning from the cross (esp.

Matthew and John). Still earlier, the kingdom is dawning in Jesus's public ministry, even his work through his disciples, so much so that he sees Satan fall from heaven (Luke 10:18). In fact, Jesus is born king of the Jews (Matt. 2:2). Even though there are more texts that tie Jesus's kingly reign to his resurrection and ascension, the range of options as to when the messianic kingdom dawned is actually a good thing, an evocative thing, laced with imagination-stirring complexity. Similarly, the question as to when the church began can be answered with some pretty straightforward exegeses of particular texts—but then, when one has taken a deep breath and looked around again, one finds layers of God-given and imagination-stirring subtlety that demands slightly different answers in different contexts.

9

The Beauty of Biblical Balance

WHEN I WAS A YOUNG MAN in pastoral ministry, I wrote a book-length manuscript under the title shared with this essay. I sent it to only one publisher. That publisher turned it down with more grace than the manuscript deserved. He gently pointed out major exegetical and logical flaws in one of the arguments. I could see he was right, and, suitably humbled and foolishly discouraged, I couldn't bring myself to expend the time and energy to fix the problem. I moved on to other things.[1]

Decades later, however, I remain convinced that, even if one particular error needed repair, the main thesis of the book was right: the Bible depicts the importance of balance along quite a few quite different axes, and it is important not to confuse them.

Before I list some of these different axes, I should acknowledge that balance is not always a virtue. For example, when Scripture commands us to love God with our whole being (Deut. 6:4–5; Mark 12:29–30), it does not add, "Of course, all things in moderation: one must balance love for God with other priorities." Applied in the wrong contexts, the appeal for balance may be a mask for moral indifference and spiritual compromise. But let me assume that we have heeded the warning and turn to some of the different axes around which we need to maintain balance.

---

1   This chapter was originally published as D. A. Carson, "The Beauty of Biblical Balance," *Themelios* 37, no. 2 (2012): 178–81.

Balance in the Use of Our Time, While We Attempt to Be Faithful to Scripture

The Bible exhorts us to discharge many responsibilities, all of them time-consuming: to work, love our neighbor, love our spouse, bring up our children in the nurture and admonition of the Lord, pray, meditate on God's word, meet together with other believers for mutual edification and corporate praise, bear witness to the gospel with unbelievers, and much more. If we are elders/pastors/overseers, the work of teaching demands careful study, while the teaching itself extends indefinitely beyond Sunday morning sermons to include one-on-one Bible study, small group study, training others, and counsel of many kinds for the people in our flock, including the members of our own family. All of these are good things; all of them require time. The same Scriptures insist on proper cycles of rest: God gives his beloved sleep. Add to this pile the peculiar rush of duties that befall us in peculiar circumstances: a family member falls critically ill; two children are graduating from university about the same time that a third is getting married; the family business is on a knife-edge between a great leap forward and going belly-up—and all of these circumstances are under God's providential arrangement.

The needed balance in the face of such demands turns on right priorities in using the time God has given us, along with refusing to feel like dismal failures because we cannot squeeze thirty hours of living into twenty-four. We have all the time that God has wisely allotted; there is no more. We can work away at making our use of time more efficient; above all, we can pursue godly priorities. And we can trust the wisdom of our good and wise heavenly Father.

Balance in Integrating Complementary Biblical Emphases

What I have in mind are such paired exhortations as the injunction to speak the truth coupled with the injunction to do so in love. This kind of balance is quite different from the first kind. The first kind is what the gaming theorists call a zero-sum game: no matter how hard we hope otherwise, our daily distribution of time always sums up all the discrete blocks of time to achieve the same total: twenty-four hours. One cannot allot more time and energy to one responsibility without correspondingly diminishing one or more of the other blocks. But this second kind of balance is not a zero-sum game. One must not diminish the obligation to speak the truth by appealing to the priority of love; one must not diminish the obligation to speak in love by appealing to the priority of truth. There is no zero-sum game.

In the case of the claims of truth and love, these twin virtues have roughly parallel claims: God mandates both of them. Both "truth" and "love" carry slightly different overtones in different contexts, of course, but there is no intrinsic reason that we should think that either diminishes the other.

Other pairs in this category of balance are more complicated yet. For example, Christians must constantly recognize that they are saved by grace; Christians must perform the good deeds that God has created us to discharge (cf. Eph. 2:8–10). In this case, although neither pole should diminish the other, they are not quite parallel and certainly not reciprocal. In many respects the good deeds are the necessary fruit and even the demonstration of the grace; the converse is not true.

It is easy to think of other polarities under this heading that sustain relationships that are more complex yet. For example, the Bible urges Christian unity (think John 17), and the Bible insists on the nonnegotiability of sound doctrine (think Gal. 1), even if this means the most fundamental disruption of unity, namely, excommunication. The two desiderata are not quite parallel: one, the truth of the gospel, is *always* nonnegotiable; the other, the virtue of unity, is *often* presented as something eminently desirable, but sometimes as an act of compromise (e.g., the alliances of Jehoshaphat). In other words, to achieve balance in polarities of this sort, one must study how Scripture holds them up, if and how each relates to the other, whether both are equally nonnegotiable, and so forth.

The Balance of a Healthy Biblical Diet

This could be cast as something important for almost all Christians, but I shall cast it in terms of the responsibility of pastors to feed the flock of God with the whole counsel of God. There are at least three components to this balanced diet.

First, pastors should be teaching and preaching from all parts of the Bible—from both the Old and the New Testaments, and from the different genres of the Bible: history, lament, chronicle, psalm, epistle, proverb, apocalyptic, wisdom, and so forth. Pastors should keep looking back over their shoulders to see what they have covered and what they have not covered recently.

Second, pastors should be checking up on themselves to see if they are covering all the major biblical themes. It is sadly possible for a preacher to choose texts from many different parts of the Bible and yet overlook major themes of the Bible. For example, it is possible to handle text after text with a tone and an application that are invariably denunciatory, even angry, sometimes self-righteous, and devoid of much grace; alternatively, it is possible to handle text after text in such a way that underscores God's love and grace but without a word about God's jealousy, wrath, and judgment. When I was in pastoral ministry, every six or nine months I'd skim the index of a systematic theology or two so as to alert me to themes I had not so much as touched on.

Third, because the Bible is not a collection of miscellaneous religious texts that the preacher is honor-bound to cover but a God-breathed collection that establishes trajectories—trajectories of both narrative and theme—the balanced preacher will so trace out these trajectories to demonstrate how rightly handling the word of truth follows innercanonical lines that bring us to Jesus and the gospel. Failing to do this regularly is simply not faithful, balanced, biblical preaching. In other words, balanced biblical preaching does not take place where the preacher unpacks sentences in the narrow focus of the immediate context without keeping an eye peeled for the biblical-theological storyline, for the entire canonical context.

Balance as the Product of a Spiritual Diagnostician

I suppose I might have included this fourth point with the third. Yet there is a fundamental difference. The balance that the third point calls for gathers around the nature of Scripture itself; the balance that this fourth point calls for demands spiritual discernment so as to know which biblical emphases the lives of specific people most urgently need. Small wonder that the Puritans called their pastoral care "the cure of souls." Like the medical doctor who must make an accurate diagnosis before prescribing something, so the pastor must make an accurate diagnosis before closely applying particular biblical truths and themes. The ministry of Jesus shows us that we should not treat the cocksure and the self-righteous the same way as the broken, the contrite, and the desperate.

Balance in Integrating Complementary Truths that Lie on the Edge of Great Mysteries, Not Least Complementary Truths about God

God is unfathomably loving, yet his wrath reflects his perfect justice. He is utterly sovereign, yet he personally interacts with other persons, not least the human beings he has made in his own image, such that he holds them accountable for what they say and do and feel and imagine; for sovereign though he is, he never treats them as insensate robots. God is one, yet he exists as three persons who interact with one another. Even when one begins to make sense of these complementary truths, it is not long before one is wrestling with the relationships between time and eternity, with the nature of secondary causality, with the nature of the will and the nature of freedom, with the notions of person and substance. Part of the aim of biblical balance in these cases is to learn to state the complementary truths in such a way that one is not unwittingly undermining something else that Scripture says. One refuses to draw inferences from one facet of the truth that endangers some other facet of the truth. One learns to let each truth function in our lives and in our theology in the same ways they function in Scripture, and in no other ways.

It would be easy to add more axes where Christians need to achieve biblical balance. For example, the Bible itself establishes something of a hierarchy of truths, so part of maturity in pastoral ministry is tied up with maintaining a similar sense of proportion and priority, aligned with the Bible itself. Moreover, it would also be easy to expand each of the five points listed above into an entire chapter replete with examples and pastoral applications. What should be clear even from these short paragraphs, however, is that biblical balance requires thought, self-examination, ongoing study of Scripture, humility of mind, and a continuing resolution to bring every thought captive to Christ.

10

Subtle Ways to Abandon the Authority of Scripture in Our Lives

RECENTLY EERDMANS PUBLISHED *The Enduring Authority of the Christian Scriptures.*[1] It is a rather big book, with thirty-seven contributors, all of them experts in their fields.[2] The hope and prayer that guided the project were that this volume of essays would be used by God to stabilize worldwide evangelicalism—and not only evangelicals, but all who hold to confessional Christianity. More recently, however, I have been pondering the fact that many Christians slide away from full confidence in the trustworthiness of Scripture for reasons that are not so much intellectual as broadly cultural. I am not now thinking of the college student brought up in a confessional home who goes to university and is for the first time confronted with informed and charming intellectuals whose reasoning calls into question the structure and fabric of his or her Christian belief. Clearly that student needs a lot more information; the period of doubt is often a rite of passage. No, in these jottings I'm reflecting on *subtle* ways in which we may reduce Scripture's authority *in our lives*—and the "we" refers to many Christians in the world, especially the Western world, and not least pastors and scholars. If they then introduce intellectual and cognitive objections to the authority of Scripture in order to bolster the move toward skepticism that they

---

1 D. A. Carson, ed., *The Enduring Authority of the Christian Scriptures* (Grand Rapids, MI: Eerdmans, 2016).

2 This chapter was originally published as D. A. Carson, "Subtle Ways to Abandon the Authority of Scripture in Our Lives," *Themelios* 42, no. 1 (2017): 1–12. It is a condensed version of a talk given to the Council of TGC in May 2016.

have already begun, a focus on such intellectual and cognitive objections, however necessary, is in danger of addressing symptoms without diagnosing the problem.

It might be useful to try to identify some of these subtle factors.

1. An Appeal to Selective Evidence

The most severe forms of this drift are well exemplified in the teaching and preaching of the health, wealth, and prosperity gospel. Link together some verses about God sending prosperity to the land with others that reflect on the significance of being a child of the King, and the case is made—provided, of course, that we ignore the many passages about taking up our cross, about suffering with Christ so that we may reign with him, about rejoicing because we are privileged to suffer for the name, and much more. These breaches are so egregious that they are easy to spot. What I'm thinking of now is something subtler: the simple refusal to talk about disputed matters in order to sidestep controversy in the local church. For the sake of peace, we offer anodyne treatments of hot topics (poverty, racism, homosexual marriage, distinctions between men and women) in the forlorn hope that some of these topics will eventually go away. The sad reality is that if we do not try to shape our thinking on such topics under the authority of Scripture, the result is that many of us will simply pick up the culture's thinking on them.

The best antidote is systematic expository preaching, for such preaching forces us to deal with texts as they come up. Topical preaching finds it easier to avoid the hard texts. Yet cultural blinders can easily afflict expositors too. A Christian preacher I know in a major Muslim nation says he loves to preach evangelistically, especially around Christmas, from Matthew 1 and 2 because these chapters include no fewer than five reports of dreams and visions—and dreams and visions in the dominant culture of his country are commonly accorded great respect. When I have preached through Matthew 1 and 2, I have never focused on those five dreams and visions (though I haven't entirely ignored them), precisely because such dreams and visions are not customarily accorded great credibility in my culture. In other words, ruthless self-examination of one's motives and biases, so far as we are aware of them, can go a long way to mitigating this problem.

2. Heart Embarrassment before the Text

This is a more acute form of the first failure. Not infrequently preachers avoid certain topics, in part because those topics embarrass them. The embarrassment may arise from the preacher's awareness that he has not yet sufficiently studied the topic so as to give him the confidence to tackle it (e.g., some elements of eschatology, transgenderism), or because of some general unease at the topic (e.g., predestination), or because the preacher knows his congregation is sharply divided on the topic (any number of possibilities), or because the preacher really does not like the subject even though it surfaces fairly often in the Bible (e.g., hell, eternal judgment). In its ugliest form, the preacher says something like this: "Our passage this morning, Luke 16:19–31, like quite a number of other passages drawn from the life of Jesus, depicts hell in some pretty shocking ways. Frankly, I wish I could avoid these passages. They leave me distinctly uncomfortable. But of course, I cannot ignore them entirely, for they are right here in the Bible, after all." The preacher has formally submitted to Scripture's authority while presenting himself as someone who is more compassionate or more sensitive than Jesus. This is as deceptive as it is wicked—and it is easy to multiply examples.

Contrast the apostle Paul:

> Therefore, since through God's mercy we have this ministry, we do not lose heart. Rather, we have renounced secret and shameful ways; we do not use deception, nor do we distort the word of God. On the contrary, by setting forth the truth plainly we commend ourselves to everyone's conscience in the sight of God. (2 Cor. 4:1–2)

3. Publishing Ventures that Legitimate What God Condemns

Recently Zondervan published *Two Views on Homosexuality, the Bible, and the Church*;[3] this book bills these two views as "affirming" and "non-affirming," and two authors support each side. Both sides, we are told, argue "from Scripture." If the "affirming" side was once viewed as a stance that could not be held by confessional evangelicals, this book declares that not

---

3 Preston Sprinkle, ed., *Two Views on Homosexuality, the Bible, and the Church*, Counterpoints (Grand Rapids, MI: Zondervan, 2016).

only the non-affirming stance but also the affirming stance are represented within the evangelical camp, so the effect of this book is to present alternative evangelical positions, one that thinks the Bible prohibits homosexual marriage, and the other that embraces it.

All who read these lines will of course be aware of the many books that proffer three views or four views (or two, or five) on this or that subject: the millennium, election, hell, baptism, and many more. Surely this new book on homosexuality is no different. To this a couple of things must be said.

(a) The format of such volumes, "x views on y," is intrinsically slippery. It can be very helpful to students to read, in one volume, diverse stances on complex subjects, yet the format is in danger of suggesting that each option is equally "biblical" because it is argued "from Scripture." Of course, Jehovah's Witnesses argue "from Scripture," but most of us would hasten to add that their exegesis, nominally "from Scripture," is woefully lacking. The "x views on y" format tilts evaluation away from such considerations, baptizing each option with at least theoretical equivalent legitimacy. In short, the "x views on y" format, as useful as it is for some purposes, is somewhat manipulative. As I have argued elsewhere, not all disputed things are properly disputable.[4]

(b) Otherwise put, it is generally the case that books of the "x views on y" format operate within some implicit confessional framework or other. That's why no book of this sort has (yet!) been published with a title such as "Three Views on whether Jesus is God." We might bring together a liberal committed to philosophical naturalism, a Jehovah's Witness, and a confessional Christian. But it's hard to imagine a book like that getting published—or, more precisely, a book like that would be tagged as a volume on comparative religion, not a volume offering options for Christians. Most books of the "x views on y" sort restrict the subject, the y component, to topics that are currently allowed as evangelical options. To broaden this list to include an option that no evangelical would have allowed ten years ago—say, the denial of the deity of Jesus, or the legitimacy of homosexual practice—is designed simultaneously to assert that Scripture is less clear on the said topic than was once thought, and to redefine, once again, the

---

4   See chapter 32, "On Disputable Matters," originally published in *Themelios* 40, no. 3 (2015): 383–88.

borders of evangelicalism. On both counts, the voice of Scripture as the *norma normans* ("the rule that rules"), though theoretically still intact, has in fact been subtly reduced.

Inevitably, there have been some articulate voices that insist that adopting an "affirming" stance on homosexual marriage does not jeopardize one's salvation and should not place such a person outside the evangelical camp. For example, in his essay "An Evangelical Approach to Sexual Ethics," Stephen Holmes concludes,

> Sola Fide. I have to stand on that. Because the Blood flowed where I walk and where we all walk. One perfect sacrifice complete, once for all offered for all the world, offering renewal to all who will put their faith in Him. And if that means me, in all my failures and confusions, then it also means my friends who affirm same-sex marriage, in all their failures and confusions. If my faithful and affirming friends have no hope of salvation, then nor do I.[5]

But this is an abuse of the evangelical insistence on *sola fide*. I do not know any Christian who thinks that salvation is appropriated by means of faith plus an affirmation of heterosexuality. Faith alone is the means by which *sola gratia* is appropriated. Nevertheless, that grace is so powerful it transforms. Salvation by grace alone through faith alone issues in a new direction under the lordship of King Jesus. Those who are sold out to the "acts of the flesh . . . will not inherit the kingdom of God" (Gal. 5:19–21). The apostle Paul makes a similar assertion in 1 Corinthians 6:9–11:

> Or do you not know that wrongdoers will not inherit the kingdom of God? Do not be deceived: Neither the sexually immoral nor idolaters nor adulterers not men who have sex with men nor thieves nor the greedy nor drunkards nor slanderers nor swindlers will inherit the kingdom of God. *And that is what some of you were. But you were washed, you were sanctified, you were justified in the name of the Lord Jesus Christ and by the Spirit of our God.*

---

5   Stephen Holmes, "An Evangelical Approach to Sexual Ethics," *Shored Fragments*, November 19, 2016, http://steverholmes.org.uk/.

In the context of Paul's thought, he is not saying that without sinless perfection there is no entrance into the kingdom, but he is saying that such sins—whether greed or adultery or homosexual practice or whatever— no longer characterize the washed, sanctified, and justified. In other words, it is one thing to affirm with joy that *sola fide* means that we appropriate the merits of Christ and his cross by faith alone, not by our holiness—that holiness is the product of salvation, not its condition—and it is quite another thing to say that someone may self-consciously affirm the nonsinfulness of what God has declared to be sin, of what God insists excludes a person from the kingdom, and say that it doesn't matter because *sola fide* will get them in anyway. The Scriptures make a lot of room for believers who slip and slide in "failures and confusions," as Holmes put it, but who rest in God's grace and receive it in God-given faith; they do not leave a lot of room for those who deny they are sinning despite what God says. *Sola gratia* and *sola fide* are always accompanied by *sola Scriptura*, by *solus Christus*, and by *soli Deo gloria*.

Or again, one really must question the recent argument by Alan Jacobs, from whose books and essays I have gained a great deal over the years. In his essay "On False Teachers: Bleat the Third,"[6] however, Jacobs argues that when we warn against doctrine that is so dangerous it must be labeled and condemned, one naturally thinks of 2 Peter 2, where Peter warns against false teachers analogous to false prophets in the old covenant, and 1 Timothy 4, where Paul warns us against doctrines of demons. What is remarkable, Jacobs argues, is that when Paul rebukes Peter in Antioch (Gal. 2:11–14), he tells him he is not walking in line with the gospel, but he does not label him a "false teacher." If Paul can be so restrained in rebuking Peter over conduct that challenged the very heart of the gospel, then should we not allow a very wide swath of what we perceive to be inappropriate conduct before we assert someone is a false teacher and expounding doctrines of demons? As Jacobs summarizes:

> So if we can be as wrong as Peter was about something as foundational for the Gospel and still not be denounced as a false teacher, then I think it

---

6   Alan Jacobs, "On False Teachers: Bleat the Third," *The Homebound Symphony*, November 22, 2016, https://blog.ayjay.org/.

follows that if people do not "walk correctly" in relation to biblical teaching about sexuality, they likewise should not be treated as *pseudodidaskaloi* [false teachers] but can be seen as brothers and sisters whom those who hold the traditional views patiently strive to correct, without coming out from among them, speaking with the patience and gentleness commended in 2 Timothy 3:14–15.[7]

Against this, the following must be said.

(a) In Galatians 2:11–14, Paul is building off his argument (2:1–13) that Paul and Peter enjoy theological agreement. Peter's problem, Paul thinks, is that Peter's conduct is inconsistent with his theological commitments. This is all the clearer when we see that Peter's preference for eating with "those from James" has to do not with any alleged confusion in his mind about justification, but with this concern for the persecution his fellow Jews are enduring back home in Jerusalem at the hands of "the circumcision group."[8] In any case, this is rather different from the current situation in which some voices are insisting that homosexual marriage is not wrong. Paul is not saying that Peter's theology is wrong, but that his conduct is not in line with his theology. Incidentally, Jacobs assumes, probably correctly, that the Jerusalem Council (Acts 15) occurs *after* this episode in Antioch, prompting him to comment, "and of course Paul's view won out at the Council of Jerusalem (where, I have always thought comically, Peter presents it as his own view, with no reference to Paul having corrected him)."[9] But there is nothing comical about Peter's stance at the Council: Paul himself insists that so far as their theological understanding goes, he and Peter are in agreement, so it is neither surprising nor comical to find Peter saying the same thing.

(b) It is not clear to me why Jacobs rests so much weight on the "false teacher" passage in Peter and the "doctrines of demons" passage in Paul. There are plenty of other passages that deploy quite different terminology and that insist that false doctrine or untransformed behavior keep one

---

7   Jacobs, "On False Teachers."

8   D. A. Carson, "Mirror-Reading with Paul and against Paul: Galatians 2:11–14 as a Test Case," in *Studies in the Pauline Epistles: Essays in Honor of Douglas J. Moo*, ed. Matthew S. Harmon and Jay E. Smith (Grand Rapids, MI: Zondervan, 2014), 99–112.

9   Jacobs, "On False Teachers."

out of the kingdom: Matthew 7:21–23; 11:21–24; Luke 16:19–31; Romans 1:18–3:20; Galatians 1:8–9; Revelation 13–14, to name but a few.

(c) Despite the best efforts of bad exegesis, the Bible makes it clear that treating homosexuality as if it were not a sin but a practice in which people should feel perfectly free to engage keeps one out of the kingdom (as we have seen: e.g., 1 Cor. 6:9–11). There is nothing more serious than that, and the seriousness is present whether or not a particular term, such as ψευδοδιδάσκαλος ("false teacher") is used.

From time to time, expansion of the frame of reference of what has traditionally been called evangelicalism has been influenced by William J. Webb's trajectory hermeneutic, which argues that sometimes it is not what Scripture actually says that is authoritative but rather the direction to which it points.[10] His favorite example is slavery; his favorite application of that example is the role of women. This trajectory hermeneutic has been adequately discussed elsewhere;[11] it would be inappropriate to rehearse the hermeneutic here. What cannot be denied, however, is that this way of reading the Bible diminishes the authority of what the Bible actually says in favor of what the interpreter judges to be the end goal of the Bible's trajectory after the Bible has been written and circulated. One of the latest examples is the defense mounted by Pete Briscoe and his elders as the Bent Tree Bible Fellowship in Dallas embraces egalitarianism, a defense that specifically references Webb's work.[12] Further, Briscoe says he has moved the debate over egalitarianism and complementarianism into the "agree to disagree" category, which may function well enough in the cadre of evangelicalism *as a movement*, but can only function practically at the level of the local church if one side or the other is actually being followed at the expense of the other. In any case, the "agree to disagree" argument nicely brings us to my fourth point.

---

10 See especially William J. Webb's *Slaves, Women and Homosexuals: Exploring the Hermeneutics of Cultural Analysis* (Downers Grove, IL: InterVarsity, 2001).

11 Wayne A. Grudem, "Review Article: Should We Move Beyond the New Testament to a Better Ethic? An Analysis of William J. Webb, *Slaves, Women and Homosexuals: Exploring the Hermeneutics of Cultural Analysis*," *Journal of the Evangelical Theological Society* 47 (2004): 299–346. See also Benjamin Reaoch, *Women, Slaves, and the Gender Debate: A Complementarian Response to the Redemptive-Movement Hermeneutic* (Phillipsburg, NJ: P&R, 2012).

12 Bent Tree Bible Fellowship, *The Future of Leadership at Bent Tree: A Statement from the Board of Elders*, April 2016, https://benttree.org.

4. "The Art of Imperious Ignorance"

The words are in quotation marks because they are borrowed from Mike Ovey's column in a 2016 issue of *Themelios*.[13] This is the stance that insists that all the relevant biblical passages on a stated subject are exegetically confusing and unclear, and therefore we *cannot* know (hence "imperious") the mind of God on that subject. The historical example that Ovey adduces is the decision of a church council during the patristic period whose decisions have mostly been forgotten by nonspecialists. At a time of great controversy over Christology—specifically over the deity of Christ—the Council of Sirmium (AD 357), which sided with the pro-Arians, pronounced a prohibition against using terms like *homoousios* (signaling "one and the same substance") and *homoiousios* (signaling "of a similar substance"). In other words, Sirmium prohibited using the technical terms espoused by *both* sides, on the ground that the issues are so difficult and the evidence so obscure that we *cannot* know the truth. Sirmium even adduced a biblical proof text: "Who shall declare his generation?" (Isa. 53:8 KJV; in other words, "It is all too mysterious").

Nevertheless, the Orthodox fathers Hilary of Poitiers and Athanasius of Alexandria assessed the stance of Sirmium as worse than error: it was, they said, blasphemy. They decried the element of compulsion in Sirmium's decree and insisted that it was absurd: how is it possible to legislate the knowledge of other people? But the blasphemous element surfaces in the fact that the decree tries to put an end to the confession of true propositions (e.g., the eternal generation of the Son). Practically speaking, the claim of dogmatic ignorance, ostensibly arising from Scripture's lack of clarity, criticizes Scripture while allowing people to adopt the positions they want.

This art of imperious ignorance is not unknown or unpracticed today. For example, both in a recent book and in an article,[14] David Gushee argues that homosexual marriage should be placed among the things over which we agree to disagree, what used to be called "adiaphora," indifferent things. He predicts that "conservatives" and "progressives" are heading for an unfortunate divorce over this and a handful of other issues precisely because they cannot agree to disagree. He may be right. In all fairness, however, in

---

13 Michael J. Ovey, "The Art of Imperious Ignorance," *Themelios* 41, no.1 (2016): 5–7.

14 David Gushee, *A Letter to My Anxious Christian Friends: From Fear to Faith in Unsettled Times* (Louisville: Westminster John Knox, 2016); Gushee, "Conservative and Progressive US Evangelicals Head for Divorce," *Religion News Service*, February 12, 2016, http://religionnews.com/.

addition to the question of whether one's behavior in the domain of sexuality has eternal consequences, it must be said, gently but firmly, that the unified voice of both Scripture and tradition on homosexuality has not been on the side of the "progressives" (see especially the book by S. Donald Fortson III and Rollin G. Grams, *Unchanging Witness: The Consistent Christian Teaching on Homosexuality in Scripture and Tradition*).[15] As Trevin Wax has pointed out, on this subject the "progressives" innovate on teaching and conduct and thus start the schism, and then accuse the "conservatives" of drawing lines and promoting schism instead of agreeing to disagree.[16]

A somewhat similar pattern can be found in the arguments of Jen and Brandon Hatmaker. Most of their posts are winsome and compassionate, full of admirable concern for the downtrodden and oppressed. Their recent move in support of monogamous homosexual marriage has drawn a lot of attention: after devoting time to studying the subject, they say, they have come to the conclusion that the biblical texts do not clearly forbid homosexual conduct if it is a monogamous commitment, but condemn only conduct that is promiscuous (whether heterosexual or homosexual), rape, and other grievous offenses.[17] In his explanation of their move, Brandon testifies that after seeing so much pain in the homosexual community, the Hatmakers set themselves "a season of study and prayer," and arrived at this conclusion: "Bottom line, we don't believe a committed life-long monogamous same-sex marriage violates anything seen in scripture about God's hopes for the marriage relationship."[18] Quite apart from the oddity of the expression "God's hopes for the marriage relationship," Brandon's essay extravagantly praises ethicist David Gushee, and ends his essay by citing John 13:34–35 (Jesus's "new command" to his disciples to "love one another").

Among the excellent responses, three deserve mention here.[19]

---

15 S. Donald Fortson III and Rollin G. Grams, *Unchanging Witness: The Consistent Christian Teaching on Homosexuality in Scripture and Tradition* (Nashville: B&H Academic, 2016).

16 Trevin Wax, "Can We 'Agree to Disagree' on Sexuality and Marriage?' Gospel Coalition, February 25, 2016, https://www.thegospelcoalition.org/.

17 See, for example, Jen Hatmaker's interview with Jonathan Merritt, "The Politics of Jen Hatmaker," *Religion News Service*, October 25, 2016, http://religionnews.com/.

18 Brandon Hatmaker, "Where I Stand on LGBTQ," Facebook, November 1, 2016, https://www.facebook.com/.

19 See also Justin Taylor, "The Only Four Things You Need to Read in Response to the Hatmakers," Gospel Coalition, November 2, 2016, https://www.thegospelcoalition.org/. Taylor highlights the articles by Butterfield and DeYoung mentioned below.

(a) Speaking out of her own remarkable conversion, Rosaria Butterfield counsels her readers to love their neighbors enough to speak the truth.[20] "Love" that does not care enough to speak the truth and warn against judgment to come easily reduces to sentimentality.

(b) With his inimitable style, Kevin DeYoung briefly but decisively challenges what he calls "the Hatmaker hermeneutic."[21] To pick up on just one of his points:

> I fail to see how the logic *for* monogamy and *against* fornication is obvious according to Hatmaker's hermeneutic. I appreciate that they don't want to completely jettison orthodox Christian teaching when it comes to sex and marriage. But the flimsiness of the hermeneutic cannot support the weight of the tradition. Once you've concluded that the creation of Adam and Eve has nothing to do with a procreative *telos* (Mal. 2:15), or the fittedness of male with female (Gen. 2:18), or the joining of two complementary sexes into one organic union (Gen. 2:23–24), what's left to insist that marriage must be limited to two persons, or that the two persons must be faithful to each other? Sure, both partners may agree that they *want* fidelity, but there is no longer anything inherent to the ontology and the *telos* of marriage to insist that sexual fidelity is a must. Likewise, why is it obvious that sex outside of marriage is wrong? Perhaps those verses were only dealing with oppressive situations too. Most foundationally, once stripped of the biological orientation toward children, by what internal logic can we say that consensual sex between two adults is wrong? And on that score, by what measure can we condemn a biological brother and sister getting married if they truly love each other (and use contraceptives, just to take the possibility of genetic abnormalities out of the equation)? When marriage is redefined to include persons of the same sex, we may think we are expanding the institution to make it more inclusive, but in fact we are diminishing it to the point where it is something other than marriage.[22]

---

20 Rosaria Butterfield, "Love Your Neighbor Enough to Speak Truth: A Response to Jen Hatmaker," Gospel Coalition, October 31, 2016, https://www.thegospelcoalition.org/.
21 Kevin DeYoung, "A Few Brief Thoughts on the Hatmaker Hermeneutic," Gospel Coalition, November 2, 2016, https://www.thegospelcoalition.org/.
22 DeYoung, "A Few Brief Thoughts."

(c) And finally, I should mention another piece by Kevin DeYoung, presented as a breakout session at Together for the Gospel on April 13, 2016, titled, "Drawing Boundaries in an Inclusive Age: Are Some Doctrines More Fundamental Than Others and How Do We Know What They Are?"

I have devoted rather extended discussion to this topic because nowhere does "the art of imperious ignorance" make a stronger appeal, in our age, than to issues of sexuality. By the same token, there are few topics where contemporary believers are more strongly tempted to slip away from whole-hearted submission the Scripture's authority in our own lives.

The rest of my points, although they deserve equal attention, I shall outline more briefly.

5. Allowing the Categories of Systematic Theology to Domesticate What Scripture Says

Most emphatically, this point is neither belittling systematic theology nor an attempt to sideline the discipline. When I warn against the danger of systematic theology domesticating what Scripture says, I nevertheless gladly insist that, properly deployed, systematic theology enriches, deepens, and safeguards our exegesis. The old affirmation that theology is the queen of the sciences has much to commend it. The best of systematic theology not only attempts to bring together all of Scripture in faithful ways but also at its best enjoys a pedagogical function that helps to steer exegesis away from irresponsible options that depend on mere linguistic manipulation by consciously taking into account the witness of the entire canon. Such theology-disciplined exegesis is much more likely to learn from the past than exegesis that shucks off everything except the faddish.

So there are ways in which exegesis shapes systematic theology and ways in which systematic theology shapes exegesis. That is not only as it should be; it is inevitable. Yet the *authority* of Scripture in our lives is properly unique. Systematic theology is corrigible; Scripture is not (although our exegesis of Scripture certainly is).

Failure to think through the implications of this truth makes it easy for us to allow the categories of systematic theology to domesticate what Scripture says. The categories we inherit or develop in our systematic theology may so constrain our thinking about what the Bible says that the Bible's own voice is scarcely heard. Thus diminished, the authority of the Bible is insufficient to reform our systematic theology. Recently I was rereading Exodus 7–11. After each of the first nine "plagues" with which God chastened the Egyptians, we read variations of "Pharaoh hardened his heart" and "God hardened Pharaoh's heart" and "Pharaoh's heart was hardened." I could not help but remember with shame and regret some of the exegetical sins of my youth. Barely twenty years old at the time, I was invited to speak to a group of young people, and carefully explained the three stages: first, Pharaoh hardens his own heart; second, as a result, Pharaoh's heart is hardened; and finally, God imposes his own final sanction—he judicially hardens Pharaoh's heart. Of course, I was aware that the narrative did not display those three expressions in this convenient psychological order, but the homiletical point seemed to me, at the time, too good to pass up— it simply is the way these things develop, isn't it? So my theology of the time, shallow as it was, domesticated the text. Only later did I learn how commonly the Bible juxtaposes human responsibility and divine sovereignty without the smallest discomfort, without allowing the slightest hint that the affirmation of the one dilutes belief in the other (e.g., Gen. 50:19–20; Isa. 10:5–19; Acts 4:27–28). It is the part of humility and wisdom not to allow our theological categories to domesticate what Scripture says.

6. Too Little Reading, Especially the Reading of Older Commentaries and Theological Works

The more general failure of too little reading contributes, of course, to some of the paths that tend with time to hobble the authority of Scripture, paths already articulated. The obvious one is that we do not grow out of youthful errors and reductionisms; we prove unable to self-correct; our shallow theology becomes ossified. Thus too little reading is partly to blame for my irresponsible exegesis of Exodus 7–11 (point 5 above), or to downplaying the cultural importance of dreams and visions in other parts of the world (cf. point 1 above). But a more focused problem frequently surfaces, one that requires separate notice. Too little reading, especially the reading of older confessional material, not infrequently leads to in an infatuation with current agendas, to intoxication by the overimbibing of the merely faddish.

Of course, the opposite failure is not unknown. Many of us are acquainted with ministers who read deeply from the wells of Puritan resources but who have not tried to read much contemporary work. Their language, thought categories, illustrations, and agendas tend to sound almost four centuries old. But that is not the problem I am addressing here, mostly because, as far as I can see, it is far less common than the failure to read older confessional materials, not least commentaries and theological works.

The problem with reading only contemporary work is that we all sound so contemporary that our talks and sermons soon descend to the level of kitsch. We talk fluently about the importance of self-identity, ecological responsibility, tolerance, becoming a follower of Jesus (but rarely becoming a Christian), and how the Bible helps us in our pain and suffering, and conduct seminars on money management and divorce recovery. Not for a moment would I suggest that the Bible fails to address such topics—but the Bible is not primarily *about* such topics. If we integrate more reading of, say, John Chrysostom, John Calvin, and John Flavel (to pick on three Johns), we might be inclined to devote more attention in our addresses to what it means to be made in the image of God, to the dreadfulness of sin, to the nature of the gospel, to the blessed Trinity, to truth, to discipleship, to the Bible's insistence that Christians will suffer, to learning how to die well, to the prospect of the new heaven and the new earth, to the glories of the new covenant, to the sheer beauty of Jesus Christ, to confidence in a God who is both sovereign and good, to the nonnegotiability of repentance and faith, to the importance of endurance and perseverance, to the beauty of holiness and the importance of the local church. Is the Bible truly authoritative in our lives and ministries when we skirt these and other truly important themes that other generations of Christians rightly found in the Bible?

7. The Failure to be Bound by Both the Formal Principle and the Material Principle

The distinction between these two principles was well-known among an earlier generation of evangelicals. The *formal* principle that constrains us is the authority of Scripture; the *material* principle that constrains us is the substance of Scripture, the gospel itself. And we need both.

That the formal principle by itself is inadequate is obvious as soon as we recall that groups such as Jehovah's Witnesses and Mormons happily and unreservedly affirm the Bible's truthfulness, reliability, and authority, but their understanding of what the Bible *says* (the material principle) is so aberrant that (we insist) they do not in reality let the Bible's authoritative message transform their thinking. On the other hand, today it is not uncommon to find Christians saying that they refuse to talk about biblical authority or biblical inerrancy or the like, but simply get on with preaching what the Bible says. History shows that such groups tend rather quickly to drift away from what the Bible says.

In other words, to be bound by only one of these two principles tends toward a drifting away from hearty submission to the Bible's authority. If one begins with adherence to the formal principle, thus nominally espousing the biblical authority of the formal principle, and adds penetrating understanding of and submission to what the Bible actually says, the result is much stronger, much more stable. Conversely, if one begins with an honest effort to grasp and teach what the Bible says, thus nominally espousing the material principle, and adds resolute adherence to the formal principle, one is much more likely to keep doing the honest exegesis that will enrich, revitalize, and correct what one thinks the Bible is saying.

8. Undisciplined Passion for the Merely Technical or Unhealthy Suspicion of the Technical

By the "technical" I am referring to biblical study that deploys the full panoply of literary tools that begin with the original languages and pay attention to syntax, literary genre, textual criticism and literary criticism, parallel sources, interaction with recent scholarship, and much more. An exclusive focus on technical study of the Bible may, surprisingly, dilute the "listening" element: manipulation of the tools and interaction with the scholars of the guild are more important than trembling before the word of God. Conversely, some so disdain careful and informed study that they seduce themselves into thinking that pious reading absolves one from careful and accurate exegesis. In both cases, the Bible's real authority is diminished.

A variation of this concern surfaces when students arrive at the seminary and begin their course of study. Often they enter with boundless love for the Bible and a hunger to read it and think about it. Soon, however, they are enmeshed in memorizing Greek paradigms and struggling to work their way through short passages of the Greek New Testament. What they are doing now, they feel, is not so much reading the word of God as *homework*, and it is hard. Instead of simply reading the Bible and being blessed, they are required to make decisions as to whether a verb should be taken this way or that, and whether an inherited interpretation really can withstand accurate exegesis. Confused and not a little discouraged by the demand to memorize defective Hebrew verbs, they talk to sympathetic professors and ask what is wrong, and what they can do about the coldness they feel stealing over their hearts.

It is not helpful to tell such students that, on the one hand, they simply need to get on with the discipline of study, and, on the other, they need to preserve time for devotional reading of the Bible. That bifurcation of tasks suggests there is no need to be devotional when using technical tools and no need for rigor when reading the Bible devotionally. Far better to insist that even when they are wrestling with difficult verbal forms and challenging syntax, what they are working on is the word of God—and it is always imperative to cherish that fact and treat the biblical text with reverence. And similarly, if when reading the Bible for private edification and without reference to any assignment, one stumbles across a passage one really does not understand, one is not sinning against God if one pulls a commentary or two off the shelf and tries to obtain some technical help.

In short, one should not be seduced by merely technical disciplines, nor should one eschew them. In every case, the Bible remains the authoritative word of God regardless of the "tools" one deploys to understand it better, and it functions authoritatively in our lives when we manage a better integration of technical study and devotional reading.

9. Undisciplined Confidence in Contemporary Philosophical Agendas

Many examples could be provided. For example, some of the choices offered by analytic philosophy wrongfully exclude structures of thought the Bible maintains.[23] Or again, the recent book by Charles Taylor,[24] written in the heritage of some forms of deconstruction and, like all his work, inevitably stimulating, argues that language is in some measure cut off from reality: it is not so much something that designates as it is the medium in which

---

23 For an example, see my essay, "Biblical-Theological Pillars Needed to Support Faithful Christian Reflections on Suffering and Evil," *Trinity Journal* 38 (2017): 55–77.

24 Charles Taylor, *The Language Animal: The Full Shape of Linguistic Capacity* (Cambridge, MA: Belknap, 2016).

we exist. There is no fixed "meaning" to texts (which is very hard to square with the conviction expressed in Jude 3). One form of this approach to texts, often dubbed American pragmatism,[25] thinks of readers as "users" of the text. A "good" reading, for example, is one that meets specific needs in the reader or the community. There is much to be said in favor of this stance, but it becomes self-defeating when it says, in effect, that a "good" reading meets particular needs on the part of the reader or community *and must not be thought of as conveying timeless truth.* Occasionally entire commentaries are today written out of this philosophical commitment. Yet as many have pointed out, the stance is self-defeating: American pragmatism defends itself with an ostensible timeless truth about the virtues of American pragmatism. Pretty soon the commentaries that work out of this tradition do not so much help us think about God and his character and work, as about what we think we need and how the biblical texts meet those needs. The door is opened to interpretations that are exploitative, merely current, sometimes cutesy, and invariably agenda driven, but only accidentally grounded in responsible exegesis.

Not for a moment should we imagine that this is the first generation to make such mistakes. Every generation in this sin-addled world experiments with a variety of philosophical stances that can easily (sometimes unwittingly) be used to subvert what Scripture says—and thus the authority of Scripture is again domesticated. Students of history have learned to appreciate the contributions of, say, Aristotelianism, Platonism, Gnosticism, Thomism, Cartesianism, rationalism—but also to allow Scripture's voice to stand over them. It is more challenging to avoid the pitfalls lurking in the "isms" that are current.

10. Anything that Reduces Our Trembling before the Word of God

"These are the ones I look on with favor: those who are humble and contrite in spirit, and who tremble at my word" (Isa. 66:2). "All people are like grass, and all their glory is like the flowers of the field; the grass withers and the flowers fall, but the word of the Lord endures forever." And this is the word that was preached to you" (1 Pet. 1:24–25; cf. Isa. 40:6–8).

---

25 For a brief introduction, see Benjamin Sargent, "Using or Abusing the Bible? The Hermeneutics of American Pragmatism," *Churchman* 130 (2016): 11–20.

The things that may sap our ability to tremble before God's word are many. Common to all of them is arrogance, arrogance that blinds us to our need to keep reading and rereading and meditating upon the Bible if we are truly to think God's thoughts after him, for otherwise the endless hours of data input from the world around us swamp our minds, hearts, and imaginations. Moral decay will drive us away from the Bible: it is hard to imagine those who are awash in porn, or those who are nurturing sexual affairs, or those who are feeding bitter rivalry to be spending much time reading the Bible, much less trembling before it. Moreover, our uncharitable conduct may undermine the practical authority of the Bible in the lives of those who observe us. Failure to press through in our studies until we have happily resolved some of the intellectual doubts that sometimes afflict us will also reduce the fear of the Lord in us, a subset of which, of course, is trembling before his word.

Concluding Reflections

So that concludes our list of subtle ways to abandon the authority of Scripture in our lives. I'm sure these ten points could be grouped in other ways, and other points could usefully be added.

But I would be making a serious mistake if I did not draw attention to the fact that this list of warnings and dangers, an essentially negative list, implicitly invites us to a list of positive correlatives. For example, the first instance of subtle ways to trim the authority of Scripture was "an appeal to selective evidence"—which implicitly calls us to be as comprehensive as possible when we draw our theological and pastoral conclusions about what the Bible is saying on this or that point. If "heart embarrassment" before this or that text (the second example) reduces the authority of Scripture in my life, a hearty resolve to align my empathies and will with the lines of Scripture until I see more clearly how God looks at things from his sovereign and omniscient angle will mean I offer fewer apologies for the Bible while spending more time making its stances coherent to a generation that finds the Bible profoundly foreign to contemporary axioms. It would be a godly exercise to work through all ten of the points so as to make clear what the positive correlative is in each case.

11

But That's Just Your Interpretation

IN MID-JUNE OF 2019, a former theology student (let's call him Demas) posted the following. Demas had successfully completed his MDiv at a well-known evangelical seminary and then had served a few years as a fruitful pastor of a growing church in a metropolitan area while pursuing a PhD in New Testament studies.[1] He was a pretty good student, a steady preacher, and was invariably warm and personable with people. Sadly, he entered into an adulterous relationship and ended up selling real estate. Mercifully, he and his wife held their marriage together. So this is what Demas posted on social media in June of this year, several years after resigning his pastorate:

> Here's my public contribution during #PrideMonth: Whenever I talk with a conservative Christian or pastor (who [sic] I love and esteem, and whom I believe good things about, and which I used to be) about homosexuality now, whatever I actually end up saying to them—what I'm actually THINKING is, "Look. I've done biblical and theological training at a very high level. At least as high if not higher than you (for 99.9% of the population). And I'm telling you: *You. don't. know. for sure.*" You don't know for sure that your reading of the Bible is right. Or if your hermeneutics are correct. You do not know for sure how interwoven or weighted the divine and human authorship(s?) of the Bible is. You do not know that. You don't know 100% for certain which ancient books are actually God

---

1   This chapter was originally published as D. A. Carson, "But That's Just Your Interpretation!," *Themelios* 44, no. 3 (2019): 425–32.

Almighty's eternal Word. Because there were a lot of books. And we rely on these particular books because they're the ones the Church happened to be using when the Church first put a "Bible" together. Moses did not bring the whole Bible down the mountain from God. We love these books, but we have very thin understandings of how this collection of books came together and why and on who's [sic] authority. We do not know. We don't know for absolutely certain how God wanted us to use these books. How he wanted them applied to the 21st century western world. We do not know for certain. We cannot know for certain. Believing in the Bible is an act of faith. For everyone. And I believe in the Bible. But when my eyes are open to the fact that I can say BOTH "This book is holy" AND "There is a lot of uncertainty about how it should be applied to our society" I immediately realize that I could get the "answer" to the homosexuality question wrong—one way or the other. I could end up approving something God hates or hating something God loves. Could go either way. Because the issue is not certain. It's not. We know the same facts. You know it's not certain. So, if my potential mistake it [sic] to love something God hates, then I'm going to err on the side of what looks and feels to me most like love. Because whatever else I believe about God, I believe that God Is Love. So, I should try to approve of the things that look most like love. Which makes me an LGBTQ+ affirming Christian. And I should be willing to say that more. Happy Pride Month.

In the past, Christians who spoke about the status of the Bible tended to speak of the Bible's truthfulness, reliability, sufficiency, inspiration, inerrancy, and so forth. In line with many contemporaries, however, Demas, without overtly calling into question any of these more familiar categories, has undermined several of them by raising epistemic and hermeneutical questions: How can I know with certainty what the Bible is saying? How can I be certain what books really belong in the Bible? How can I be sure that my interpretation of any text is correct and, still more, what its proper application is when I draw lines from texts that are two or three thousand years old and written in another language and in another culture to our life in the early twenty-first century?

At a milder level, many preachers who are not entertaining the sweep of the epistemic challenges that Demas raises may nevertheless face somewhat similar challenges as they prepare their Sunday morning sermons. Which interpretation of the text in front of me is correct? How can I declare what the word of the Lord is saying if I cannot be certain what it is saying? Or which of us have tried to explain what the Bible says on some sensitive topic or other, only to be dismissed with the line, "But that's just your interpretation"?

The subject is much too large and multifaceted for a brief reflection, but it may not be inappropriate to lay down a handful of markers, the first four in a little more detail than the final entry.

First, it is deceptive, and even idolatrous, to set up omniscience as the necessary criterion for "certain" or "sure" knowledge. Recall that Demas keeps saying that you cannot know "for sure" or "for certain" or "for 100% certain" and the like. His argument seems to be that if you do not know something "for 100% sure," then you do not *truly* know it. In other words, you must possess omniscient knowledge about something before you can legitimately say that you know that thing well enough to build life decisions on your putative knowledge. In the concrete example that is the focus of Demas's concern, unless you know with omniscient knowledge that the Bible really does condemn homosexual behavior, and unless you know with omniscient knowledge that the books of the Bible with those passages in them really do belong to the canon of God-inspired books, and unless you know with omniscient knowledge that this is the way God himself wants those ancient texts to be interpreted and applied today, then you have no right to speak as if these things are truly known at all. According to Demas, you are free to choose some other path.

But it is deceptive to set up omniscience as the necessary criterion for "certain" or "sure" knowledge, and this for at least four reasons.

1. We commonly speak of human knowing without making omniscience the criterion of true knowing. This is true even in the Bible. For example, Luke tells Theophilus that although many people had undertaken to hand down reports of Jesus's life and ministry as reported by the eyewitnesses, he himself carefully "investigated everything from the beginning" and then "decided to write an orderly account for you, most excellent Theophilus, so that you may *know the certainty* of the things you have been taught" (Luke 1:3–4). Luke uses words that are entirely appropriate to human knowing, to human certainty; he is not promising omniscient knowledge to Theophilus.

Again, John tells his believing readers that he is writing his first epistle "so that you may *know that* you have eternal life" (1 John 5:13): he is not writing so that they may become omniscient with respect to their knowledge of their status. When Paul encourages Timothy to become "a worker who does not need to be ashamed and who correctly handles the word of truth" (2 Tim. 2:15), he is anticipating that Timothy will become a faithful interpreter of Scripture, but not that he will become an omniscient interpreter of Scripture.

2. If Demas's arguments are valid for the issues that concern him—that is, if because we do not enjoy 100 percent certain knowledge about what the Scriptures are saying regarding these ethical issues, therefore we cannot legitimately adjudicate their rightness or wrongness—then to be consistent we must adopt the same agnostic position on everything the Bible says, including what it says about the most deeply confessional Christian truths. For example, Christians hold that Jesus is truly to be confessed and worshiped as God. But the deity of Christ is denied by Arians old and new, including Jehovah's Witnesses: one cannot say that there is universal agreement that this is what the Bible teaches. Must we therefore say that because we don't know "for sure" what the Bible says about these things, therefore we should leave the matter open?

3. Believing in the Bible, Demas asserts, "is an act of faith." True enough. It appears, however, that Demas pits faith over against knowing. If I understand him correctly, his argument is as follows: You may *believe* that the Bible says such and such about LGBTQ+ issues, but you cannot *know* "for 100% sure," and therefore you are not warranted to pronounce that LGBTQ+ behavior is disapproved by God. This, however, buys into not only a misguided view of knowledge but also contemporary secular definitions of "faith." On the streets of New York or Montreal, "faith" has one of two common meanings: either it is a synonym for "religion" (there are many "religions"; there are many "faiths"), or it refers to a personal, subjective, religious commitment without any necessary connection to truth. Something like the latter is what Demas appears to accept, even though "faith" is never used that way in the Bible. In the Bible, faith is intimately connected with truth. The Bible never asks you to believe or trust what is not true or trustworthy. Indeed, in the Bible one of the most common means of strengthening faith is by articulating and defending the truth. What is to be believed or trusted is often propositional, sometimes not, but it is never

*un*truth. To pit the truth of what the Bible says against the beliefs that the Bible elicits, makes, from the Bible's perspective, no sense at all.

4. One cannot help but ask how Demas knows that God is a loving God. Many so-called "new atheists" viscerally deny that God is great or good.[2] The Bible itself depicts God as standing behind judgments that amount to genocide, and many people wrestle with God's "goodness" because of such passages. So why does Demas base his ethical decisions on his conviction that God is good? To be consistent, shouldn't he say that we cannot know "for 100% sure" that God is good? Isn't he making ethical decisions on the basis of what (his own logic must tell him) he cannot know?

It appears, then, that Demas has succumbed to the categories of this present evil world to arrive at, or at least support, his conclusions. Essentially, Demas is undermining the clarity and the authority of Scripture on the ground that we cannot truly know what Scripture is saying because we don't enjoy omniscient knowledge, and that even our view of the Bible is grounded not in knowledge but in (his understanding of) faith. But I have tried to show that this appeal is deceptive, for our common use of language shows that, whether in the Bible or in general usage, we commonly speak of human knowing even though such knowing is not anchored in omniscience. But the ploy is not only deceptive, it is idolatrous. It demands of human beings that they enjoy an attribute that belongs to God alone if they are to know ("for certain"—i.e., well enough to make ethical decisions) anything at all. Of course, Demas and his friends are claiming we *don't* enjoy omniscient knowledge: we are *not* to pretend we have the attributes of God. So why am I charging them with idolatry? It is because by claiming we cannot know anything ("for certain") we are being forbidden to think about human beings and human knowing in a biblical fashion? The Bible demonstrates, often implicitly but sometimes explicitly, that human beings *can* grow in knowledge, with appropriate certainty, responding to God's revelation with thought and active faith and obedient submission to our Maker and Redeemer. The ideal of *knowing* God and making him *known* is traded in for dogmatic focus on what we cannot know without reference to what God says about human knowing and by the forging of

2   E.g., Christopher Hitchens, *God Is Not Great: How Religion Poisons Everything* (New York: Hatchett, 2007).

epistemological chains that make us deaf to and careless about what God has disclosed of himself, of our world, of moral and ethical conduct. God has been de-godded. The name of this game is idolatry.

Second, we must at all costs avoid being manipulated by what a friend has called "the art of imperious ignorance."[3] Returning for a moment to the digital post of the man I've called Demas, the thing to note about his argument is that he not only claims that he himself does not know whether the relevant texts are from God, and/or what they mean (which is an admission of *his own* ignorance), but he also claims no one else may legitimately claim that they know (which is a dogmatic declaration of their ignorance). This is "imperious ignorance"—that is, an imperial declaration that they must be ignorant whether or not they admit it.

The example of imperious ignorance that Ovey provides has to do with the Council of Sirmium (AD 357). The theological debate concerned Jesus's nature: was he homoousios, of the same substance as the Father, or homoiousios, of a similar substance as the Father? The former word would be a confession that Jesus is truly God; the latter would be an indication that he is godlike, but not God. Sirmium was pro-Arian—it sided with the view that Jesus is less than God. But instead of coming out and saying so clearly, the council came to the conclusion that the arguments on each side were so finely drawn that we can't know which is right. Their conclusion was that it was wrong to affirm one side or the other; indeed, their decision was an implicit prohibition against claiming anything specific, because, after all, we can't know. The orthodox theologians Athanasius of Alexandria and Hilary of Poitiers criticized the decision of Sirmium not only because, they insisted, it was wrong, but because it was blasphemous. The decree, they said, had an element of compulsion—but how can you legislate against someone else's knowledge? Indeed, because it prohibited the confession of the truth, it was blasphemous. The claim of imperious ignorance means, in practice, that people are allowed to adopt whatever position they prefer.

I thought of Sirmium when I read Andrew Bartlett's book, *Men and Women in Christ: Fresh Light from the Biblical Texts*.[4] The book contains many astute exegetical observations. But more than once (e.g., on 1 Cor.

---

3   Michael J. Ovey, "The Art of Imperious Ignorance," *Themelios* 41, no. 1 (2016): 5–7.
4   Andrew Bartlett, *Men and Women in Christ: Fresh Light from the Biblical Texts* (London: Inter-Varsity, 2019).

14:34–35) the author argues for the view that the arguments are so finely drawn that it is impossible to decide one way or the other. This is more than an admission that Bartlett himself cannot decide; rather, it is an argument that the exegetical evidence is such that it is impossible to decide, so that others are implicitly forbidden to decide under risk of being charged with careless exegesis. This is a fine example of an appeal to imperious ignorance. I think that in every case some *can* decide, with varying degrees of certainty, even if others confess that *they* cannot decide. But that is quite different from legislating ignorance in order to avoid conclusions one wants to avoid.

Third, we should be careful to sniff out publishing ploys that seem designed to introduce new waves of uncertainty. Consider a recent book edited by Preston Sprinkle titled *Two Views on Homosexuality, the Bible, and the Church.*[5] Most of us are familiar with the "two (or three, or four) views" books. Many of them are very helpful, presenting multiple positions on, say, the millennium, or the rapture, or whatever. In the past, the "views" books have usually dealt with debates within the constraints of evangelicalism. Such books are usually not of the sort that claim to offer "two views on the deity of Christ." Sprinkle's book, published by an evangelical publisher, now makes the debate about the legitimacy of homosexual practice an intraevangelical matter. The advertising for the book maintains that both sides argue their case "from Scripture"—though of course, Jehovah's Witnesses argue their case "from Scripture" too. The point is that if there is such a thing as orthodoxy, then not all disputed things are properly disputable. Sometimes the Christian church is built up and strengthened by farsighted publishing ventures; sometimes it is being manipulated by publishers with little or no confessional loyalty or ecclesiastical discipline.

Fourth, become informed as to the nature of some postmodern epistemologies that, though now rarely teased out, are very widely assumed. Twenty or twenty-five years ago, it was required that most students of the arts—English, history, social studies, politics, journalism, and the like—become familiar with the ideas (and, in the better universities, the writings) of Jacques Derrida, Michel Foucault, Jean-François Lyotard, and a host of other writers of related persuasion. In other words, it became necessary

---

5   Preston Sprinkle, ed., *Two Views on Homosexuality, the Bible, and the Church* (Grand Rapids, MI: Zondervan, 2016).

to learn and defend the *theory* that lay behind postmodernism, especially postmodern epistemology. Today relatively few study these authors but nevertheless many have drunk deeply from the effluent of the movement. In other words, many still think in transparently postmodern ways, even though their grasp of underlying theory is relatively thin. In some cases they no longer know what Foucault meant by totalization, but they deploy a similar argument if someone makes an exclusive religious claim.

It may help to begin with an example that was much more current in the middle of the twentieth century. When I was a seminary student, one of the books on hermeneutics we had to read was Bernard Ramm's *Protestant Biblical Interpretation*.[6] I was exposed to the book in its first and second editions where there was no interaction with postmodern hermeneutics. The third edition added some material to tip the hat in that direction, but most of it shared the assumptions of the first two editions. The task of biblical hermeneutics is to develop skills to enable "me," the interpreter, to ask questions of "it," the text. I, the knower/interpreter, direct appropriate questions to the text, and the text, as it were, answers me back with equal directness. But the "new" hermeneutic (now quite old!), that is, postmodern hermeneutics, points out, quite tellingly, that the "I" who is asking the questions is never neutral, never reliably objective. Perhaps the "I" is a white, middle-class, Western, well-educated male looking for tenure at a fine university. Probably the questions he asks won't be the same as the questions of an impoverished, semiliterate street urchin in a Lagos slum who is becoming interested in a health, wealth, and prosperity gospel preached in a nearby tabernacle. Apparently neither of us asks a purely neutral question. Our social and cultural locations guarantee that my question is not a direct hit; it's more of a glancing blow that reflects an angle that says more about the "I," the knower-interpreter, than it does about the text. So similarly, the text does not answer back directly either. It responds with an answer that is substantially determined by the kind of question that has been directed to it, which itself is determined by who the "I" is. So "I" hit the text with a glancing question, and it responds with a glancing answer. The "I" is doubtless affected in some way by the answer he or she has received, so that when the "I" fires off another question, it is subtly different from

---

6   Bernard Ramm, *Protestant Biblical Interpretation*, 3rd ed. (Grand Rapids, MI: Baker, 1980).

the previous question, as is the answer provided by the text. And thus text and interpreter have set up a "hermeneutical circle" with no obvious way of escaping the subjectivity. Insofar as this model is valid, it affects how we interpret literature, how we shape the history that we write and read, how we evaluate evidence, and so forth. And suddenly, we have tumbled into some profound reasons, some postmodern hermeneutical reasons, for justifying the skeptical charge, "But that's just your interpretation."

The result is a cornucopia of innovative interpretations that transform personal beliefs and (if enough people buy into them) cultural assumptions. As Richard Topping has pointed out, "Remember we live in a time when six of the seven deadly sins are medical conditions—and pride is a virtue."[7] When enough people absorb the interpretations that postmodernism has authorized, it is easy for a traditional Christian to feel excluded. Topping goes on to remind us of the well-known line from Flannery O'Connor, who said, "You will know the truth, and the truth will make you odd."[8] By contrast, if with Demas you decide you cannot know the truth, then in the culture steeped in the effluent of postmodernism, you will not be odd. And neither do you know the truth.

The beginnings of an answer might be summarized in several points.

1. It is important to avoid a response that is needlessly polarizing, for transparently no interpreter, no "I," no knower, is perfectly objective. The only way to achieve perfection in that department is (here we go again!) by becoming omniscient. In other words, traditional hermeneutics owes a debt of gratitude for reminding all of us how we cannot escape our subjectivity, our finiteness, our cultural blind spots.

2. Yet it does not follow that all interpretations are equally valid or invalid. Experience shows us our efforts at interpretation do not consign us to a hermeneutical circle; rather, our knowing, our interpretations, are rather more akin to the movement of a hermeneutical spiral: as we circle in on the text again and again, we get closer and closer to faithful understanding, even if it is never the understanding available only to Omniscience.[9]

---

7   Richard Topping, "Theological Study: Keeping It Odd," *Scottish Bulletin of Evangelical Theology* 37 (2019): 5.

8   Topping, "Theological Study," 5.

9   Cf. Grant R. Osborne, *The Hermeneutical Spiral: A Comprehensive Introduction to Biblical Hermeneutics*, 2nd ed. (Downers Grove, IL: InterVarsity, 2006).

Or to change the mathematical model, persistent attempts to understand something, not least biblical texts, regularly place us on an asymptotic approach to perfect knowledge (i.e., we will never get there [for that is the prerogative of Omniscience], but we may sidle up so closely that it's "as good as" or "as if" we managed to get all the way, much like the approximations in a discipline like calculus).[10]

3. The appropriateness of these models of learning and knowing (i.e., we grow closer to faithful knowing with time) is confirmed by the way we learn, whether the subject is Greek, Spenserian verse, statistics, microbiology, or biblical studies. Our first attempts at knowing any subject expose how large the distance is between what we think we know and what is actually there (as measured by those whose diligent study has brought them asymptotically close). Us human beings learn; we come to know by degrees; we self-correct; we compare notes with others. None of this supports the notion that by diligent hermeneutical discipline we may obtain perfect (i.e., omniscient) knowledge, but it surely excludes the conclusion that all putative knowledge is no better and no worse, neither more faithful nor less faithful, than any competing putative knowledge. Along similar lines, while we ought to excoriate those condescending cultures that are dismissive of all other cultures, we find it hard to justify the view that all cultures are of equal value and worth to all other cultures. Is the culture of Nazism of equal value and worth to the culture of, say, Mother Teresa?

> At last we know all truth is gray: no more
> Faith's raucous rhetoric, this blinding trap
> Of absolutes, this brightly colored map
> Of good and bad: our ocean has no shore.
> Dogmatic truth is chimera: deplore
> All arrogance: the massive gray will sap
> The sparkling hues of bigotry, and cap
> The rainbow, mask the sun, make dullness soar.
> Yet tiny, fleeting hesitations lurk
> Behind the storied billows of the cloud

---

10 I have tried to work out these models in *The Gagging of God: Christianity Confronts Pluralism* (Grand Rapids, MI: Zondervan, 1996).

Like sparkling, prism'd glory in the murk:
The freedom of the gray becomes a shroud.
Where nothing can be false, truth must away—
Not least the truth that all my world is gray.[11]

4. And finally, the models change again if we become convinced that Omniscience has kindly spoken to us in the words of human language. That does not mean that God gives us the capacity to enjoy omniscient knowledge ourselves: for that, we would have to be God. But surely it is reasonable to assume that this omniscient God knows which words and idioms and syntax and figures of speech to use so as to best communicate with his image bearers, however lost and blind they may be. And on all the topics on which he most wants us to be informed, in love he says the same thing again and again, in the words of different human authors, in different contexts. Not only so, but he liberally bestows his Spirit to enlighten their understanding. He expects his readers to be like believers in Berea who "received the message with great eagerness and examined the Scriptures every day to *see if what Paul said was true*" (Acts 17:11)—a marvelous example of growing in knowledge without ever claiming to possess omniscient knowledge. In other words, it is possible (as well as urgent) to press toward what Paul elsewhere calls "the pattern of sound teaching" (2 Tim. 1:13; cf. Rom. 6:17), lest we find ourselves in the place of inverting what God declares to be the case (cf. Isa. 5:20–21). The notion of a "pattern of sound knowledge" flags how much our understanding of this or that text or theme is itself shaped and reshaped by the "givens" of our own worldview, of our preunderstandings. But that would demand at least another article.

Finally, this special character of the word of God, in which the omniscient God stands behind it, however faulty our interpretive efforts of it, calls us to humility and godly fear whenever we engage the sacred text. God declares, "These are the ones I look on with favor: those who are humble and contrite in spirit, and who tremble at my word" (Isa. 66:2). For our purposes, there are two lessons to be drawn from this assertion.

1. The prophecy of Isaiah repeatedly makes it clear that God loathes all forms of religion that are largely for show, a veneer to mask greed, lust,

---

11 D. A. Carson, "The Postmodern," *First Things* 93 (May 1999): 51. Used by permission.

and idolatry. Cognitive skills, as important as they are, guarantee nothing, for idolatry in our cognitive powers is still idolatry. So we rightly look for teachers and preachers who unambiguously place themselves under the word in transparent humility, while we remain highly suspicious of those who try to be too clever by half, who with a smirk and a wink seek rather to domesticate the Scriptures than to be mastered by them.

2. This stance also grants the interpreter a certain kind of humble boldness. Not long ago I was speaking at a Christian meeting along the lines developed in this essay. At the end of the session, someone approached me in anger and tears, saying that I had repeatedly hurt her deeply. It turned out that she had a lesbian daughter, and by condemning homosexuality (unlike Demas) I had wounded her badly. She was in no condition to be told that I brought up homosexuality simply because that was the hinge in Demas's argument. I might have told her that elsewhere I have tried on occasion to talk at length about this complex subject; I might have mentioned some excellent and thought-provoking authors such as Rosaria Butterfield. But the woman was determined to make herself the victim, and me the abuser and victimizer. So finally I asked her, rather quietly, if her anger and hurt sprang from what I said, or from what God says in Scripture. Was she angry with me or with God? I make it a practice to listen to alternative interpretations, and I am happy to be corrected: I too must want to be a good worker who does not need to be ashamed as I handle the Bible. But if I tremble before the word of God, I will not duck what it has to say just because it is culturally uncomfortable. To tremble before the word of God leaves me content to be odd in a culture that fails to recognize the authority of that word. But it also affords me a place to shelter.

"But that's just your interpretation." Well, yes, it is my interpretation. Whose else could it possibly be? Yet, in today's climate, the question is not designed to offer a superior or better-warranted interpretation, but to relativize all interpretations. And that plea for imperious ignorance must not be allowed to stand. It is, finally, incoherent and idolatrous. A far better approach to Holy Scripture is preserved for us in Psalm 119.

12

Kingdom, Ethics, and Individual Salvation

IN RECENT YEARS A NUMBER of stances have arisen that have set themselves over against traditional evangelicalism and traditional Reformed thought, not a few of them arguing, in part, on the basis of a particular understanding of the kingdom. These stances claim to be more biblical and thus more faithful than traditional stances. To some extent they overlap; to some extent each is identifiably different from the others. What are these stances, what can we learn from them, and what should be resisted—and why?[1]

1. The kingdom, especially as emphasized in the Synoptic Gospels, is often tied to communitarian ethics rather than individual ethics. By contrast, Paul downplays the kingdom and focuses rather more on individual salvation. This has played into the individualism of the West, which must be resisted by restoring a return to Jesus himself, achieving a better balance with Pauline emphases.

2. The kingdom is bound up with a way of looking at reality that undermines the perceptions of the fallen and broken world order. Many of the "parables of the kingdom" have this fundamental reversal at their core, so it turns out that the last are first and the wild and wayward son is given the party. In this kingdom, we do not govern the way the world does: the one who wishes to lead must be the slave of all, even as Christ came not to be

---

1 This chapter was originally published as D. A. Carson, "Kingdom, Ethics, and Individual Salvation," *Themelios* 38, no. 2 (2013): 197–201.

served but to serve (Matt. 20:20–28). The kingdom cross has more to do with ethics, especially the ethics of reversal, than with atonement.

3. With the triumph of Christ achieved on the cross and through his resurrection, the kingdom has dawned—a glorious anticipation of the spectacular glory of resurrection existence in the new heaven and new earth. That means Christ's people are mandated to begin now to work out the dimensions of righteousness and justice that will be consummated at the end: saying "no" to raw power, caring for the poor and needy, reversing discrimination, being good stewards of the created order that anticipates the consummated created order. All of this is the mission of Jesus.

4. The clear command of Jesus is to seek the kingdom of God and his righteousness—and Jesus makes clear, not least in the Sermon on the Mount, that this entails a range of shocking ethical transformations: turning the other cheek to violence, recognizing that the heart is more fundamental than mere action, and forgiving others (because, quite frankly, we will not be forgiven unless we do). This stance is often associated with the Anabaptist movement, whether in its more traditional guise or in its Hauerwas form. The broad pacifism Jesus mandated finally means that the church in some measure, in some way, must withdraw from the world: our job is not to transform culture, but to constitute a new people, to live by the shaping constraints and privileges of the kingdom. It is not our job to tell the world what to do, or even to figure out how to interact with the broader culture; it is simply our job to be the people of God.

5. A postmillennial anticipation of the coming of the kingdom, combined with either a soft sphere sovereignty (think Kuyper) and/or with some form of theonomy, develops its own ways of thinking about the transformation of the culture.

6. At a popular level (think *Left Behind*), it is still not uncommon for some to think of the kingdom as virtually an exclusive reality so that terms like "gospel" and "church" may be nicely tied to this generation while "kingdom" has to do with the future, millennially conceived or not.

These are all distinguishable ways of thinking about the dawning of the kingdom. Four of the six devote a lot of thought to the challenge of transforming culture; one (the fourth option, Hauerwas) specifically sets itself against such reflection, but devotes a lot of thought to the challenge of being a distinct society over against the surrounding culture. All but the last tend to depreciate individual salvation, while the last tends to emphasize it to the depreciation of large-scale communitarian and ethical reflection (i.e., where it focuses on ethics, it tends to emphasize the ethics of the priorities of individuals). By contrast, many in these camps who align themselves with social and communitarian ethics would take umbrage at the charge that they downplay individual salvation since they acknowledge that individuals must repent and believe. Nevertheless, the focus of their frame of reference is one or another of these large visions, usually tied to a distinctive understanding of the kingdom, heavily leaning toward societal transformation (either of the entire society or, in the Anabaptist heritage, the ecclesial society). Individual supporters of these movements tend to emphasize different needs: the overwhelming challenges of poverty, of AIDS and other diseases, of abuse of power, of ecological responsibility, of reconciliation of various sorts (racial, ethnic, religious).

Preliminary Responses

First, like most positions that claim to right a wrong, there is some level of truth in these proposals. Nevertheless, in each case there is something reductionistic about the proposal, or just plain exegetically wrong, or both. For instance, with respect to the first proposal, which tends to pit Jesus and the kingdom over against Paul: once one has noted the difference in both literary genre and temporal location of Gospels and Epistles, one can nevertheless trace out the many theological connections between Jesus and Paul.[2] Or again, with respect to the second proposal, which elevates ethics in the Gospels above the atonement, it painfully overlooks just how central the cross is to the entire Bible's storyline. Even in the Gospels, to abstract the ethics passages from the narrative that drives toward the passion and resurrection (one of Brian McLaren's approaches) ultimately distorts both the ethics and the narrative—as the better commentaries invariably show,

---

2 See esp. David Wenham, *Paul: Follower of Jesus or Founder of Christianity?* (Grand Rapids, MI: Eerdmans, 1995); or, more briefly, Wenham's *Paul and Jesus: The True Story* (Grand Rapids, MI: Eerdmans, 2002); or older, short books on this topic by Herman Ridderbos (*Paul and Jesus: Origin and General Character of Paul's Preaching of Christ* [Philadelphia: P&R, 1957]) and by F. F. Bruce (*Paul and Jesus* [Grand Rapids, MI: Baker, 1974]); or Paul Barnett, *Jesus and the Rise of Early Christianity: A History of New Testament Times* (Downers Grove, IL: InterVarsity, 1999).

and as Peter Bolt, for instance, has dramatically demonstrated in Mark.[3] So much of the exegesis in this camp is slightly distorted, but this "slightly" turns out to be massively corrupting. For instance, I recently heard a well-known New Testament scholar argue that the famous utterance in Mark 10:45 and Matthew 20:28 is not *really* about the atonement at all, but about politics and the nature of leadership. Well, yes and no: the entire *pericope* is about the nature of leadership among Christ's disciples, but the fundamental ground and standard is Christ and his atoning cross-work. Far from pitting ethics and the atonement against each other, the passage grounds the former in the latter. Or again, the third proposal, though not superficially wrong, becomes deeply wrong because (a) the storyline on which it is based is reductionistic, and (b) the applications commonly pursued are merely hyped echoes of contemporary agendas that compared with Scripture are at best decentered and at worst naive. And so we could work through all the proposals.

Second, several of these proposals depend on reductionistic approaches to the nature of the "kingdom" in the New Testament. The easiest way to demonstrate this is by outlining some of the uses of "kingdom."

(a) In many uses, the kingdom of God is virtually coextensive with God's sovereignty: God's kingdom rules over all, and he does what he wills. Everyone is in the kingdom in that sense—atheists, Buddhists, Christians, and so forth. It is impossible *not* to be in the kingdom. In this sense, the kingdom is neither something to pursue nor something that can be avoided.

(b) On the other hand, in many uses the kingdom of God is that subset of God's total reign under which there is acceptance with God and eternal life. For example, one can neither see nor enter the kingdom (in this sense) unless one is born again (John 3). One is either in the kingdom or one is not.

(c) Very frequently the Gospels present the kingdom as coming—either in process of dawning now or promised for the future and yet already inaugurated. Often this tension is implicitly cast over against the anticipation of some Jews that the kingdom of God would come in a climactic burst that would usher in righteousness and destroy the ungodly. Instead, it comes like seed sown in various soils, like yeast transforming dough.

---

3   See Peter G. Bolt, *The Cross from a Distance: Atonement in Mark's Gospel*, New Studies in Biblical Theology 18 (Downers Grove, IL: InterVarsity, 2004).

(d) This coming or dawning kingdom can itself, at the moment, include both wheat and weeds. That makes it like (a) above—except God's sovereignty cannot be said to "come" or to be anticipated. That it is not to be identified with all of God's providential reign makes it akin to (b) above—except that this usage includes both wheat and weeds.

(e) Increasingly in the New Testament, the kingdom is distinctively Christ's kingdom. In many of the parables, Jesus speaks of the kingdom *of God*. In some, however, such as the parable of the sheep and the goats (Matt. 25:31-46), the king is clearly Jesus. That raises the question as to when Jesus *becomes* king. At one level, Jesus is born a king (e.g., Matt. 2); at another, he enters into his kingship with the onset of his public ministry; at yet another, in deepest irony he reigns from the cross (e.g., Matt. 27:27-53); very frequently in the New Testament his kingship is thematically connected with his resurrection, ascension, and session at the Father's right hand, assuring him that all authority is given to him in heaven and on earth (e.g., Matt. 28:18). Paul sums up this vision by insisting that all of God's sovereignty is currently mediated through Christ and that this will continue to be the case until the last enemy has been destroyed (1 Cor. 15). That means that Jesus's mediatorial kingship is contested. The consummation of the ages finally arrives when his foes, including death itself, have been utterly vanquished.

(f) None of this descriptive analysis mentions Matthew's preference for "kingdom of heaven" over "kingdom of God." Of the various proposals advanced to explain the semantic difference, that of Jonathan Pennington is as believable as any.[4] The difference is not one of referent, but of emphasis or perspective: the kingdom, we might say, is viewed a little more focally from heaven's vantage point.

(g) In no instance is kingdom to be *identified* with church, as if the two words can on occasion become tight synonyms. Even when there is a referential overlap, the domain of "kingdom" is reign, and the domain of "church" is people.

(h) The kingdom is sometimes associated with certain virtues or conduct (e.g., Matt. 5:3, 8), even with righteousness (Matt. 6:33). Sometimes such passages seem to relish a certain eschatological tension: Does "your

---

4   Jonathan T. Pennington, *Heaven and Earth in the Gospel of Matthew*, Supplements to Novum Testamentum 126 (Leiden: Brill, 2007); Pennington, "The Kingdom of Heaven in the Gospel of Matthew," *Southern Baptist Journal of Theology* 12, no. 1 (2008): 44–51.

kingdom come, your will be done, on earth at it is in heaven" (Matt. 6:10) envisage the consummation, the presence of the future (to take up Ladd's unforgettable title), or both? Certainly there is nothing in the New Testament quite like the current infatuation for expressions like "kingdom ethics," in which "kingdom" is reduced to a mere adjective.

One could extend this analysis quite a bit further, but this is enough to flag the dangers of reductionism.

Third, several of the proposals mentioned at the beginning of this editorial are difficult to evaluate in short compass because they depend on debatable assumptions regarding the meanings of several other biblical terms or theological themes. Nowhere is this more notable than in current debates over the meaning of "gospel." Someone brings up the expression "the gospel of the kingdom," assures us that the kingdom has to do primarily with ethics, and then assures us that the only way to develop a really "robust" gospel is to integrate kingdom ethics into our gospel. The methodological missteps bound up with such word association games are too complex to be untangled here. But if "gospel" refers primarily to the great news of what God has done in Christ Jesus to redeem and transform his people, we ought to distinguish what God has done from its entailments in how his people will respond. One could do a lot worse than read Greg Gilbert's *What Is the Gospel?*[5]

Fourth, there is a huge need to test all of these proposals and systems by *all* the great turning points in redemptive history, keeping in mind *all* of them *all* the time.[6]

Four Concluding Reflections

Here I wish to do no more than prime the pump.

First, there are important and sometimes neglected things to learn from the actual practice and focus of the New Testament documents. For example, we cannot help but observe that some of the priorities of these stances do not seem to be the first priorities of the Book of Acts or of any of the Epistles, Pauline or otherwise. One wonders why, if Paul had been focally concerned about being a good steward of creation in his own time, he did not say a bit

---

5 Greg Gilbert, *What Is the Gospel?* 9Marks (Wheaton, IL: Crossway, 2010).

6 This is one of the larger themes of my *Christ and Culture Revisited* (Grand Rapids, MI: Eerdmans, 2007).

more about cleaning up the horse poop in Rome. There is plenty of biblical warrant for thinking through our stewardship of creation on the broadest canvas, but one should be careful to make the first things the first things.

Second, in much of the contemporary discussion, there is an alarming lack of eternal perspective—or, better put, a mere tipping of the hat toward the eternal, but not any acknowledgement that viscerally and powerfully affects conduct and priorities. "Do not be afraid of those who kill the body but cannot kill the soul. Rather, be afraid of the One who can destroy both soul and body in hell" (Matt. 10:28).

Third, doubtless some in the broad evangelical camp overreact and think exclusively of saving souls as opposed to people in all the complexities of their existence (whether because they spring from an older dispensation-alism or because they have been burned by the heritage of a 1920s social gospel). But somewhere along the line Christians have to wrestle with what it means to do good to all, even if our first responsibility is toward the house-hold of God, serving as salt in a decaying world, as light in a dark world.

Finally, it is desperately important not to try to slaughter the complexity and balance of biblical mandates on all these fronts by the simple expedient of universalizing *our* slot in history and culture. Many of us are quick to identify the ostensible imbalances and errors of Christians in other genera-tions without adequately reflecting on our own blind spots or on the blind spots of our heroes. One wonders what stances Kuyper would have adopted had he been born in China in 1940.

13

A Biblical Theology of Education

THE TOPIC AT HAND—a biblical theology of education—is like an oversized, underinflated beach ball: you can't miss it, and it's easy to swat around, but it's very difficult to control.[1]

Nevertheless, let me try to impose at least a little order on the topic. Begin with the expression "biblical theology." Although there are many variations, today's use of the expression commonly conjures up one of two ideas.

First, whereas "systematic theology" tends to order its treatment of the theology of the Bible along logical and hierarchical lines (see, for example, a standard systematic theology like that of Bavinck or a more popular one like that of Grudem), biblical theology tends to order its treatment of the theology of the Bible along temporal lines, focusing on the contribution of each book and corpus along the path of the Bible's storyline. The distinction between systematic theology and biblical theology is never absolute, of course, but it is strong enough to warrant recognition. Thus, a biblical theology of, say, the temple, traces out temple themes in the early chapters of Genesis, follows their trajectories all the way to the Apocalypse, and observes how these trajectories are not random but interrelated, constituting the warp and woof of interwoven themes, unfolding across time. Similarly, one can speak of the biblical theology of creation/new creation,

1 This chapter was originally published as D. A. Carson, "A Biblical Theology of Education," *Themelios* 46, no. 2 (2021): 257–68. It is a slightly revised version of a paper delivered at the International Alliance for Christian Education (IACE) annual conference on February 3, 2021 at Southwestern Baptist Theological Seminary in Fort Worth, Texas, and tweaked in light of questions and comments at the conference and in light of suggestions made by the editor of *Themelios*.

of priesthood, of exile, and of much more. But in this sense of "biblical theology," can one legitimately speak of a biblical theology of education?

I don't think so. It's not as if there is a theological development of the theme of education from one end of the canon to the other. Of course, one could cheat a little and insist that all of God's self-disclosure across human history constitutes an education of those humans. In that sense, education is biblical theology. But no one uses the term "education" today in precisely that way. Consider the definition of education advanced by Wikipedia: "Education is the process of facilitating learning, or the acquisition of knowledge, skills, values, morals, beliefs, and habits".[2] This static vision of education is not following the storyline of redemptive history. To put it another way, it is difficult to discern that the canon provides developing reflection on education. So, in this sense of "biblical theology" we may reasonably doubt that there is such a thing as a biblical theology of education.

A second common contemporary meaning of "biblical theology" is theology that is found in or based upon the Bible—a way of referring to systematic theology that is biblically faithful. On this view, our title makes education a subset, in effect, of systematic theology. This is conceptually less problematic. To talk of the biblical theology of education, in this sense of biblical theology, is akin to talking about the biblical theology of ecology or the biblical theology of angels. Ecology, angels, and, I would say, education, are not central biblical themes akin to Christology, atonement, and theology proper, but enough is said about each of them that if we assemble these bits carefully and inquire as to how they fit into the Bible as a whole, it is surprising how much can be learned. So, let us assemble some of the bits and pieces of what the Bible says about education. Then we shall briefly survey how those bits and pieces have worked themselves out in a handful of historical arrays before we explore the peculiar challenges of putting these pieces together at the beginning of the twenty-first century in the Western world.

Observations on Some Biblical Bits and Pieces

One of the first passages cited by writers who survey what the Bible says about education is Deuteronomy 6:6–9:

---

2 Wikipedia, s.v. "Education," accessed 2020, http://en.wikipedia.org/.

> These commandments that I give you today are to be on your hearts. Impress them on your children. Talk about them when you sit at home and when you walk along the road, when you lie down and when you get up. Tie them as symbols on your hands and bind them on your foreheads. Write them on the doorframes of your houses and on your gates.

Indeed, in the future when a new generation asks what this is all about, the older generation is to fill them in on the entire exodus history, the history of the redemption of God's covenant people and the bedrock that warrants the call to obedience (6:20–25). The concern is to educate each new generation. Three details stand out: (1) the primary responsibility lies with the parents who are called to shape their children, (2) the focus is not on education broadly conceived, but on knowing their own God-shaped history and the covenantal structure and stipulations that rest on that history, (3) the context in which this theological formation takes place is not a formal educational institution but family life—sitting at home, walking along the road, answering questions in the intimacy of the family. A millennium and a half later, the same family structure is presupposed in the Olivet Discourse: "Two men will be in a field; one will be taken and the other left. Two women will be grinding with a hand mill; one will be taken and the other left" (Matt. 24:40–41). In the economic culture of the time, the two men were likely to be two brothers, or a father and a son; the two women were likely to be two sisters, or a mother and a daughter. That is why the separation brought about by the Lord's return is so shocking. But that is also where education takes place.

Of course, some training takes place outside family lines: Eli mentors Samuel, and Elijah mentors Elisha, to cite two obvious instances. Nevertheless, recall the importance of the family in the wisdom literature:

> My son, do not forget my teaching, but keep my commands in your heart, for they will prolong your life many years and bring you peace and prosperity. . . . Listen, my sons, to a father's instruction; pay attention and gain understanding. I give you sound learning, so do not forsake my teaching. For I too was a son to my father, still tender, and cherished by my mother. Then he taught me, and he said to me, "Take hold of my words with all your heart; keep my commands, and you will live." . . . My son,

keep your father's command and do not forsake your mother's teaching.
(Prov. 3:1–2; 4:1–4; 6:20; cf. 1:8)

Family instruction lays emphasis on conduct: "Start children off on the way they should go, and even when they are old they will not turn from it" (Prov. 22:6). The role of the mother in educating her son in the faith surfaces unforgettably in the influence of Lois and Eunice on Timothy (2 Tim. 1:5) and, sometimes regrettably, in the influence of Rebekah on her son Jacob. All of such transgenerational education is, of course, informal.

The importance of the written materials that make up what we today call the Bible surfaces in both personal and institutional contexts. When an Israelite came to regal power, his first responsibility was not to audit the books of his predecessor, nor to appoint a full slate of cabinet officers, but to copy out, by hand, "this law" (scholars continue to debate how much is included in the expression), then read it every day for the rest of his life (Deut. 17:14–20)—a stipulation more commonly observed in the breach than in the performance, or all of Israel's history would have been different. Psalm 119 is a sustained meditation on the law of the Lord and its shaping power. Times of reformation and revival are driven by the rediscovery of the written word (Josiah) or by the exposition of that word (Nehemiah). Although the exact referents are disputed, Paul's desire to be reunited with the books and the parchments disclose a similar priority (2 Tim. 4:13), as do affirmations of the unyielding importance of Scripture (2 Tim. 3:16; 2 Pet. 1:19–20). In recent years, scholars have shown how during the patristic period Christians stood out from their pagan peers, not least by being people of a book: their teaching, evangelism, catechizing, and worship were all shaped by written documents, by Scripture. All of this presupposes a sustained interest in *learning* what texts say, that is, in theological education. Whether early Christians read, say, 1 Corinthians for themselves, or accessed it primarily by hearing it read at length in the congregation, they stood out for their desire to become educated in their sacred texts.

The roots of such priorities lie deep within Old Testament soil. Unlike the other tribes, the Levites did not settle in one tribal area but were scattered among the tribes, not least because their responsibilities included teaching the word of God to their fellow Israelites. In other words, there was an *institutional* pattern of educating the people in Holy Scripture. This side of the exile, that pattern morphed into the synagogue system, with its heavy emphasis on memory and recitation. In the New Testament, under the new covenant, assemblies were to be led by pastors/teachers/overseers, and one of the qualifications demanded of such leaders was that they be "able to teach" (1 Tim. 3:2). The Pastoral Epistles devote quite a lot of space to spelling out what the teachers must aim to accomplish: they must ground the believers in sound doctrine, warn divisive people, provide encouragement, and so forth. More broadly, Christians are to admonish one another. All of these are forms of education—Christian education. And, after all, even Christian proclamation of the gospel is a form of education.

The Bible also lays some stress on the lessons to be learned from history—or, more precisely, the lessons to be learned from history as interpreted by God. The entire book of Judges overflows with the point: when the covenant people slide into idolatry, God sends judgment until there is repentance and a desperate call for help. The book as a whole teaches that the people are incapable of long-term faithfulness without a godly king to keep them in line. The juxtaposed blessings and curses of Deuteronomy are designed to educate the people along similar lines. The seven churches of Revelation 2–3 are threatened with the dire consequences of prolonged sin: the candlestick is removed, the church is destroyed.

Although there is very little reflection in the Bible on how each new generation was educated in the broader knowledge and science of the day, there are adequate glimpses of the range of expertise. Genesis 4 identifies nomadic herders, musicians, and technical folk with rising mastery of tools made from bronze and iron. David was a poet; Solomon set himself to master proverbs; scribes collected and compiled them; and all of these skills require training of some sort or other—education, if you will. The word "wisdom" covers a wide range of competencies, of course, but in some contexts it refers to something like a technical skill. Bezalel and Oholiab are "wise" men because they are endowed "with knowledge and with all kinds of skills—to make artistic designs for work in gold, silver and bronze, to cut and set stones, to work in wood, and to engage in all kinds of crafts" (Ex. 31:3–5). When David reflects on the sky, he declares, "The heavens declare the glory of God; the skies proclaim the work of his hands. Day after day they pour forth speech; night after night they reveal knowledge" (Ps. 19:1–2; cf. vv. 1–6). Like Paul in his reflection on what can be learned about God from the natural order (Rom. 1:19–20), David runs quickly to theological implications, but we cannot fail to note that these theological structures are anchored in observations of the natural order. Job knows about constellations such as Pleiades and Orion: presumably someone educated him in elementary astronomy. Once again, there is little reflection on the processes, structures, and methods of education, but quite regularly the biblical writers spell out nature's theological implications.

I cannot abandon this survey without saying something about the Lord Jesus. One of the dominant ways by which his disciples referred to him was as "the Teacher." After Jesus and Martha have finished their quiet exchange in John 11, Martha, we are told, "went back [to her house] and called her sister Mary aside. 'The Teacher is here,' she said, 'and is asking for you'" (11:28). Jesus himself ratifies the appropriateness of the designation when he instructs his disciples how to prepare for the Passover: "Go into the city to a certain man and tell him, 'The Teacher says: My appointed time is near'" (Matt. 26:18). Or again, in John's Gospel, Jesus tells his disciples, "You call me 'Teacher' and 'Lord,' and rightly so, for that is what I am" (13:13). In Matthew's Gospel, the apostle provides five large teaching blocks, the first of which is the Sermon on the Mount, which begins with the comment, "His disciples came to him, and he began to teach them" (5:1–2), and ends with the observation that "the crowds were amazed at his teaching, because he taught as one who had authority, and not as their teachers of the law" (7:28–29). Mark's Gospel reports much less teaching, but the evangelist has a predilection for referring to Jesus as the Teacher.[3] Certainly the canonical Gospels depict Jesus teaching in a variety of modes: lecturing, mentoring those closest to him, coining one-liners, interacting with opponents, illustrating some element of his teaching with parables or with symbol-laden miracles, unpacking grace, faith, obedience, and more. None of this is presented as a disquisition on education. The focus, rather, is on the content—Jesus himself, the kingdom, his path to the cross and resurrection, eternal life—and that content is presented by a master teacher. One may legitimately learn some things about education by watching Jesus, but it would rather miss the point to come away and say, "After studying Jesus

---

3 "Teacher" (διδάσκαλος) refers to Christ twelve times in Mark (4:38; 5:35; 9:17, 38; 10:17, 20, 35; 12:14, 19, 32; 13:1; 14:14).

in Luke's Gospel, I see how copying Jesus's teaching styles will improve my performance in my classes teaching students the challenges of how nuclear fusion might one day contribute to the electrical grid."

A Miscellany of Historical Observations

Before trying to pull some of these strands together to see what kind of biblical theology of education we might weave, it might be worth our while to offer a potted miscellany of historical observations. This survey quickly discloses how almost none of the controlling features of what we mean by "education" today share any substantive overlap with the elements of education that surfaced in our survey of Scripture. When today we talk about education, we unwittingly smuggle into our discussion such categories as colleges and universities, private Christian institutions versus public options, K–12 schools, the value (or otherwise) of SAT exams, two-year associates degrees, technical colleges, distance learning, digital courses, universal access to libraries (hardcopy or digital) or, more broadly, access to the internet—and not one of these categories, not one, had any place in the mind of Solomon, of Hezekiah, of Doctor Luke, or of Thomas Aquinas. To think about some of these categories for a moment enables us to ponder what we may and may not legitimately infer about education from the biblical texts.

In the first century, there was no ideal of government-supported, universal education. Some governments trained some of their employees or slaves: we catch glimpses of this as early as the time of Daniel and his three friends. Most Jewish lads in the time of Paul learned how to read, but most would not have owned any of their own books. There was nothing akin to a modern Western university. Lecturers/preachers often wandered from town to town, giving addresses in the public marketplace. If they were good enough, local nobility might pay them to educate their sons—and this could lead to the establishment of a one-man local academy, such as the school of Tyrannus. In relatively rare cases, a learned scholar attracted other would-be scholars who gathered around their master. The focus could be as broad as all philosophy or much more narrow (e.g., mathematics). One of the results of this diversity is that although these so-called schools could argue among themselves, there was no government-mandated curriculum. Of course, government pressure came in other ways: read the

Apocalypse or 1 Peter. But it was not usually exerted through the rather slender first-century institutions of education. There were no trade schools. People who learned a trade did so in a master-apprentice relationship, in some cases controlled by the guilds (the ancient version of trade unions). Not infrequently the son learned his father's trade from his father. That is why Jesus was labeled "the carpenter's son" and, in one remarkable passage, simply "the carpenter" (Mark 6:3)—probably because Joseph had died and Jesus had taken over the family business before embarking on his public ministry. Thus, the moral and theological education envisaged in Deuteronomy 6 took place on the same platform, in the same fields and shops, as the formation needed to become a farmer or a carpenter.

In the early Middle Ages, because clergy were the citizens most likely to be able to read, and because collections of books (which were very expensive) could usually be accumulated only by institutions substantial enough to pay for them, cathedrals and monasteries became the preservers of learning and often ran their own schools. In his book *How the Irish Saved Civilization*,[4] what Thomas Cahill really means is "how the Irish monasteries saved civilization." Certainly there were other monasteries than Irish ones. The first three European universities—at Paris, Oxford, and Cambridge—were first of all monkish enclaves, and the trappings of Christendom, to say no more, continue in them from the twelfth century to the present day. Eventually these institutions became quite powerful. You can still visit the room in Queen's College, Cambridge, where Erasmus did much of his work. John Owen (1616–1683) was an administrator at the University of Oxford and an advisor to Oliver Cromwell, the Lord Protector. By and large, however, Oxford sided with the Catholics, and Cambridge with the Protestants— no college more so than Emmanuel College ("Emma"), Cambridge, whose support of the Puritans meant that Cromwell wanted to replace the masters of the other colleges by Emma men. Meanwhile the fall of Constantinople to the Muslims (1453) sent many scholars and their manuscripts to the West, strengthening the Renaissance by the recovery of ancient learning.

At this period in history, a university was indeed a *university*: it was *one* body, an organization given to research and teaching, with something approaching a unified vision, with God at the center. In the late medieval

---

4 Thomas Cahill, *How the Irish Saved Civilization* (New York: Doubleday, 1995).

period, even the university libraries were organized in such a way as to demonstrate that theology is the unifying queen of the sciences. Today, for many reasons, there is little that is conceptually and vibrantly unifying in most universities.

From where did those students come who were admitted to Oxbridge (as Oxford and Cambridge together have come to be called) and other universities? Parents with means often paid for a part-time or even a live-in tutor to prepare their sons (and at this historical juncture, only sons went to university) for the leap to Oxbridge. But meanwhile another movement had sprung up. Eton College, a boarding school for boys ages thirteen to eighteen, was founded in 1440 as a sister "feeder school" for King's College, Cambridge, and other colleges with similar purposes followed in its train. They were called "public schools" because they were open to any young man with the money and the gifts to get in—unlike students who made their way by relying on private tutors. Transparently, they were not public in the sense that they were sustained and controlled by public funds. As measured by those standards, England's "public schools" were, and are, not public but private and elitist.

Five more steps completed the transformation to something akin to what we have today. First, in 1751 William King, followed very closely by Robert Raikes, started the first Sunday school. This was designed to provide basic education for children in the workforce who had had no educational opportunities at all. Sunday schools grew very rapidly. They taught reading, writing, ciphering (arithmetic), and a basic knowledge of the Bible. This was Christian education organized by Christians and some others to provide basic content to the disadvantaged.

Second, the Education Act of 1870 provided elementary education to everyone at government expense. Eventually this cut out the need for most Sunday schools as they had operated and gradually transformed them into what we mean by Sunday schools today. At the same time, the same move brought the powerful force of government into play. The reach of government soon extended through secondary schools, technical colleges, and universities. The power of the purse is often velvet gloved, but it can be formidably coercive. I shall return to this reality in a moment.

Third, Britain's demographics changed, especially after World War II. The polite but anemic Judeo-Christian perspective that had dominated the culture for centuries gave way to massive multiculturalism. London currently boasts somewhat more than 460 languages spoken on its streets. Some of us love the racial, cultural, and linguistic diversity; others are frightened by it. Meanwhile, in such a population, where is the consensus on history, social studies, culture, religion, ethics, sexuality and gender identity, controlling literature, sense of humor, courtesy, justice, economics? How will the disagreements that undergird such diversity play out in government and in education at every level? What is clear is that the widespread attempts in government and the media to advocate a neutral ground called secularism is simultaneously naive and dangerous.

Fourth, we cannot ignore the impact on education of the Industrial Revolution. New skills were needed, and many of them could not be acquired at home. Gradually the knowledge and skills needed in a scientific and technological society were taught by colleges and universities. The benefits were many, but the pattern of sending large numbers of eighteen-year-olds away from home to acquire an "education" tended with time to weaken the influence of the home and to modify what we mean by education.

Fifth, James Tunstead Burtchaell's book *The Dying of the Light*[5] carefully traces (in almost nine hundred pages) the common steps taken by colleges and universities as they departed from the confessional convictions and organizational control of the denominations that founded them. One of these common steps is a change in the kind of leadership. Very often these educational institutions were founded by visionary pastor-theologians. As the institutions grew in numbers, however, boards sought out leaders with administrative, financial, and legal skills. The controlling pursuit of secularism was the result. The administrative skills are necessary, of course, but the question is whether they should be allowed to displace or domesticate the founding vision.

Obviously, with the exception of the last couple of points, I've slanted my potted history toward Britain, but with remarkably little modification I might have told the story of the United States, of France, of Germany, of Canada, and so forth. The bearing of such historical realities on the topic of this paper is obvious. There is no straight-line development from what

---

5 James Tunstead Burtchaell, *The Dying of the Light: The Disengagement of Colleges and Universities from Their Christian Churches* (Grand Rapids, MI: Eerdmans, 1998).

might pass as education in the Bible to what has developed as education across the last half millennium. By the same token, it may be useful to cast a glance over a handful of recent cultural developments that certainly add to the challenge of trying to think biblically about education.

Some Recent Developments

If we are to interact with the culture in which God has placed us, we must try hard to understand it, especially as it has a bearing on our understanding of education. One of the most striking features of Western culture is how fast it is changing. It is hard to keep up; indeed, there is a danger that some of us will try so hard to keep up with the changing face of the culture that we spend too little time in the Bible, leaving ourselves with little more than a Sunday-school grasp of what the Bible actually says. So, at the risk of considerable presumption, permit me to list a handful of authors whose insight has helped me.

Thomas Sowell

Sowell has written many shrewd books over the past several decades, all of them graced with clear thinking and exceptionally clear writing. The volume I mention here is his *Quest for Cosmic Justice*.[6] Sowell claims that the demand for a perfect solution on every known inequity soon coughs up doctrinaire "solutions" that are not only simplistic but also damn anyone who disagrees. Worse, to qualify for the benefits of the "solution," it is necessary to be a victim, which results in long-term dependence on those claiming to have the "solution."

> On issue after issue, the morally self-anointed visionaries have for centuries argued as if no honest disagreement were possible, as if those who opposed them were not only in error but in sin. This has long been a hallmark of those with a cosmic vision of the world and of themselves as saviors of the world, whether they are saving it from war, overpopulation, capitalism, genetic degradation, environmental destruction, or whatever the crisis du jour might be.[7]

6   Thomas Sowell, *The Quest for Cosmic Justice* (New York: Touchstone, 1999).
7   Sowell, *Quest for Cosmic Justice*, 103.

The number and intensity of such movements are escalating, along with the corresponding arrogance. The demand for perfect justice turns out to be impossible in this broken world and turns out to disenfranchise and belittle those who successfully make merely ameliorating improvements. Genuine modest improvements are sacrificed on the altar of reductionistic but absolutist visions to which all must bow, not least in the fields of education. By contrast, in the name of King Jesus, Christians are educated to do good to all people, to confront wickedness and injustice, while knowing full well that perfection awaits the return of the King.

Charles Taylor

Of his many books, doubtless the most important for our purposes is *A Secular Age*.[8] His cultural analysis cascades onto his readers in prose that is sometimes dense but invariably enlightening. One of his most insightful notions is that our age has, for a number of complex reasons, elevated the notion of "authenticity." A person is to be held in high regard and celebrated if he or she is *authentic*—that is, living in conformity with what he or she claims to value. It matters little what that siren vision is; what matters is the authenticity of the pursuit. Traditional voices of authority against which we measured ourselves in the past—family traditions, religious commitments, social and governmental demands, sexual conformity—now have no intrinsic authority unless for some strange reason I choose to adopt them as mine. What makes me an admirable person is not the vision I choose to pursue, but that my pursuit, in whatever direction, is authentic. It is difficult to imagine a stance more calculated to baptize my opinions with public approval. It is equally difficult to imagine a stance more antithetical to what Jesus teaches us: our Lord wants us to follow him, die to self-interest, and take up our cross and die daily, not in a pique of self-flagellation but because we have been educated to recognize that it is in dying that we live, in giving that we receive, that the plaudits of a passing world are not to be compared with the glory to come and with the "Well done!" of the Teacher. In other words, in large parts of "our secular age" the traditional goals of education have been turned on their head. Once the new goals have been widely adopted, education in any classical sense means challenging the culture.

8   Charles Taylor, *A Secular Age* (Cambridge, MA: Belknap, 1997).

A second insightful contribution is Taylor's exposition of what he calls the modern social imaginary. By this expression he refers to the web of values, morals, direction, institutions, laws and symbols by which a society imagines itself and even realizes itself. The social imaginary of the Western world of five hundred years ago included belief in a (more or less) Christian God; the social imaginary of today's Western world is functionally atheistic, even while many espouse belief in some kind of God (not uncommonly the moralistic, therapeutic, deistic god described by sociologist Christian Smith).[9] That fundamental shift in the social imaginary means it is far more difficult to talk about the God of the Bible, far more difficult to educate people in the Christian way.

Douglas Murray

A provocative essayist with many contributions to his credit, Douglas Murray came to prominence with the publication of his previous book, *The Strange Death of Europe: Immigration, Identity, Islam*.[10] His more recent volume, and the one about which I wish to say a few words here, is *The Madness of Crowds: Gender, Race and Identity*.[11] Some of it could have been written only by someone self-described as gay. What he brings to the table are two things: a remarkable degree of clarity as he discusses four of our culture's most disputed terms (namely, *gay, women, race,* and *trans*), and, above all, a passionate plea for sane discourse over against the carefully engineered mass hysteria of our time, "the madness of crowds."

To illustrate: It is a remarkable fact that when Hillary Clinton ran against Barack Obama in 2008, both of them declared that marriage should be between one man and one woman. How short is the time it took to make homosexual marriage the law of the land, with penalties for those who dare to disagree! Once again, "the madness of crowds." Millennia of convictions as to what marriage *is* were jettisoned. Precisely how should an informed and compassionate—yes, and dispassionate—confessional

9   See Christian Smith with Melinda Lundquist Denton, *Soul Searching: The Religious and Spiritual Lives of American Teenagers* (Oxford: Oxford University Press, 2005), 118–71.

10 Douglas Murray, *The Strange Death of Europe: Immigration, Identity, Islam* (London: Bloomsbury Continuum, 2017).

11 Douglas Murray, *The Madness of Crowds: Gender, Race and Identity* (London: Bloomsbury Continuum, 2019).

stance educate the culture? How shall we recapture clarity, reason, sanity, in order to declare the logic and coherence of the gospel, when we are competing with the madness of crowds?

Christopher Caldwell

His book *The Age of Entitlement: America Since the Sixties*[12] offers a reading of the past half century that is thought-provoking and must be at least partially right. In brief, he argues that the attempt to resolve all of our cultural disputes by legislation has generated a citizenry characterized by a deep sense of entitlement, complete with whining and a knee-jerk reliance on the courts to right all wrongs.

Mary Eberstadt

She has become one of the most insightful cultural commentators that we have. Among other contributions, she wrote *It's Dangerous to Believe: Religious Freedom and Its Enemies*.[13] More recently she wrote *Primal Screams: How the Sexual Revolution Created Identity Politics*.[14] In some ways this book is akin to Robert Putnam's *Bowling Alone: The Collapse and Revival of American Community*, first published in 2000.[15] She argues that with the arrival of the pill and the sexual revolution it helped to spawn, personal identity was no longer tied to family and community. Individualism was tied to freedom, not least sexual freedom, and if there was community, it was arbitrary community incapable of sustaining well-being. In the wake of what Eberhardt calls "the great scattering," it is small wonder that teenage psychological problems are on the rise, along with loneliness studies, a loss of social learning, and "the infantilized vernacular of identity politics itself."[16] The "primal scream" of the title is the desperate cry, "Who am I?" and "Where do I belong in the world?"

---

12 Christopher Caldwell, *The Age of Entitlement: America Since the Sixties* (New York: Simon and Schuster, 2020).

13 Mary Eberstadt, *It's Dangerous to Believe: Religious Freedom and Its Enemies* (New York: Harper, 2016).

14 Mary Eberstadt, *Primal Screams: How the Sexual Revolution Created Identity Politics* (West Conshohocken, PA: Templeton, 2019).

15 Robert Putnam, *Bowling Alone: The Collapse and Revival of American Community*, revised ed. (New York: Simon and Schuster, 2020).

16 Eberstadt, *Primal Screams*, 11.

Other Contributions

Constraints of space forbid that I comment on other contributions, including those of Jordan Peterson and Rod Dreher. Roger Trigg may be taken as a fine exemplar of those who argue that our mediating institutions—family, clubs, trade unions, professional societies, schools, universities, and the like—are gradually being displaced or progressively being controlled by the state.[17] The result is more and more control by the state—not least in the domain of education. Perhaps the most comprehensive and convincing analysis is the recent book by Carl Trueman, *The Rise and Triumph of the Modern Self: Cultural Amnesia, Expressive Individualism, and the Road to Sexual Revolution.*[18] If you have time to read only one of the books I have mentioned, let that be the one.

The point of this survey is to remind ourselves that if we are to interact with the culture in which God has placed us, we must try hard to understand it and be discerning. The challenge is captured in the well-known and strangely prescient lines of T. S. Eliot, drawn from the opening stanza of his "Choruses from 'the Rock,'" now nearly a century old:

Where is the Life we have lost in living?
Where is the wisdom we have lost in knowledge?
Where is the knowledge we have lost in information?[19]

Conclusions

First, the center of what the Bible intimates about education is that nothing is more important than the knowledge of God mediated by the Lord Jesus Christ. That is as true for the diesel mechanic, the window washer, and the neurosurgeon as it is for the pastor-theologian. What shall it profit anyone to gain the whole world, including a Nobel prize or two, and lose their own soul? For those of us laboring in the fields of education, that axiomatic truth ought to shape not only our curriculum but our relationships with one another and with our students, our adorning of the gospel as well as our articulation of it.

---

17 Roger Trigg, "Equality and Freedom of Religion," *Theology* 124 (2021): 32–39.

18 Carl Trueman, *The Rise and Triumph of the Modern Self: Cultural Amnesia, Expressive Individualism, and the Road to Sexual Revolution* (Wheaton, IL: Crossway, 2020).

19 T. S. Eliot, *Collected Poems, 1909–1962* (New York: Harcourt, 1963), 147.

There are many implications. For a start, it means we could not possibly be satisfied with a return to broad Judeo-Christian values, even if we could arrange their return (and of course, we cannot). A Dickensian Christmas, complete with a turn-over-a-new-leaf Scrooge, doesn't bring us any closer to "the real meaning of Christmas" than a bacchanalian frenzy. In fact, Dickens may be more dangerous, since his sentimentality tends to swamp our discernment. Attempts to adhere to the second greatest command become thin when the first of the two greatest commands is ignored. The first thing to hold on to is that nothing is more important than the knowledge of God, mediated by the Lord Jesus Christ.

Second, it follows that, owing to the very nature of what it means in Scripture to know God, our educational priorities can never be merely curricular. It is not enough to train students to recite the Nicene Creed and identify who the left-handed judge is; they must learn to integrate their knowledge of the Bible and theology with personal faith, ethics (including personal, sexual, and social ethics), with goals, use of time and money, and relationships with fellow believers in the life of the church. They must learn how to conduct themselves with those of different faiths and with unbelievers whose carefree abandonment of all religious claims is utterly alien to us. All these things, and more, flow out of what Scripture and theology teach—that is, how Scripture educates us.

Third, the piecemeal nature of what Scripture says about education and the highly diverse patterns in which the institutions of education have played out across the centuries alert us to the danger of thinking that the Bible provides us with a thoroughgoing handbook of the dos, don'ts, and how-tos of educational practice. The Bible does provide us with broadly comprehensive educational goals and incentives; but it cannot be said to determine the shape of our educational institutions. We must never fall into the trap of thinking that provided we educate people in line with the best current educational fads, all will be well. I have said too little, except implicitly, about the moral dimensions of education, and I have not teased out the profound assumptions embedded in the words, "The fear of the Lord is the beginning of wisdom" (Prov. 9:10) and "of knowledge" (Prov. 1:7), or considered the work of the Spirit and of regeneration and the place of the life of the church in any truly Christian education. Such considerations take us well beyond techniques and institutions.

Fourth, a responsible strategy of education must be shaped by the place where God has placed us. I recently read a book by John and Bonnie Nystrom with the title *Sleeping Coconuts*,[20] relating their work of overseeing the translation of the Bible into Arop and nine other languages in Papua New Guinea. Part of their task of education entails the formation of tribal translators, teaching people what an alphabet is, teaching people how to read. All of that is Christian education, even though it is very different from the courses taught by a Christian university. Closer to home, in the United States when heavy-handed opposition tries to shut down Christian groups on campus, students appeal to freedom of religion and to constitutional rights. They cast their meetings as worship, which is constitutionally protected. That argument won't fly in France, where students, to preserve a hearing, insist that their meetings are *not* religious but academic and educational: the French Revolution had a different shape to the American Revolution. The former mandated freedom *from* religion, while the latter opted for freedom *of* religion. My point is that the Bible does not provide a detailed protocol for how education should properly and appropriately engage each culture, whether in Papua New Guinea, France, the United States, or anywhere else. That is why in trying to outline the fundamentals of a biblical theology of education and applying them to the Western cultures I know best, I have avoided universalizing the practical outworkings. While we debate whether (for instance) it is wiser to stay in the public schools and exercise influence there or to withdraw and build independent Christian schools, the shape of this debate is very different in, say, Hungary, or China, or Bahrain, or first-century Athens. A faithful biblical theology of education will provide us with the framework for thinking through such questions but will not give us formulaic universals.

Fifth, this does not mean that all of our relationships with the unconverted world must be adversarial. Those in the Reformed tradition often appeal to "common grace"—the grace that God distributes commonly, to the redeemed and the unredeemed alike. It is not for nothing that Jeremiah tells us to seek the good of the pagan city in which we reside. At the end, according to Revelation, the kingdoms of this world are depicted as bringing their

20 John Nystrom and Bonnie Nystrom, *Sleeping Coconuts* (Orlando: Wycliffe Bible Translators, 2012).

treasures into the new Jerusalem. The summary exhortation of the apostle Paul is striking: "Finally, brothers and sisters, whatever is true, whatever is noble, whatever is right, whatever is pure, whatever is lovely, whatever is admirable—if anything is excellent or praiseworthy—think about such things" (Phil. 4:8). The implication is obvious: there are many fields of study where we may, and sometimes ought to, share the educational endeavors of our lives with others. That this will demand wisdom and discernment should drive us to James 1:5: "If any of you lacks wisdom, you should ask God, who gives generously to all without finding fault, and it will be given to you." If we are not to be conformed to this world but to be transformed (Rom. 12:2), it will be by the renewal of our *mind*, by what and how we think, which presupposes sound formation, sound education.

In one of his recent books,[21] Tim Keller outlines what the Bible teaches Christians to observe and practice in the way they treat others. He highlights key features of the early church's social vision, which should inform Christians' vision today: (1) be multiracial and multiethnic, (2) care for the poor and marginalized, (3) choose to forgive and not retaliate, (4) stand strongly against abortion and infanticide, (5) insist on and practice what is today considered a revolutionary sexual ethic. At the risk of generalization, political liberals typically support 1 and 2, political conservatives typically support 4 and 5, and neither practices 3. That means the thoughtful Christian cannot totally align with political (and educational!) parties other than the kingdom of God. That does not mean there is no place for working with some such entities, as Daniel worked for the government of Babylon. Similarly in the field of education: doubtless there is a place for working with others, but we are called to do so in such a posture of faithfulness that we risk being cast into a den of lions. It is a dubious exercise to predict the future—there are too many unknowns. But it is not unthinkable that our commitment to (the relatively little of) what the Bible says about education could drive us to the educational equivalent of the Revocation of the Edict of Nantes or to the Great Ejection.

Finally, although the Bible provides no biblical theology of education of the sort that runs along a clear trajectory to climax in a resounding

---

21 Timothy Keller, *How to Reach the West Again: Six Essential Elements of a Missionary Encounter* (New York: Redeemer City to City, 2020), 25–29. I am grateful to my pastor, Steve Mathewson, for tracking down this reference.

typological consummation, it provides biblical theology of education in the shape of many pieces that enrich our thinking about the substance, goals, and means of truly Christian education—what the French rightly call *formation*. Coupled with informed surveys of the changing shape of educational institutions across the centuries, the biblical mandates and examples take form in various ways and make us aware of how urgently we need to become insightful "readers" of the present culture. Here the outworking of faithful gospel proclamation, surely including biblically faithful education, will carry us to renewed influence, or to painful persecution, or perhaps both.

14

The Changing Face of Words

ANYONE WHO READS thoughtfully knows that words often change their meaning with time and context. Christians are a "peculiar people," the King James Version tells us (1 Pet. 2:9), only "peculiar" did not mean in 1611 what it means today. Sometimes an older meaning of a word continues in a restricted sector of the culture, even though most people use it in quite a different way: for example, for most readers today, God's gift is not "unspeakable" but "indescribable" (2 Cor. 9:15), even though a conservative fringe of the populace confuse the two words. Sometimes a difference in meaning or overtone is triggered not by the passage of time, but by a different context. "Redemption" in the arcane legal terminology of a mortgage document does not conjure up exactly the same images as the use of the word in the New Testament.[1]

All of this is common knowledge. These examples are innocuous precisely because the change in meaning is widely recognized. Far more inimical to careful conversation are those expressions whose meanings, or whose associations, are frequently unrecognized. Here are a few of them.

Guilt

For many decades now, "guilt" has sometimes referred to culpability but very commonly referred to what might better be thought of as feelings of guilt. Our judicial systems try to establish the guilt or innocence of accused

---

1 This chapter was originally published as D. A. Carson, "The Changing Face of Words," *Themelios* 43, no. 3 (2018): 339–42.

parties, regardless of whether those parties feel guilty; by contrast, our counselors often focus their attention on the guilt feelings of their clients, taking relatively little notice of the extent to which guilt feelings may be grounded in guilt. All of this, as I indicated, has been understood for a long time. When preachers talk about "penal substitutionary atonement," they understand that the punishment is merited: before God the party is guilty and deserves the penalty that, in the case of substitutionary atonement, is discharged by another. This does not mean that wise pastors overlook the terrible burden of guilt feelings. Guilt feelings may be the psychological result of real guilt. Sometimes, however, people feel terribly guilty over things that have no valid tie to real guilt (as, for example, when a woman is sexually assaulted as she walks home from work, yet labors for years under guilt feelings [or shame? See further below]). The careful application of passages about the cross of Christ rightly addresses both our guilt and our feelings of guilt. Efforts to expunge the latter without addressing the former may leave a sinner feeling better about themselves but still unreconciled to God; and exclusive emphasis on addressing the real guilt before God may generate a cerebral grasp of the nature of penal substitution without providing much comfort.

All of this is common discourse in evangelical and Reformed circles, and in some others as well. The reason for bringing it up again is that current cultural pressures are making the potential misunderstandings worse, and harder to clear up. To incur guilt, one must have committed an offense, whether against another individual, against the state (or the law, or the crown, or the like), or against God. Some offenses (e.g., theft) against individuals can be addressed by restitution (perhaps with an additional percentage, as in the Old Testament); some cannot (e.g., rape). Traditionally, to avoid a swamp of subjectivity or, worse, a vendetta, most cultures have established a codification of personal offenses and the corresponding punishments for the guilty. Steal someone's cow, and this is what will happen to you. Today, however, even though much of such codification still prevails, so much emphasis in Western culture is laid on the individual and his or her "rights" that new offenses against the individual are being discovered (or invented) every day. Who decides when an "offense" against an individual has been committed? When the individual feels offended? There is now not only tension between being guilty and feeling guilty, but between being guilty according to some codification of law and feeling the other party is guilty even though no code has been breached (or it has been breached only by the most egregiously creative legal extensions).

More serious is the culture's increasing suspicion of external authority, whether that of God, of the state, or of traditional values. The broad sweep of what that looks like, for good and ill, has been discussed endlessly and need not be canvassed again here. For our purposes it is enough to observe that the traditional understanding of guilt, of culpability, over against guilt feelings, requires the authority of a God or a state or an adopted statute to transgress. If I become my own authority for right and wrong, it is difficult to see how there can be any form of "guilt" that transcends guilt feelings. In that case, there is no need for a sacrifice to deal with that guilt, either.

So in our evangelism, we simply must reserve space for talking about the God who is offended, and thus the nature of guilt, and thus God's solution to this guilt. The gospel provides more than psychological comfort.

Shame

For several decades, missionaries and other culture commentators have pointed out that while much of the Western world fastens its attention on guilt, most of the Eastern world fastens its attention on shame. In such a context, if you present Christ as the one who deals with our guilt, the argument will not resonate as much as an argument that asserts Jesus deals with our shame.

Anyone who has spent time in, say, Southeast Asia, knows there is something to this analysis. One may go further and say that our increasing cross-cultural awareness in this global world affords Christians the opportunity to study the Bible afresh and recognize the place that *both* guilt *and* shame play in its pages. Certainly both guilt and shame surface at the introduction of sin (Gen. 3); indeed, they are so entangled that it is sometimes difficult to separate them, except in analytical terms.

Once again, however, just as there is "guilt" and "guilt"—the Bible focuses on guilt before God while we tend to focus on guilt feelings—so also is there "shame" and "shame." As far as I can see, most shame cultures worry about loss of face before family and friends. People worry about doing something that brings shame on the family, lets down the side, makes it difficult to face neighbors. The fear of bringing shame on yourself or your family becomes a powerful motivation to conform to accepted norms. Of course, both guilt and shame operate in both the East and the West, but there is a preponderant emphasis on shame in the East.

Yet the emphasis on shame in the Bible is not first and foremost with reference to peers and to family, but to God. Adam loses face before God and hides from him in the garden. In other words, our deepest shame is the loss of face we bear before God, not before our parents. Because God himself tells us we are to honor our parents, shaming our parents cannot be entirely separated from shaming God. Yet where a shame culture focuses almost entirely on horizontal relationships, it is still not ready to learn how the gospel addresses our shame. Instead of glorifying God, we have brought shame to his name. In a shame culture, it is necessary to demonstrate that, in the light of what the Bible says about God, our deepest shame humbles us before the living God, who alone can raise us up.

Conscience

The best concise recent treatment of conscience is doubtless that of Andrew David Naselli and J. D. Crowley.[2] My interest here is a little more historically focused: How has one's understanding of conscience changed with the changing of the worldview in which it is embedded?

In the second half of the sixteenth century, Richard Hooker (1554–1600) sought a path between the Catholic churchmanship of the past and the Calvinist churchmanship influenced by Geneva. After 1588 and the destruction of the Spanish Armada, the dangers from the Catholic side were substantially dissipated. Doctrinally, Hooker largely disagreed with Trent but was more open to the late medieval theologians than some of his Calvinist peers. This led to complex discussions about the desirability (or otherwise!) of freedom of conscience. At a time when church and state together imposed the standards of churchmanship and worship that the ruling parties thought acceptable throughout the state, to argue that it could be good for the nation to allow some flexibility grounded in the conscience of the individual believer was innovative. But note well that this was not freedom to choose anything; one's conscience was constrained by the given revelation, by the

---

2   Andrew David Naselli and J. D. Crowley, *Conscience: What It Is, How to Train It, and Loving Those Who Differ* (Wheaton, IL: Crossway, 2016).

authority of God. The question was how to interpret it. Even a century later, when John Locke (1632–1704) advocated a much broader freedom of conscience, it was in some ways constrained by deist assumptions.

By contrast, freedom of conscience today is not far from an appeal to let everyone do that which is right in their own eyes. There is no eternal referent to which appeals might be made for a different interpretation; conscience is individualistic and self-referring.

Tolerance

It has often been pointed out that in the past every culture displays both tolerance and intolerance. There may be less tolerance where a regime is more dictatorial, or where the plausibility structures are copious and interlocking,[3] but every regime allows a certain amount of dissent, perhaps because it is impossible to control everything, perhaps because of a belief that it is good for the society to permit and perhaps even foment differences of opinion.

All of this is simply a clumsy way of saying that in the past, whether in the time of Tiglath-pileser III, the time of Louis XIV, the time of Queen Victoria, or the time of Teddy Roosevelt, tolerance presents itself as a parasitic virtue. By this I mean that it is a virtue that necessarily feeds off larger cultural values and virtues: it was always a question of how much deviation from the cultural norms could be considered good for the culture. Tolerance was neither an independent virtue nor an independent vice; it was always perceived as either a good or at least a useful deviation from larger norms, or a wicked and dangerous deviation from those norms—but in any case, it had no meaning apart from those norms that gave it shape.

But in some calls for tolerance today, tolerance seeks to project itself as an independent virtue, perhaps the most important virtue. I have argued elsewhere that this turns out to be intellectually confusing and morally perverse. It is intellectually confusing because it makes little sense to speak of *tolerating* something or other unless one disagrees with it: one cannot meaningfully say that a Christian tolerates an atheist, or vice versa, until one establishes that they disagree. It is not tolerance *unless one first disagrees*; if there is no disagreement, one may speak of moral indifference, or ignorance of the other's position, or carelessness, but not of tolerance. This elevation

---

3 Cf. the discussion in my *Intolerance of Tolerance* (Grand Rapids, MI: Eerdmans, 2012).

of tolerance to the level of independent virtue is not only intellectually confusing, however, but morally perverse. It is morally perverse because it proves to be spectacularly intolerant toward those who claim certain other positions are wrong. In the name of tolerance, this new so-called tolerance adopts intolerance.

What should be clear by now from all four of these examples is that the dramatic differences in meaning is a correlative of the loss of God, or at least the loss of an external standard. Guilt becomes guilty feelings with special ease when there is no God or law before whom or which we are objectively guilty; shame becomes loss of face before peers if there is no God before whom to be ashamed. Freedom of conscience becomes sanction to do whatever I want to do, instead of the right to interpret what God has given. And tolerance becomes either an incoherent mess, or, at best, nothing more than a poorly grounded plea to be nice.

The urgency of thinking and speaking worldviewishly presses on us ever harder.

15

One of the Saddest Texts
in the Old Testament

THREE OLD TESTAMENT PASSAGES devote considerable space to the life and times of King Hezekiah and disclose what a good and faithful man he could be (2 Kings 18–20; 2 Chron. 29–32; Isa. 36–39). We gladly remember his far-reaching efforts to lead the nation into reformation in line with the Torah, and we are moved by Hezekiah's stunning courage and faithful trust when he is forced to confront Sennacherib.[1]

None of these three Old Testament documents glosses over Hezekiah's moral failures. But two of the three, namely, 2 Kings and Isaiah, treat one of his failures in a distinctive way that generates a narrative of surpassing sadness. For the sake of simplicity, I shall focus attention on Isaiah 39:1–8 and draw attention to three details.

First, like many biblical narratives, this chapter provides the capstone to stunning moral contrast. After witnessing Hezekiah's faith and courage in Isaiah 36–37, and after meditating on his extraordinary prayer in 37:14–20, we cannot help but feel let down when we learn about his whining self-pity in chapter 38 and his foolish boasting to the Babylonian emissaries in 39:1–2, which leads to the staggering divine rebuke of 39:5–7. How can the same man be so good and so bad, so wise and so foolish, so God-centered and so self-focused? We like our heroes and models to be a little more consistent. The moral contrast is not only startling, it is discouraging.

---

1 This chapter was originally published as D. A. Carson, "One of the Saddest Texts in the OT," *Themelios* 47, no. 3 (2022).

Yet this is not what makes Isaiah 39 one of the saddest texts in the Old Testament. Even as it provides the capstone to stunning moral contrast, it is entirely in line with many biblical narratives, as I stipulated. There is no warrant to extract a superlative out of this narrative: so far, it is sad enough, but certainly not the "saddest." Abraham, that great man of faith and father of the faithful, lies so shamefully that he endangers his wife; Moses, that most humble of men, vents his frustration in self-righteous anger when he strikes the rock; David, a man after God's own heart, is not only a blameworthy father but an adulterer and a murderer. And if we look for New Testament examples, we soon think of Peter, the apostle who is shown by the Father who Jesus is, yet thinks he knows enough he can correct Jesus's theology and, worse, three times denies knowing who Jesus is, bringing himself to tears; and so on, and so on. True, there is a handful of characters in the Bible about whom nothing negative is recorded (e.g., Joseph, Daniel, Esther), but their numbers are vastly exceeded by those whose lives betray discouraging moral contradictions, deep moral contrasts. And Hezekiah falls into their number.

Second, while holding to some form or other of the doctrine of providence, Hezekiah twists it to no good purpose. To put it a slightly different way, Hezekiah tips his hat to honor God's sovereignty but applies it to his life with a perverse willfulness: he commits himself to wholehearted submission to God's will in order to secure his own selfishness. When in the name of God the prophet Isaiah rebukes Hezekiah for the way he stooped to disgraceful bragging before the envoys from Babylon, thereby endangering the kingdom, the prophet spares Hezekiah no details of the disastrous judgment ahead: the wealth of the kingdom will be "carried off to Babylon. Nothing will be left" (Isa. 39:6). Moreover, the impending disaster will have a personal dimension: "And some of your descendants, your own flesh and blood who will be born to you, will be taken away, and they will become eunuchs in the palace of the king of Babylon" (39:7). Hezekiah's response? "The word of the LORD you have spoken is good," he replies (39:8a). A superficial initial glance might lead the reader to think that Hezekiah wants nothing more than the will of God, even if that will spells judgment. But the last line of verse eight betrays the utterly selfish heart of this spent king. The reason Hezekiah can sound so sanguine about the terrible justice hanging over him and his dynasty is that he thinks, "There will be peace and security in my lifetime" (39:8b).

Contrast the response of David to the threat of judgment. In the wake of the adultery and murder he committed, David is told not only of the judgment that will befall the nation, but of the death of his son born to Bathsheba. David repents of his sin, and Nathan the prophet declares, "The LORD has taken away your sin. You are not going to die. But because by doing this you have shown utter contempt for the LORD, the son born to you will die" (2 Sam. 12:13–14). For the next week, as the child fights for his life, David clothes himself in dust and ashes and refuses to eat. When the infant finally dies, David's attendants are hesitant to tell their master: "While the child was still living, [David] wouldn't listen to us when we spoke to him. How can we now tell him the child is dead? He may do something desperate" (2 Sam. 12:18). But the tragic news is soon made clear, whereupon David washes himself, puts on clean clothes and lotions, worships the Lord, and then sits down to a good meal. David's attendants make no sense of this: "Why are you acting this way? While the child was alive, you fasted and wept, but now that the child is dead, you get up and eat!" (2 Sam. 12:21). It is in his reply that David shows himself to be so different from Hezekiah. David tells his attendants, "While the child was still alive, I fasted and wept. I thought, 'Who knows? The LORD may be gracious to me and let the child live.' But now that he is dead, why should I go on fasting? Can I bring him back again? I will go to him, but he will not return to me" (2 Sam. 12:22–23).

David hears the pronouncement of God's judgment and knows it is deserved, but he also recognizes that God is more than raw will. God interacts with his people, and he is very merciful: despite the divine decree, perhaps the child will be spared. Hezekiah too recognizes the will of God, and he too knows that the pronounced judgment is deserved, but his affirmations of God's will are blindingly selfish. He offers no intercession for the people over whom he rules. Even when he is told that some of his own descendants will be castrated in the wretchedness of war, he remains unmoved. "The word of the LORD you have spoken is good," he tells the prophet Isaiah—not because he throws himself on the mercy of God, but because the judgments that God has ordained are scheduled to hit after Hezekiah is dead: "There will be peace and security in my lifetime" (39:8). This king who could face down Sennacherib now cares for no one, not even his children and grandchildren, more than he cares for himself. It was once said of this king,

Hezekiah trusted in the LORD, the God of Israel. There was no one like him among all the kings of Judah, either before him or after him. He held fast to the LORD and did not stop following him; he kept the commands the LORD had given Moses. And the LORD was with him; he was successful in whatever he undertook." (2 Kings 18:5–7)

But Hezekiah ends up with no horizon larger than his own comforts. There is a poignancy in this narrative that is immeasurably sad.

Third, Hezekiah serves as a tangible demonstration of one of the great themes of Isaiah 40–66. In some ways, the sad chapter, Isaiah 39, announces one of the drumming themes of the rest of this prophecy. In the rest of his book, the prophet keeps flipping back and forth between a focus on spiritual vitality and a focus on catastrophic condemnation. God is immeasurably merciful; Israel is immeasurably unfaithful (Isa. 43:14–28). Israel is chosen by God; Israel cherishes worthless idols (Isa. 44) and pursues iniquity and injustice (Isa. 59). Jerusalem will be restored (Isa. 44:24–28; 51:1–16; 54) and Israel will be freed (Isa. 48:12–15; 49:8–21), but with salvation comes judgment (Isa. 65). Even in the closing two chapters, there is both judgment and hope: new heavens and a new earth, along with ghastly failure and death.

Whether in the profile of one individual leader or in the profile of the covenant people of God, we are called to press on—to emulate the examples of courageous faith and to grieve bitterly over the examples of blistering selfishness. The voice of the exalted Master still says, "Be faithful, even to the point of death, and I will give you life as your victor's crown" (Rev. 2:10).

PART 4

REFLECTIONS ON CHRIST
AND CULTURE

16

Do Not Be Conformed to the World

THE APOSTLE PAUL WRITES, "Do not conform to the pattern of this world, but be transformed by the renewing of your mind" (Rom. 12:2). Elsewhere he tells the Corinthians, "We demolish arguments and every pretension that sets itself up against the knowledge of God, and we take captive every thought to make it obedient to Christ" (2 Cor. 10:5).[1]

Thinking differently from the "world" has been part of the Christian's responsibility and agenda from the beginning. The language Paul uses intimates that this independence of thought will not be easy. The assumption seems to be that the world has its own patterns, its own structured arguments, its own value systems. Because we Christians live in the world, the "default" reality is that we are likely to be shaped by these patterns, structures, and values unless we consciously discern how and where they stand over against the gospel and all its entailments and adopt radically different thinking. Moreover, our response must not only be defensive (Rom. 12:2) but offensive, aiming to "demolish arguments and every pretension that sets itself up against the knowledge of God," aiming to "take captive every thought to make it obedient to Christ" (2 Cor. 10:5).

Neither Scripture nor experience suggests that this will be an easy task. Transparently, one of the things needed is substantial discernment, since some things the world thinks are not intrinsically bad (in the Reformed heritage, this is commonly seen to be the fruit of "common grace"). More

---

1 This chapter was originally published as D. A. Carson, "Editorial," *Themelios* 33, no. 3 (2008): 1–4.

difficult yet, the challenges are not vanquished once, enabling us to coast. Until the end of the age, the "world" continues to exist, and it keeps launching its challenges from constantly changing angles. When Christians who had suffered through two centuries of waves of Roman persecution faced the stunning reality that the emperor now declared himself to be a convert, they were faced with the temptation to rethink what political "victory" looked like, what structures controlling Christian influence in the corridors of power might achieve—and thus to rethink the nature of the kingdom. Doubtless Matthew 20:20–28 seemed less relevant than reflections on the life and times of King David. Moreover, decisions of the same sort played out again and again, across centuries, until there was an imperial papacy, and beyond.

Choose your own historical examples. Probably the most difficult "patterns" of thought to identify as things we should not be "conformed" to are those in any culture that the overwhelming majority in the culture think are pretty obvious, but which stand either tangentially skewed with respect to, or totally opposed to, the gospel. Most of us look back on the temptations toward ascetic and gnostic movements in the second and third centuries and marvel that so many people who called themselves Christians were taken in. But the most dangerous movements in any age are those that are so widely assumed that it is very hard to see them. It is easy to discern and denounce yesteryear's blind spots, and even feel vaguely superior because we are able to do so; it is far more difficult to discern our own. And to these big "worldviewish" structures of thought must be added the rippling recurrence of the many temptations to avarice, pride, sexual libertinism, and lust for power.

All this is the common reflection of Christians across the centuries. Certainly I have tried to think about these matters periodically throughout my adult life; most of us have. Recently, however, two things have forced me to probe them more than I have before.

First, writing the book *Christ and Culture Revisited*[2] forced me to ponder a little more seriously the way Christians are simultaneously part of a culture and set over against it, how they are influenced by the culture for good and ill and influence it in return, likewise for good and ill.

---

2 *Christ and Culture Revisited* (Grand Rapids, MI: Eerdmans, 2008).

Second, increasing reflection on the sheer speed, volume, and democratic openness of the Internet prompts guarded thanks for access to useful information and sheer horror at the potential for abuse and corruption.

(a) One cannot help but be thankful for the way the Internet can disseminate vast quantities of useful information, how books and other sources once available only in the best libraries are now, for countless hundreds of millions of people, only a click away.

(b) Equally we ought to be thankful for the way independent voices on the Internet sometimes puncture the pretentious or plainly false claims of the major traditional media. Granted, as Lord Acton insisted, that all power corrupts, and that absolute power corrupts absolutely, one does not like to see too many news sources falling into too few hands. The Internet is gloriously irreverent to the major traditional media. I am not suggesting that Internet information is intrinsically more reliable than information disseminated on television or in newspapers and weekly journals; I'm merely saying that multiplication of sources of information is more likely to ensure freedom and truth than entrusting all the sources of information distribution into too few hands.

(c) But there are many downsides as well. The sleaze and trash on the net are stupefying. Porn, for example, was certainly not invented by the Internet, but the Internet makes it constantly accessible to everyone. Some reports say that more money is now spent in Western countries on porn than on tobacco, alcohol, and hard drugs combined. What is this doing to human relationships, to marriages, to the gift of godly imagination?

(d) Because the Internet is spectacularly accessible, almost anyone can voice an opinion or make a claim. In this sense, it is the most "democratic" of the media. Occasionally this means that voices otherwise silenced, voices that should be heard, are indeed heard. Much more commonly, voices multiply that are ill-informed, opinionated, often pretentious and arrogant. A higher percentage of these voices were weeded out when the distribution was via print, radio, or television; by democratizing the delivery system, every voice can be published, and it becomes culturally unacceptable even to suggest that some voices are not worth publishing. This does nothing to enhance either discernment or self-discipline. As Michael Kinsley likes to ask, "How many blogs does the world need?"[3]

(e) Much more interesting, and more difficult to predict, is the phenomenon called "groundswell."[4] Opinions and responses coagulate and drive topics and evaluations in uncontrollable and largely unpredictable directions. This can foster openness; alternatively, what is perceived to be a cultural consensus on some matter or other may simply be wrong.

(f) The speed of the Internet is stunning. A few years ago I was attending a meeting of pastors, most of us with our laptops out taking notes during the complex discussions, when the chap next to me turned his screen to me and invited me to read what was there. About fifteen minutes earlier he had said something to the group. What he had said was summarized and sent by another member of the group to his associate back home. The associate blogged the information, and that blog was picked up by an RSS feed that brought the information to the blog of one of the assistants of the chap beside me. That assistant emailed his boss, and there was the question on the screen: "Did you really say that?" Amusing, even fun—but such speed is encouraging us to bash out responses before we've heard another side, before we've had time to evaluate, before we've pondered whether or not it is wise and godly to respond at all, before we've cooled down and been careful in our choice of words. When you set out to write a book, a good editor fosters such virtues, but most blogs pass through the hands of no editors, and graceful communication is not thereby enhanced.

(g) Scarcely less important than speed of access is the Internet's sheer intoxicating addictiveness—or, more broadly, we might be better to think of the intoxicating addictiveness of the entire digital world. Many are those who are never quiet, alone, and reflective, who never read material that demands reflection and imagination. The iPods provide the music, the phones constant access to friends, phones and computers tie us to news, video, YouTube, Facebook, and on and on. This is not to demonize tools that are so very useful. Rather, it is to point out the obvious: information does not necessarily spell knowledge, and knowledge does not necessarily spell wis-

---

3   Michael Kinsley, "How Many Blogs Does the World Need?," *Time*, November 20, 2008, https://content.time.com/.

4   See esp. Charline Li and Josh Bernoff, *Groundswell: Winning in a World Transformed by Social Technologies* (Boston: Harvard Business Press, 2008).

dom, and the incessant demand for unending sensory input from the digital world (says he, as he writes this on a computer for an electronic theological journal) does not guarantee we make good choices. We have the potential to become world citizens, informed about every corner of the globe, but in many western countries the standards of geographical and cross-cultural awareness have seriously declined. We have access to spectacularly useful information, but most of us diddle around on ephemeral blogs and listen to music as enduring as a snowball in a blast furnace. Sometimes we just become burned out by the endless waves of bad news and decide the best course is to turn the iPod volume up a bit.

One more example of a slightly different sort: Joseph Bottum and Ryan T. Anderson write a fascinating essay in *First Things* titled "Stem Cells: A Political History."[5] They carefully chart the way the story has been told by the media since 2001 when President Bush *allowed* the use of federal funds for embryonic stem cell research. That's right, he *allowed* it; no president before him, including Clinton, had done so. Bush did restrict the use of federal funds to previously established stem cell lines, largely because he was afraid of the dehumanizing effects of simply harvesting stem cells from embryos. Meanwhile, private companies could experiment as they wanted. The next six years stirred up a torrent of opprobrium. Bush was against science, people were not going to be cured if he continued to have his way, and so forth. The detailed documentation provided by Bottum and Anderson is captivating. Then, using mice, Shinya Yamanaka demonstrated that fully pluripotent stem cells could be created directly from adult cells. By November 2007, two independent teams published the results of their work showing that human pluripotent stem cells could be produced without using embryos, cloning, or human eggs. The story dropped away from the front pages of the media. And these same media do not now report how the small but genuine advances made in stem cell research (for instance, in multiple sclerosis, lupus, and scleroderma), at least in the United States, have almost without exception sprung from work with adult stem cells. The "spin" on the story has shaped public opinion: conservatives oppose stem cell research, and liberals are for it. What Carl Trueman calls "the wages of

---

5   Joseph Bottum and Ryan T. Anderson, "Stem Cells: A Political History," *First Things*, November 2008, https://www.firstthings.com/.

spin" shape not only what we think is newsworthy, but our ethical reflection and our perception of what is for the public good.[6]

These precise challenges never faced Paul, Augustine, Aquinas, Luther, and Turretin. But what does it mean not to let the world squeeze us into its mold in the opening decade of the twenty-first century?

I shall not here review the Christian resources God has kindly lavished on us to enable us not to conform to the pattern of this world. If we are to be transformed by the renewing of our mind, then we must be reading the Scriptures perennially, seeking to think God's thoughts after him, focusing on the gospel of God and pondering its implications in every domain of life. We need to hear competing voices of information from the world around us, use our time in the digital world wisely, and learn to shut that world down when it becomes more important to get up in the morning and answer emails than it does to get up and read the Bible and pray. We may also learn much from church history, where we observe fellow believers in other times and cultures learning the shape of faithfulness. We begin to detect how easily the "world" may squeeze us into its mold. We soon learn that adequate response is more than mere mental resolve, mere disciplined observance of the principle "garbage in, garbage out" (after all, we are what we think), though it is not less than that. The gospel is the power of God issuing in salvation. Empowered by the Holy Spirit and living in the shadow of the cross and resurrection, we find ourselves wanting to be conformed to the Lord Jesus, wanting to be as holy and as wise as pardoned sinners can be this side of the consummation.

---

6   Carl Trueman, *The Wages of Spin: Critical Writings on Historical and Contemporary Evangelism* (Fearn, UK: Mentor, 2011).

17

Words and Deeds

IN MANY PARTS OF THE evangelical world, one hears a new debate—or, more precisely, new chapters in an old debate—regarding the precise place that "deeds of mercy" ought to have in Christian witness. I am not talking about the perennial debate between left-wing and right-wing economic solutions, that is, between those who think there will be more social justice and less poverty if the government takes a greater share of the nationally produced wealth and distributes it more equitably, and those who think there will be more social justice and less poverty where government legislation offers carrot-and-stick incentives to help people get off welfare rolls and become less dependent on initiative-killing generosity while providing a safety net for those truly incapable of helping themselves. I am talking, rather, about the debate between those Christians who say that we should primarily be about the business of heralding the gospel and planting churches, and those who say that our responsibility as Christians extends to the relief of oppression, suffering, and poverty in all their forms.[1]

Both sides cite impressive historical precedents. Under the ministry of Howell Harris, George Whitefield, John and Charles Wesley, and those associated with them, the gospel, faithfully preached, transformed the social face of England. What receives the most press is the work of Wilberforce in driving through parliament legislation that shut down the slave trade and eventually abolished slavery throughout the British Empire. But movements

---

1 This chapter was originally published as D. A. Carson, "Editorial," *Themelios* 33, no. 2 (2008): 1–3.

led by Methodist converts also formed and directed trade unions that tamed the ugliest aspects of the Industrial Revolution, passed legislation that reformed prisons (not least the notorious debtors prisons), drove up the minimum age at which children could work (which took five-year-olds out of the mines), and took the first steps toward universal literacy. For about sixty years, the movement accomplished an astounding amount of social good, while preserving the primacy of preaching the gospel and winning converts.

On the other hand, the experience of many churches in the West from about 1880 to 1925 provides another trajectory that many thoughtful Christians today fear. The gospel came increasingly to be identified with progress; the gospel itself was progressively diluted. At least until the outbreak of World War I, the optimism was contagious, intoxicating, and naive. Christian mission, increasingly understood in an expansive fashion, eventually started replacing the preaching of the gospel with deeds of mercy (or, from the perspective of those adopting this stance, the gospel was increasingly redefined). To preserve a show of unity, the Edinburgh Conference of 1910 simply didn't bother with tough-minded and biblically framed notions of the gospel. Unity was preserved; substance was lost. Once the confessional evangelicals picked themselves up and reorganized, many of them vowed not to make the same mistake again. They tended to underline the proclamation of the word and downplay, or in some instances disown, the responsibility to engage in deeds of mercy in Christ's name.

That, at least, is the way the story is regularly told. Recent studies both in the United Kingdom and the United States modify the account somewhat. Apparently, a disproportionate number of conservative evangelicals give their time to organizations such as UNICEF, World Relief, and Save the Children, so when it comes to actual boots on the ground, the polarity between conservatives and liberals is not, in practice, what is often portrayed.

Recently these and related matters were discussed over three days by a group of about fifty pastors. These pastors approached the subject out of the conviction that gospel proclamation must occupy pride of place in our priorities, but they represented quite different positions on what follows from this, some of them hoping for a new Evangelical Awakening and others fearful of a new round of gospel-destroying liberalism. A fair bit of time was then devoted to scanning relevant biblical passages: the parable of the good Samaritan, serving as salt and light in a world that is both corrupt and dark, doing good to all people (especially those of the household of faith), and so forth. And finally there was, I think, a broad consensus that Christians who understand the priority of preparing people for eternity must also help people here and now, and that gospel proclamation must not be set antithetically against deeds of mercy. Far from it: many of the pastors and the Christians they served were heavily involved in an array of strategic ministries. It was, of course, immediately recognized that how one discharges such responsibilities will vary enormously from community to community, from country to country, for the needs vary hugely, almost beyond comprehension. Still, we returned again and again to this pointed question: Granted that we ought to be engaged in acts of mercy, what safeguards can be set in place so as to minimize the risk that the deeds of mercy will finally swamp the proclamation of the gospel and the passionate desire to see men and women reconciled to God by faith in Christ Jesus and his atoning death and resurrection?

Two stood out.

First, it is helpful to distinguish between the responsibilities of the church qua church and the responsibilities of Christians. Some writers flip back and forth between references to "Christians" and references to "church" as if there is no difference whatsoever. But many Christian thinkers, from Kuyperians to Baptists, have argued that if the church qua church is responsible for some of these substantial works of mercy, such works of mercy ought to come under the leaders of the church. It is very difficult to find any warrant for that step in the New Testament. Even before there were pastors/elders/overseers, the apostles themselves, according to Acts, recognized that they should not be diverted from the ministry of the word and prayer, even by the inequities of food distribution among the faithful, so they saw to it that others were appointed to tackle the problem. Ministers of the gospel ought so to be teaching the Bible in all its comprehensiveness that they will be raising up believers with many different avenues of service, but they themselves must not become so embroiled in such multiplying ministries that their ministries of evangelism, Bible teaching, disciple making, instructing, baptizing, and the like somehow get squeezed to the periphery and take on a purely formal veneer.

Second, one pastor astutely urged, "Preach hell." Two things follow from this. (1) By adopting this priority we remind ourselves that as Christians we desire to relieve all suffering, from the temporal to the eternal. If we do not maintain such a panoramic vision, the relief of immediate suffering, as important as it is, may so command our focus that we fail to remind ourselves of Jesus's rhetorical question, "What good will it be for someone to gain the whole world, yet forfeit their soul?" (Matt. 16:26). Read the closing lines of Revelation 14 and Revelation 20 when your vision becomes myopic. (2) As long as you are prepared to plead with men and women to be reconciled to God and to flee the coming wrath, you are preserving something that is central in the Bible, something that is intimately and irrefragably tied to the gospel itself—and those who want to shunt such themes aside and focus only on the relief of present suffering will not want to have much to do with you. Thus you will be free to preach and teach the whole counsel of God and to relieve all suffering, temporal and eternal, without being drawn into endless alliances in which people never focus on anything beyond threescore years and ten.

18

Contrarian Reflections on Individualism

NOT MANY VOICES are raised these days in support of individualism.[1] The left will not help, of course, for rugged individualism is associated in their minds with nineteenth-century robber barons and other greedy swine. Goodness surely lies in communitarianism, not individualism. Those like Thomas Sowell who complain that this popular analysis of the nineteenth century does not stand up very well to sober facts are not paid much attention.[2] If the right rejoices in the individualism that ostensibly characterizes an uptick in Western productivity and bemoans increasing statism, it is soon told that those early years were far more communitarian than people imagine; it is the present that is disturbingly individualistic.[3] Sociologists like Wuthnow and Bellah chart our individualism, and many conclude that Generation X is particularly individualistic.[4] Individualism has debased evangelicalism into a kind of syncretism;[5] spiritually, we need instruction

---

1   This chapter was originally published as D. A. Carson, "Contrarian Reflections on Individualism," *Themelios* 35, no. 3 (2010): 378–83. It is a lightly edited manuscript of a talk delivered on November 20, 2010 in Atlanta, Georgia at the Tyndale House breakfast coinciding with the annual meetings of the Institute for Biblical Research and Society of Biblical Literature.

2   See esp. Thomas Sowell, *Intellectuals and Society* (New York: Basic Books, 2010).

3   So Barry Alan Shain, *The Myth of American Individualism: The Protestant Origins of American Political Thought* (Princeton: Princeton University Press, 1994).

4   E.g., Gordon Lynch, *After Religion: "Generation X" and the Search for Meaning* (London: DLT, 2002).

5   So Dennis P. Hollinger, *Individualism and Social Ethics: An Evangelical Syncretism* (Lanham: UPA, 1985).

on how to meet the challenges.[6] In a recent and generally excellent book on ecclesiology, Jonathan Leeman devotes not a few pages to denouncing the individualism that, as he sees it, is one of the evils that blinds many people, especially in the West, from seeing how important the church is in the Bible.[7] In short, on all sides we are being taught that individualism dominates Western thought, and it is bad.

Without doubting that there is a fair bit of truth in these analyses, I wonder if a few questions should not be raised. Are cultures widely regarded as fostering little individualism intrinsically better places for the gospel to flourish? Is it not the case that tightly knit cultures that encourage various kinds of groupthink are often less hospitable to conversion and evangelistic enterprise than the West is? These can vary quite a lot, of course. But many gospel ministers and missionaries in Japan would like to inject a little *more* individualism into the people they serve. A tightly ordered society like Saudi Arabia is pretty hard to break into. Yes, I know, the issue there is not simply cultural cohesion but the active Muslim opposition to all things Christian. But a very open country like Australia, in which the "cut down the tall poppy syndrome" flourishes, allows plenty of freedom for gospel ministry but really dislikes individuals who stand out too strongly—and it too is not very hospitable to the gospel. Isn't *something* to be said in favor of individualism?

Here at home, I wonder whether individualism is in reality as highly prized as some think. One could make a case that many people want to belong to *something*—to the first group that manages to purchase an iPhone, to the "emerging" crowd or to those who want little to do with them, to the great company that can discuss baseball or cricket or ice hockey, to those who are up-to-date in fashion sense, to those who are suitably green or those who are suspicious of the green movement, to various groups of "friends" on Facebook, to those who tweet, and so on. If you say that most of these groups do not foster deep relationships, I shall agree with you—but then the problem lies in the domain of shallow relationships of many kinds, rather than in individualism per se. Meanwhile in politics, business, and

---

6   Richard Rice, "The Challenge of Spiritual Individualism (and How to Meet It)," *Andrews University Seminary Studies* 43 (2005): 113–31.

7   Jonathan Leeman, *The Church and the Surprising Offense of God's Love: Reintroducing the Doctrines of Church Membership and Discipline*, 9Marks (Wheaton, IL: Crossway, 2010).

even religion, many voices call for leaders who can build various kinds of cohesive movements or institutions, not develop individuals. Do not many of us bemoan the massive cultural pressures toward various kinds of political correctness? By and large, individualism does not seem strong enough to laugh off the silliest of these siren calls to conformity. On most university campuses, I could devoutly wish for a little more individualism.

When we turn to the Bible, we find more balance on these matters than we find in the endless unqualified condemnations of individualism in the West. On the one hand, of course, there is plenty of material that underscores the importance of the church, the community of the new covenant. The many "one another" passages (love one another, forgive one another, bear with one another, and so on) necessarily conjure up the supreme importance of relationships, many of them reciprocal. If the world knows that we are Jesus's disciples because we love one another, then the demands of world mission are best served where we are working hard at mutual Christian love. The body metaphor in Paul functions in two rather different ways, but one of those ways emphasizes the interdependence of the various parts of the body (esp. 1 Cor. 12). One of the images of the consummated glory still to come is of a city, the new Jerusalem—and that is a *social* vision, not a vision of a rural hut in a green valley nicely removed from prying neighbors. Of course, the symbol-laden value of the new Jerusalem turns on the fact that it is the city of the great King, a city built like a cube so that it has become the Most Holy Place, with foundations and gates numbering twelve to remind us of the links to twelve tribes and twelve apostles, and more of the same. Yet the vision of a city is built into the Apocalypse at multiple levels. Multiple authors note that the entire book could be labeled "A Tale of Two Cities": one belongs to Babylon or to the new Jerusalem, both visions social. We sin together or we are righteous together, for both sin and righteousness are heavily tied to relationships. Certainly we urgently need to recapture the importance of the church in the gospel plan of God; here Jonathan Leeman makes many important contributions.

On the other hand, the Bible applauds the deeds not only of many individuals, but of a certain kind of individualism. The two spies who stand out against the opinion of the crowd, the Caleb who cries, "Give me this mountain," the heroic stances of lonely prophets who position themselves athwart their own decaying cultures, all speak of God's use of individuals who live their lives with God alone as their shield. For all the times that Jesus is sometimes mobbed by crowds and devoted to training his own disciples, there is a human aloneness to him that cuts against the grain of social conformity. If he is not alone, it is, as he says, because "my Father is with me" (John 16:32). He himself insists that those who follow him must "hate" their mother and father—an unambiguous demand that even family ties cannot be allowed precedence over allegiance to the kingdom and the King. The great apostle of the church, Paul, knows what it is to suffer rejection by some of the churches he helped to found, but this did not deter him from gospel loyalty, even if it meant confronting another apostle against the prevailing winds in the church he was then serving (Gal. 2:11–14). Both when churches press on toward faithfulness and when they drift toward lethargy or stubbornly pursue wickedness and idolatry, the exalted Christ challenges *individuals* within such churches to be "overcomers," to be faithful (Rev. 2–3). Where would the church be today without its God-given gifts of Athanasius and Luther?

Yet when I reflect on this complicated array of evidence pointing in divergent directions, four reflections come to mind.

First, I begin to suspect that the problem lies in resting so much weight on the *category* of individualism. The sad fact is that we human beings will corrupt anything and everything we touch, including *both* individualism *and* communitarianism/collectivism. To fasten all the negative associations on one pole or the other is frankly naive, biblically and historically shortsighted. Clearly an emphasis on individualism *can* be of the very essence of sin: to insist on doing things *my* way is to dethrone God, to shape myself into a twisted idol; equally clearly, an emphasis on communitarianism *can also* be of the very essence of sin, as we build a Babel and call it progress. Clearly an individualism that is sold out to Christ *can* be of the very essence of godly self-sacrifice and faithful service to the gospel; equally clearly, an emphasis on communitarianism that demonstrates the intra-Trinitarian love of God within the life of God's blood-bought people *can also* be of the very essence of faithful Christian existence (John 17), reflecting God himself in this loveless world. The fundamental issue is not the priority of the individual over against the community, or the reverse. The fundamental issue is whether individuals and communities live their lives in this broken world, by the grace of the gospel, in joyful submission to our Maker, Redeemer, providential Ruler, and coming Judge. To displace this basic theological analysis by turning individualism into the primary bogeyman—or, in some cultures, by elevating individualism as in itself a heroic good—is to lose sight of the Godward dimension that must determine Christian understanding of what is fundamentally right and wrong.

Second, another way of getting at the same thing is to distinguish individualism from selfism. In his book *The Real American Dream: A Meditation on Hope*,[8] Andrew Delbanco outlines the spiritual history of the United States in three categories: (1) "God," which in his analysis runs from Puritan New England to the rise of democracy, a period during which many men and women kept in view the vastness of God's glory; (2) "Nation," running from the rise of democracy until the Great Society visions operating after World War II, a period during which more and more people turned away from the ideal of a vast God and anchored their hopes and aspirations in a great nation; and (3) "Self," running from the Great Society to the present time, a period in which so many have lost both the vision of a vast God and the vision of a great nation, such that all their hopes narrow down to the petty horizon of Self, a goal that is vanishingly small and incapable of sustaining America's communal life. I suspect a similar analysis could be offered of the United Kingdom, stretched over a slightly different time scale, with the second category, the Great Society, displaced by the British Empire.

Like all such analyses, of course, this one, even while it is convincing on numerous fronts, is a bit too neat. Various forms of selfism can happily, or miserably, coexist with broader visions: even in the shadow of Sinai the sons of Korah may lust for Moses's role, and even while Jesus is heading to the cross his disciples may squabble over who will sit on his right hand or his left in the kingdom. Even if it is true that much of contemporary Western culture is currently self-absorbed, with few goals other than personal power, personal wealth, and personal pleasure, the fact remains that such goals were not exactly unknown under the British Empire. Conversely, in the age of Self, such goals may be repudiated by some ordinary people today, many of them Christians, who want to make their lives count for something of more transcendental significance than hedonism.

---

8   Andrew Delbanco, *The Real American Dream: A Meditation on Hope* (Cambridge, MA: Harvard University Press, 1999).

But the larger problem with this analysis is twofold. (a) Selfism is not necessarily the same as individualism, even though the latter is frequently tarred with the brush of the former. Selfism sounds intrinsically selfish; individualism may or may not be selfish. (b) In particular, the selfism of the Delbanco analysis frequently hides itself by pretending it fosters rugged individualism, whereas in fact it induces a herd mentality that has much more in common with a sort of socially encouraged communitarianism. Before cigarette advertising was all but banned, the image of the Marlboro Man—a tough, lone, tanned, fit, hunkish cowboy—appealed to all the stereotypes of the American ideal of rugged individualism, and Marlboro sold millions of cigarettes to all those would-be hunks hankering to conform to the ideal. Car manufacturers parade their products by trying to convince you that their vehicle will bring out the real you—and of course the cars in question are mass-produced. In other words, the emphasis on self-fulfillment in advertising often plays to rugged individualism that has a sort of iconic appeal, even while the brute fact is that this is an appeal to the masses to conform to a mythical, community-shared construct.

In short, we need to rethink the link between individualism and selfism. Unless your name is Ayn Rand, selfism is unlikely to be a good thing; individualism may or may not be a good thing.

Third, we need to reflect a little more on the bearing of truth on our topic. Begin with an essay by Phil Myles, "Of Truth, Tolerance and Tyranny."[9] Myles begins by outlining one of the central myths of our time. According to this myth, a society is likely to be most tolerant if it holds to flexible, nondogmatic, even multivalent notions of truth; conversely, a society is likely to be most *in*tolerant where it holds to absolute truths, truths that are inflexible, unbending. In other words, tyranny and tolerance find themselves in a perennial battle, and which pole triumphs is largely tied to the conception of truth that we sustain.

But does this myth capture reality? Is the myth true? Myles sets forth his thesis:

> The reality of the situation is just the *opposite* of what we have been led to believe. Put simply, tyranny is not the inevitable outcome of an absolutist

---

9 Phil Myles, "Of Truth, Tolerance and Tyranny," *Kategoria* 22 (2001): 7–27.

view of truth, but is, rather, the direct product of *relativism*. Likewise, tolerance arises not from relativism but from the very thing that our society anathematizes—the belief in absolutes.[10]

It would take too long to lay out the details of Myles's argument. Suffice it to say that he holds that many of our categories for thinking about these things are inappropriate. In part, he argues by case study. He begins with Japan, a country where he lived for many years. In most Western cultures, we live in the shadow of the Enlightenment, which taught us to classify our experience into two categories: the one, full of nonabsolutes, is characterized by emotion, aesthetics, the arts; the other is characterized by absolutes, objectivity, science, logical thought, and truth. These two categories are mutually exclusive. The second category is the domain of both tyranny and objective truth. By contrast, Japan brings the two categories together in ways that would be judged incompatible in most of the Western world: on the one hand, haiku poetry and delicate paintings of enchanting cherry blossoms, and on the other, ruthless business corporations and political machinations. The fact that these two categories coexist and interpenetrate each other in Japan is part of what makes Japan seem so "mysterious" to the Western observer. In reality, Myles argues, what is often called the "iron triangle"—"the triad of elected government, big business and the bureaucracy"—exerts enormous power in a frankly oppressive manner. "There is no need to picture this in terms of dictators and jackboots. Things are done a lot more subtly in Japan, but the salient fact is that those who hold power use it to control the lives of those beneath them."[11] There is little tradition of elected officials being "servants of the people"; in fact, the people exist to serve the state and culture, not to mention the company to which a person belongs. In Japanese culture, there is little notion of "right" and "wrong" in absolute terms; it is well-known that there is no Japanese word for "sin." In this sense, Japanese society is relativistic—that is, what is "right" depends on the situation in which you find yourself, determined by the social expectations of your position in the power structure. Myles writes,

---

10 Myles, "Of Truth, Tolerance and Tyranny," 8.
11 Myles, "Of Truth, Tolerance and Tyranny," 11.

Japanese are very adept at assessing what is required in a situation and acting accordingly. This is often misunderstood by Westerners as duplicity, but it is simply the way life must be lived where all is relative. Truth itself becomes merely a social construct. If everybody believes something to be true, or if the powers that be say that it is, then for the practical purposes of daily life, it is true. As the Japanese say, it's safe to cross against a red light if everyone does it together.[12]

In other words, Japan is a case study in which a kind of relativism opens up the door to a kind of social tyranny that massively discounts the significance of the individual and therefore squashes individualism. Myles argues that in this sort of culture, if there were, say, unambiguous and objective moral law to which *individuals* could appeal, there could be a critique of the unfettered deployment of social and political power. It is the *absence* of such objective standards that make the oppressiveness of the culture possible.

Though it is not part of Myles's argument, one might observe that in the twentieth century the greatest political crushing of individualism occurred under Marxism and fascism. Both deployed not only brute force but massive propaganda machines to keep people safely in line with the party dogma. Truth was what Joseph Goebbels (for instance) said it was.

In the light of such case studies, one becomes aware that individualism that can become personally tyrannical (everyone does what is right in their own eyes) may, in this broken world, alternatively serve as a bulwark standing athwart massive social and political tyrannies crying, "Enough!" But it is hard to see whence the moral fortitude for such a stance will come if we systemically lose the category of objective truth. Martyrs are not made of sponge.

Fourth, among theists, the ability to withstand the age of Self and promote a kind of Christian, countercultural individualism embedded in a profound Christian communitarianism will depend, in no small part, on what we think of God. According to Baylor University professors Paul Froese and Christopher Baker in their book *America's Four Gods: What We Say about God—and What That Says about Us*,[13] there are four dominant positions.

---

12 Myles, "Of Truth, Tolerance and Tyranny," 11–12.
13 Paul Froese and Christopher Baker, *America's Four Gods: What We Say about God—and What That Says about Us* (New York: Oxford University Press, 2010).

Although their analysis was undertaken in the United States, I suspect that similar results would show up if the same analysis were pursued in the United Kingdom and many other Western nations. To arrive at the four different "gods" they identify, Froese and Baker began by asking two questions: (a) To what extent does God interact with the world? (b) To what extent does God judge the world? "The answers to these questions," they write, "predict the substance of our worldviews much better than the color of our skin, the size of our bank account, the political party we belong to, or whether we wear white Stetsons or faded Birkenstocks."[14] Once they have analyzed their data, they set forth the four conceptions of God that dominate the American landscape:

1. the authoritative God, who both judges and is closely engaged with the world;
2. the benevolent God, who is engaged but nonjudgmental;
3. the critical God, who is judgmental but disengaged;
4. the distant God, who is neither engaged nor judgmental.

Of course, the taxonomy is limited, and perhaps a trifle manipulative. Doubtless it is heuristically useful. But suppose we reject these "gods" as sad and dangerous reductionisms. Suppose we return to the God of the Bible, the God who is fully authoritative and engaged, but also compassionate and benevolent. Suppose we return to the God who judges with perfect justice but who sends his Son to bear our sins in his own body on the tree. Suppose we take our understanding of God from revealed truth that disrupts our cultural preferences. Will we not find that the truth of who this God is enables the Christian to sift the culture and form a Christian counterculture, a community of God's people in which it is possible to be strong in the grace of God because we are weak? Will we not rejoice in the paradoxes that lie close to the heart of Christian discipleship? We take up our cross so as to be free; in dying, we live; in giving, we receive; when we are weak, we are strong. None of the pretended gods of our culture prepare us for this biblical disclosure of God. But when he captures us, he strengthens us both individually and in the context of our churches to

14 Froese and Baker, *America's Four Gods*, 10.

stand up with courage, humility, and contrition, and point away from the oppressive gods of our age.

In short, we urgently and perennially need analyses that are less indebted to clichéd visions—whether of individualism or of anything else—and more indebted to the word of God, in all its comprehensiveness and gospel focus, the word we have been called to study at Tyndale House and around the world.

19

The Postmodernism That Refuses to Die

PEOPLE AREN'T TALKING about postmodernism nearly as much as they were fifteen or twenty years ago. Thirty-five years ago, graduate students in English departments in many universities of the Western world spent more time reading Lyotard, Derrida, and Foucault than Shakespeare, Keats, and Frost. Proof of mature reading of a text was tied rather more to creative deconstruction than to trying to understand the text in its historical and cultural framework. More important than the English texts was postmodern theory.[1]

Much of this has changed. Far fewer students are assigned major readings from Jacques Derrida and Michel Foucault. The founding writers of postmodernism (understood, for the sake of this brief essay, as an epistemological enterprise) are largely sidelined from college curricula.

But that doesn't mean the impact of postmodernism has entirely dissipated. What seems to be taking place, rather, is something like this: some of the conclusions of postmodernism are now adopted with little question as cultural "givens" without a felt need to justify them. Why defend stances that large swaths of the culture accept as obviously true? So, what we find is substantial numbers of postmoderns who rarely think of themselves as postmoderns and who know next to nothing of the literature and debates that occupied so much attention a bare generation ago. They

---

1 This chapter was originally published as D. A. Carson, "The Postmodernism That Refuses to Die," *Themelios* 43, no. 1 (2018): 1–3.

understand neither the theory nor its critics, but they presuppose many of its conclusions.

A couple of examples might help. Recently, Christian students at a fine West Coast university engaged in a thoughtful survey of their fellow students, focusing on what they thought about religion in general and Christianity in particular. Some of the questions focused on the afterlife: for example, What would it take to know that there is a new heaven and a new earth to be gained? A not uncommon answer was, "How can you claim to know anything at all?" Or again, when asked how they understood the exclusive truth claims of Christianity (e.g., John 14:6; Acts 4:12), most responses fell into one of two pools: (1) "Christians are so bigoted. We all have our own distinctive approaches to spirituality. Christians don't have the right to rule out of camp the claims of other religions," or (2) "Deep down, all religions are really saying the same thing anyway, so why should one view others as distinctively different or in some way inferior?"

Of course, the adoption of such stances should not be traced exclusively to the impact of postmodernism. Other competing streams have brought to bear important influences: contemporary understanding of what "faith" means, the shifting tides of "tolerance," and the broader cultural developments that some wag has identified as "a thin crust of vehement hostility masking a vast sea of apathy." Yet we would be avoiding the obvious if we did not sniff out something of the impact of postmodernism on contemporary epistemologies.

The students at that West Coast university kindly passed on to me the results of their survey as I was preparing for an evangelistic event at the university. Those stances, I soon discovered, characterized not only a substantial number of students who labeled themselves atheists or secularists or anything other than followers of Jesus, but also surfaced in the minds of many Christians who faced these questions in their own courageous attempts to share their faith and did not quite know how to answer them. So here are a few of the answers I've found helpful in my responses to both groups.

1. Not a few of the discussions about what we can or cannot know depend on a misleading baseline. The argument is that unless we know everything about something, we cannot know anything certain about that thing. The logic depends on a rather antiquated form of the so-called

"new hermeneutic." That is an impossible standard. It means that we can legitimately speak of knowledge only if we enjoy omniscience—or, to put it another way, only Omniscience truly knows anything. Read a certain way, of course, that is true. Yet we human beings often speak of things we "know," and we are not implicitly claiming omniscience; rather, we speak of a variety of human modes of knowing that are appropriate to the human condition. That is true of human beings in the Bible; it is equally true about all human beings everywhere. We "know" the earth will rotate on its axis, and there will be a sunrise tomorrow morning; I "know" that my United flight is scheduled to leave San Francisco in just over an hour. Of course, my "knowledge" of the latter turns on what I read on the United screen and on my United app, and I confess it is a bit disconcerting to sit here and listen to an audio announcement to the effect that what the big screen says about another flight is erroneous on the screen: maybe it will turn out that the posting for mine is erroneous, too. If I were omniscient, there could be no errors of that or any other sort. Nevertheless, we continue to make our plans on the assumption that the earth will continue in its rotation and that my United flight will leave at 6:00 pm unless there is another notification. We "know" these things, as we know that King David reigned in Jerusalem and that Jesus was born in Bethlehem of Judea, not with the knowledge that belongs exclusively to God, but with the knowledge that is appropriate to our human status. To adopt the baseline of omniscience is counter to human experience and common parlance.

2. Another way of getting at the same thing—namely, that one can responsibly talk of human knowing even though our finiteness and proneness to error both ensure that human knowing is never grounded in omniscience—is to recall how learning takes place. Whenever we embark on a new discipline, whether Attic Greek, Shakespearean sonnets, or microbiology, the opening stages seem daunting: there is so very much to learn, so much to memorize. Nevertheless, the weeks and months skip past, and pretty soon the elements that seem so daunting at the beginning of the learning curve have been comfortably absorbed. There is no longer any effort expended on the present indicative paradigm of λύω, because we know that, even though there is so very much about Greek that we do not know. It is difficult to see why this should not be the case with every discipline, including biblical and theological studies. In other words, the

common experience of learning things, whether in academic courses or in the business of life, confirms that human knowledge is attainable, even if it is invariably partial.

3. That there are highly diverse interpretations of the Bible is often taken to justify the conclusion that we cannot legitimately claim to know what the Bible says. That conclusion holds if one of two conditions holds true: (a) the Bible is so multifaceted, and without a coherent message, diverse readings of it are inevitable, or (b) the Bible may in theory have a univocal message, but church history shows that we cannot agree as to what it is. Either way, how can we fairly claim to enjoy genuine knowledge of God? Neither stance holds up very well. On the first point, what is at stake is what the Bible is. I cannot delve into that subject here. On the second point, my own experience (and it is a common one) is that it is surprising how much agreement regarding what the Bible is saying can be achieved, provided there is agreement among dialogue partners that the Bible is the final authority, and that they are willing to be corrected by it. Elsewhere I have recounted my ten happy years with what was then called the World Evangelical Fellowship, coordinating highly diverse study groups where I was invariably pleasantly surprised by how much unanimity could be achieved by hard work, patient discussion, mutual criticism, humility of mind, and a greater hunger to be faithful to the text than to be thought right.

4. So far, these epistemological discussions have treated challenges to the acquisition of knowledge as essentially neutral problems. Not many experts in hermeneutics devote much space to the role of moral turpitude in trying to know the truth or to the dangers and barriers cast up by idolatry in this business of trying to know God. At some point in discussion with an atheist, isn't it worth pondering what the Bible says on this point? "The fool says in his heart, 'There is no God'" (Ps. 14:1). This is not the short-fused condescension of a knee-jerk conservative but a sober assessment of how widely God has disclosed himself and how the atheist jettisons that revelation. But in any case, it is certainly part of the biblical response to the epistemological postmodernism that will not die.

20

More Examples of Intolerant Tolerance

SINCE *THE INTOLERANCE OF TOLERANCE* was published,[1] readers have been sending me new examples they have spotted—examples of egregious intolerance masquerading in the name of tolerance.[2] Sometimes these examples have been accompanied with a plea to incorporate them in any revised edition that might be called for. Of course, I too have spotted a handful of examples myself. In this editorial I'd like to comment briefly on three of them, probing a little to uncover what we should learn from them. Although the book drew on examples in both Europe and America, the follow three have surfaced in the United States.

The first is the drama that unfolded around Chick-fil-A. By now, the bare narrative is well-known. When Dan Cathy, president of Chick-fil-A, a man known for his Christian commitments, declared that he supported traditional heterosexual marriage, he was soon attacked in the press, in blog posts, and in some talk shows as homophobic, a hate monger, and worse—despite the fact that he himself had never used the word "homosexual" and despite the fact that no one seemed able to tell of a credible instance when Chick-fil-A staff at any of their outlets had ever treated any class of customers with less than the courtesy in which the staff were trained. Protests by the LGBT crowd followed at some sites, while supporters bought countless tens of thousands of meals in a show of support. More interesting, perhaps, was the announcement by several big-city mayors, Washington

1 D. A. Carson, *The Intolerance of Tolerance* (Grand Rapids, MI: Eerdmans, 2012).
2 This chapter was originally published as D. A. Carson, "More Examples of Intolerant Tolerance," *Themelios* 37, no. 3 (2012): 439–41.

DC's Vincent Gray, Chicago's Rahm Emanuel, and San Francisco's Edwin Lee, that they would prevent Chick-fil-A outlets from opening in their cities since they did not want to encourage any business characterized by such intolerance. They were soon joined by the mayor of Boston and the mayor of Philadelphia. By contrast, Michael Bloomberg, the mayor of New York City, declared that however repellent he found Dan Cathy's views to be, government should stay clear of such pronouncements and interference with businesses that were not in any sense breaking the law.

How should we think about this little drama?

That some conservatives like Dan Cathy articulate their beliefs, while some liberals respond with their own voice, is not intrinsically problematic so far as issues of tolerance and intolerance are concerned. That the debate grabbed media attention and escalated into demonstrations against Chick-fil-A and counter movements that voiced approval for the organization by flooding the outlets with orders is part of the give-and-take of any society that cherishes free speech, no matter how much each side thinks the other is morally wrong. Somewhat troubling is the way several big-city mayors hopped on the bandwagon and declared that they would use their powers to keep Chick-fil-A out of their cities. By definition, that is a form of intolerance of the older kind, that is, use of the coercive powers of the state to punish those who step outside the norms the state approves. Of course, these mayors could argue that Dan Cathy and those he influences or represents are trying to maintain or promote laws against those who practice homosexuality—for example, laws that refuse to assign the category of "marriage" to homosexual unions. In other words, conservatives no less than liberals want to use the powers of the state to exclude behavior of which they do not approve.

There is, however, one fundamental difference. By and large the conservatives defend their position and try to advance it by arguing the merits of the case in the public arena. It must be said that in recent years, they have not made much headway, but that is what they try to do. On the other hand, the LGBT voices barely address the merits of their case or engage the substance of their opponents' arguments; rather, by and large they defend their position and try to advance it by dismissing their opponents as intolerant bigots, religious fanatics. That is one of the signs of the new tolerance. While the old tolerance was in some ways a parasitic virtue—that is, it depended for its life on decisions as to how much leeway might be allowed to a person who wished to advocate or take up a position outside the accepted norms and laws of a society, before state sanctions were imposed, and thus depended on the existence of a larger structure of accepted values and morals—the new tolerance is not parasitic on a larger structure. Rather, the new tolerance is itself the highest good, the ultimate virtue, trumping everything else, and therefore able to shunt to one side any serious moral discussion of important matters once the label "intolerant" has been attached to it.

The second example revolves around the Interdenominational Theological Center (ITC) in Atlanta. A coalition of (currently) six historically African-American seminaries from diverse denominations, ITC earned its charter in 1958. From the beginning it pursued an ecumenical focus, but in recent years it has prided itself in its gay theology, womanist theology, postcolonial theology, and liberation theology. Most of its students are African American, so a good percentage of them enter ITC with rather more conservative theology, reflecting the churches from which they spring. In 2008 ITC hired Dr. Jamal-Dominique Hopkins in its New Testament department. Administrators could happily point to Dr. Hopkins as the only African-American New Testament scholar with expertise in the Dead Sea Scrolls. In early 2008 he was promoted to associate professor. In February he invited Dr. Alice Brown-Collins, director of InterVarsity Christian Fellowship's Black Campus Ministries in the New England Region, to speak to some of the conservative students at ITC. After her presentation, Dr. Brown-Collins gave one of the students a copy of Robert Gagnon's book *The Bible and Homosexual Practice,* perhaps the best-known exegetical treatment of the relevant biblical texts, a book that reaches traditional, orthodox conclusions.

The next day Dr. Hopkins was closely questioned by the department chair, Rev. Margaret Aymer. Hopkins was accused of violating ITC's code of ethics, which upholds various diversities, including sexual orientation. Three months later, he was fired. According to Hopkins, during the interval ITC persistently sought to undermine his reputation. Moreover, he discovered that the administration had commonly changed the grades he had assigned his students. Hopkins filed a complained against ITC.[3]

---

3 Details regarding the resolution of this dispute were not publicly available at the time of the original publication of this article. Dr. Hopkins currently teaches at Baylor University's Truett Seminary.

What shall we make of this episode? From ITC's perspective, the center is defending tolerance, in particular the tolerance of a variety of sexual lifestyles. ITC does not seem to be aware how terribly intolerant it has become toward one of its employees, otherwise approved as a competent teacher and scholar, on the ground that he invited an evangelical scholar to the campus who passed out a book that disagrees with ITC's position. The stance of Robert Gagnon is in line with the overwhelming majority of Christians in the entire history of the church, but obviously that stance is too great a threat to ITC "tolerance" to be tolerated.

My final example turns on regulations issued under the United States federal government's Affordable Care Act of 2010. The regulations in question force thousands of religious organizations to violate some of their deepest religious beliefs under penalty of ruinous fines. In particular, the government has issued an administrative mandate forcing religious organizations to provide health insurance coverage for abortifacient drugs and related education and counseling, even if those organizations, on religious grounds, hold that such drugs conflict with their religiously grounded belief that abortion is wrong.[4] Moreover, the government's mandate requires that the religious organizations facilitate government-dictated speech about such matters, speech that is incompatible with its own convictions and teachings. Equally shocking, the government is happy to issue accommodations and exemptions from the Affordable Care Act for many nonreligious reasons, even to large corporations, but is unwilling to issue an accommodation in this case.[5]

The positively dangerous element in these developments needs unpacking. How does the government think its stance can withstand a First Amendment challenge, which guarantees freedom of speech and freedom

---

4   Note that some (notably Catholics) commonly hold that using any contraceptive drug is wrong, while others hold that only abortifacients are immoral. The best treatment of the topic from a theological and medical perspective is now that of Megan Best, *Fearfully and Wonderfully Made: Ethics and the Beginning of Human Life* (Kingsford: Matthias Media, 2012). This distinction is one of the reasons that the lawsuits brought against the federal government by Wheaton College and Catholic University of America, though linked, were nevertheless distinct.

5   Editor's note: In the June 2014 Burwell v. Hobby Lobby case, the Supreme Court ruled that requiring family-owned corporations to fund insurance coverage for contraception under the Affordable Care Act violated their federally protected religious freedom. In February 2018, a federal court granted Wheaton College a permanent injunction exempting the institution from the Affordable Care Act's contraceptive mandate.

of religion? As far as I can see, the government believes it can win by rede-fining what is included under the category of "religion." Corporate worship may be religion, but ethical stances about abortion are not and are therefore exempt from the protection of the First Amendment. In other words, the government is making an unprecedented move to define religion more narrowly so that it can impose by the use of coercive force its own agenda, and those who refuse on grounds that in the past would certainly have been considered religious will simply have to be crushed. In historical terms, that is called intolerance.

Three separate examples, each with its peculiar lessons to teach, but each is a troubling index of the directions being taken by our culture, and the third is frankly dangerous.

21

As If Not: Reflections on 1 Corinthians 7

I SHALL BEGIN WITH A WELL-KNOWN exegetical conundrum and then branch out to a much larger issue that none of us can afford to ignore.[1]

In a context where Paul is talking about "virgins," both men and women, and delivers his judgment as to whether they should get married, he writes, "Because of the present crisis, I think that it is good for a man to remain as he is" (1 Cor. 7:26). To what does "the present crisis" refer? The Greek word ἀνάγκη has commonly been understood in one of two ways.

First, some have taken this present "crisis" to refer to a period of major social dislocation owing to persecution or to famine induced by grain shortages or to some combination of both. The logic would be straightforward: Under normal circumstances it might make good sense to marry, but in times of social upheaval it might be the part of wisdom to remain single. If the church is going through a period of persecution, or is about to go through such a period, there is much to be said for celibacy. For a start, if you are single it is easier to be mobile and easier to hide. Moreover, malicious opponents cannot get at you through your spouse and family if you have no spouse and family.

Nevertheless, three things stand against this interpretation. (1) The various sources to which scholars appeal so as to justify a theory about grain shortages and the like, signaling famine, are notoriously difficult

---

1 This chapter was originally published as D. A. Carson, "As If Not," *Themelios* 38, no. 1 (2013): 1–3.

to date. (2) There is precious little evidence within 1 Corinthians itself that the church feels itself under threat of famine, social dislocation, or persecution. This seems to be a church that prides itself in its wisdom, a church that includes significant numbers of people who hold to some form or other of over-realized eschatology (which simply does not happen when the church is under attack: the tendency then is toward futurist eschatology), or a church that is smugly playing various internal games of one-upmanship (party spirit, claiming to possess superior χαρίσματα, God's grace gifts) rather than hunkering down to face social dislocation from outside pressures. Certainly 2 Corinthians 8–9 presuppose that the Corinthian church, far from teetering on the edge of famine, is quite well-off and jolly well ought to share its wealth with brothers and sisters in Judea who have much less. (3) Above all, this interpretation makes little sense of the peculiar list of "as if not" phrases in 1 Corinthians 7:29–31. For example, those who mourn, Paul tells the Corinthians, should live "as if they did not; those who were happy, as if they were not; those who buy something, as if it were not theirs to keep." It is not easy to fit such judgments into the first scenario.

Second, many scholars argue that what Paul has in mind by "the present crisis" (1 Cor. 7:26) is the imminence of the Lord's return—not the theological "imminence" that means only that Jesus could return at any moment yet equally could be long delayed, but the ordinary sense of imminence: Paul believed, it is argued, that Jesus's return in glory was impending, so close to being upon the church that it was the part of wisdom to serve the interests of the gospel flat-out. In the light of this impending parousia, distractions such as marriage are better put aside. After all, might not 1 Thessalonians 4:17 be understood to mean that he expected to be among the "we" who would be caught up to be with the Lord Jesus at his return?

Once again, several considerations make this an unlikely interpretation. (1) First Thessalonians 4:17 can no more be taken to mean that Paul expected to be alive at the parousia than 1 Corinthians 6:14 can be taken to mean that Paul expected to be dead at the parousia. (2) This interpretation inevitably means that Paul was wrong in his expectations. Any interpretation of Paul that, to be right, must presuppose that Paul is wrong, is inherently suspicious. (3) The strange list of "as if not" phrases in 1 Corinthians 7:29–31 does not fit this reconstruction any better than it fits the previous one.

Part of the problem is that some of our versions render ἀνάγκη by "crisis." The English word "crisis" conjures up a short-term supreme test or climax. By contrast, the first lexical definition provided by BDAG is "necessity or constraint as inherent in the nature of things, necessity, pressure of any kind."[2] None of this evokes images of crisis (such as social unrest spawned by war or famine), still less of the impending parousia. It might be less misleading to render 1 Corinthians 7:26, "Because of the present constraint, I think that it is good for a man to remain as he is." The "constraint" that is "inherent in the nature of things" is then the sum of difficult challenges coughed up by a world that is simultaneously, on the one hand, lost and subject to catastrophic judgment and, on the other, the locus of the gospel, mysteriously ruled by Christ until death itself is destroyed (1 Cor. 15:25–26). It covers the entire period between the first advent of Christ and his second. It is akin to some uses of "tribulation" in the New Testament. The time is "short" (1 Cor. 15:29) in exactly the same sense that Jesus is coming "soon" (Rev. 22:20): the last act of the old order is winding down, and the new order has already begun, though it has not yet broken out in consummation splendor.

If this is right, then all of the "as if not" phrases make sense. "From now on those who have wives should live as if they do not" (1 Cor. 7:29): this cannot mean that they should become monks or otherwise withdraw from their spouses, for in this same chapter Paul has already made it clear that this would defraud the spouse (7:1–7). Marriage itself, like celibacy, is a gracious gift from God, a χάρισμα (7:7). Each spouse has authority over the body of the other, and sexual intimacy must not be withheld except under the stringent conditions that 1 Corinthians 7:5 stipulates. Paul cannot be dismissing marriage. Rather, he means something subtler: marriage is not the summum bonum but stands under God's "as if not." Because the new age has dawned and marriage itself does not continue into the resurrection existence of the new heaven and the new earth, then, as important and as wonderful as marriage is, the thoughtful Christian will not invest it with eternal significance. Similarly, "From now on . . . those who mourn, as if they did not": our tears, however free-flowing, belong to this dying age of

---

2   Frederick W. Danker, Walter Bauer, William F. Arndt, and F. Wilbur Gingrich, *Greek-English Lexicon of the New Testament and Other Early Christian Literature* (Chicago: Chicago University Press, 2000), 61.

death. They, too, stand under God's "as if not": we sorrow, but not as those who have no hope. But exactly the same thing must be said of the inverse of mourning: "those who are happy, as if they were not" (7:30). Happiness is not banned any more than marriage is banned or mourning is banned. Rather, the happiness that the world calls forth stands under God's "as if not." Some people find their pleasure and identity in the acquisition of things, but Paul writes, "those who buy something, as if it were not theirs to keep" (7:30). Exactly so. It is not that there is no place for purchasing things, any more than there is now no place for marriage. But how can we attach overweening importance to things we cannot bring with us? They all stand under God's "as if not." More generically: "those who use the things of the world, as if engrossed in them" (7:31). It is not that we do not properly interact with "the things of the world," for this is where we live. Nevertheless, they all stand under God's as if not, so we dare not be engrossed in them. Paul puts the matter succinctly: "For this world in its present form is passing away" (7:31).

This well-known exegetical crux could be usefully discussed at much greater length. For the moment, however, I shall assume that the interpretation defended here is the most plausible one and branch out into a broader issue.

Recent years have witnessed a plethora of books and articles on the relationship between the gospel and culture, between proclamation and doing good deeds, between the gospel of Paul and the gospel of the kingdom. Some of these polarities are singularly misjudged; others are important and deserve the most patient and biblically faithful exploration. But the lesson to be learned from the passages we have been surveying in 1 Corinthians 7 is this: even when we are rightly developing faithful cultural expressions of art and music, even when we are digging wells in the Sahel and developing centers to help the homeless, even when we patiently and lovingly build solid marriages in line with God's disclosure of what marriage should be, even when we connect the use of our fiscal resources to kingdom priorities, the entire fabric of our current existence stands under God's "as if not." We cannot, we must not, be entirely engrossed even in good things that God himself labels χαρίσματα, God's gracious gifts, if those gracious gifts are tied to an order that is passing away. If we learn this lesson well, we shall better understand what it means to lay up treasures in heaven.

22

Polemical Theology

DURING THE LAST COUPLE of decades, I have had occasion to reflect a little on the ambiguities and challenges surrounding what is sometimes called "polemical theology." Here I shall offer five initial observations.[1]

1. The category is slippery. Some think of "polemical theology" in terms of a glorious heritage of serious theological engagement and debate. Others are convinced "polemical theology" can have only negative connotations, so they speak and write against it—and thus indulge in polemical theology against polemical theology. Polemical theology is nothing other than contending for a particular theological understanding (usually one that the contender holds to be the truth) and disputing those that contradict it or minimize it. It is impossible to indulge in serious critical thought without becoming enmeshed, to some degree, in polemics. Every time you include a footnote that begins "Contra" you are engaged in polemical theology; every time you assemble six reasons as to why your interpretation of a biblical passage or your formulation of a theological issue is correct and assert, or at least imply, that alternative interpretations or formulations are correspondingly incorrect, you dabble in polemical theology. The person who advances an exegetical or theological stance without reference to competing formulations may avoid polemics but will usually not be taken seriously by those who have studied any issue, precisely because there is no serious engagement with those who disagree. It is not easy for Christians

---

1   This chapter was originally published as D. A. Carson, "Editorial," *Themelios* 34, no. 2 (2009): 155–57.

to be entirely free of polemics, and it is not wise to attempt such freedom. Their arguments will inevitably attract adjectives like *ignorant, reductionistic, unengaged, naive*—and rightly so.

2. So it is not surprising that the Bible itself casts up countless examples of polemical theology. One thinks of Yahweh's sneering refutation and condemnation of the idols in Isaiah 40–45; of the direct condemnation of alternative stances in, say, Galatians or Jude, or of Jesus's condemnation of hypocrites, including what they teach (e.g., Matt. 23); of the symbol-laden destruction of imperial pretensions in the Apocalypse. One also thinks of many subtler forms of polemics. When Jesus tells parables to indicate that the kingdom dawns slowly, quietly, over time, and according to how the word is received (e.g., the soils, the yeast, the weeds and the wheat), he is implicitly challenging alternative conceptions of the kingdom, and thus he is engaged in polemical theology. When the letter to the Ephesians devotes much of its space to working out the glories and characteristics of the one new humanity that God has brought about in Christ, joining together Jew and Gentile (and, in principle, people from every tribe and language and people), it is overturning alternative views of ethnicity, of self-identification, of how to find the true locus of the covenant people of God. In other words, any robust theology that wounds and heals, that bites and edifies and clarifies, is implicitly or explicitly engaging with alternative stances. In a world of finite human beings who are absorbed in themselves and characterized by rebellion against God, polemical theology is an unavoidable component of any serious theological stance, as the Bible itself makes clear.

3. Nevertheless, there is something wrongheaded about making polemical theology the focus of one's theological identity. This can be done in many ways. There are well-known scholars whose every publication has an undertone of "everyone has got this wrong before me but here is the true synthesis." Some become far better known for what they are against than for the overflow of their worship or for their generosity to the needy or even for their affirmation of historically confessed truth. Still other Christians develop websites and ministries whose sole aim is to confute error. God knows there is plenty of error to confute. To make the refutation of error into a specialized "ministry," however, is likely to diminish the joyful affirmation of truth and make every affirmation of truth sound

angry, supercilious, self-righteous—in a word, polemical. In short, while polemical theology is just about unavoidable in theory and should not, as a matter of faithfulness, be skirted, one worries about those who make it their specialism.

4. In some ways it is convenient to distinguish polemical theology designed to challenge the stances of those who call themselves fellow Christians and polemical theology designed to challenge the stances of those who are not Christians and who may oppose Jesus. The latter goal makes polemical theology a subset of evangelism, certainly a subset of what is often called apologetics. Distinctions such as these could be teased out at considerable length, but perhaps it is enough here to make two further observations.

First, regardless of its audience and of the particular stance that is being challenged, polemical theology ought to develop a wide range of "tones." Reread Galatians. Within the space of six short chapters, Paul can be indignant with his readers, but he can also plead with them. He openly admits he wishes he could be present with them so he could better judge how he should adjust his tone. He can be scathing with respect to his opponents, precisely because he wants to protect his readers; he can devote several paragraphs to clarifying and defending his own credibility, not least in demonstrating that his core gospel is shared by the other apostles, even though he insists he is not dependent on them for getting it right. He happily connects his theological understanding to ethical conduct. All of this suggests that a mature grasp of the potential of polemical theology wants to win and protect people, not merely win arguments.

Over five decades ago a noted evangelical scholar engaged Thomas Altizer, chief voice of the "Death of God" movement, in a public debate. Most witnesses of that evening judged that at the intellectual level Altizer had been seriously trounced, but most also thought that Altizer had been the more winsome of the two.

Second, at the risk of a generalization, those who spend their lives refuting and correcting fellow believers but who rarely engage at a serious level with ideas and stances in the broader world almost always find themselves at increasing odds with more and more believers. That should be unsurprising. Those who engage in a broader polemical theology are, on the whole, more grateful to focus with gratitude on the common heritage of Christians.

5. For my last reflection, I want to recall the words of Bryan Magee, whose book *Confessions of a Philosopher* describes his own experience in polemics and what he learned from Karl Popper:

> I had always loved argument, and over the years I had become quite good at identifying weak points in an opponent's defense and bringing concentrated fire to bear on them. This is what virtually all polemicists have sought to do since ancient times, even the most famous of them. But Popper did the opposite. He sought out his opponents' case at its strongest and attacked that. Indeed, he would improve it, if he possibly could, before attacking it. . . . Over several pages of prior discussion he would remove avoidable contradictions or weaknesses, close loopholes, pass over minor deficiencies, let his opponents' case have the benefit of every possible doubt, and reformulate the most appealing parts of it in the most rigorous, powerful and effective arguments he could find—and then direct his onslaught against it. The outcome, when successful, was devastating. At the end there would be nothing left to say in favor of the opposing case except for tributes and concessions that Popper had himself already made. It was incredibly exciting intellectually.[2]

That may not always be the path of wise polemics, but few could doubt that this is the path of wisdom where the audience is already skeptical about your position. In the world of Christian apologetics, I know no one more gifted in this Popperian form of argumentation than Tim Keller. Witness his *The Reason for God: Belief in an Age of Skepticism.*[3] Keller manages to construct his opponents' arguments in such a way that they are more powerful and devastating than when the opponents themselves construct them. And then he effectively takes them apart. No one feels abused, precisely because he has treated their stances more ably than they can themselves.

The church of Jesus Christ could use more polemical theology in which the polemicists have learned such skills as the fruit of grace.

2   Bryan Magee, *Confessions of a Philosopher: A Personal Journey through Western Philosophy from Plato to Popper* (New York: Modern Library, 1999), 152–53.
3   Timothy Keller, *The Reason for God: Belief in an Age of Skepticism* (New York: Dutton, 2008).

23

Take Up Your Cross and Follow Me: Reflections on Missions Today

FOR MANY PEOPLE, the thought of missionary work sounds, at best, painfully old-fashioned.[1] It conjures up mental images of black-and-white photographs, now curled and yellowed; of intense, well-meaning men and women in dated dress, imposing their stern Victorian values on the free spirits of foreign shores. Worse, to many contemporaries missionary endeavor is not merely old-fashioned but positively mischievous, for missionaries are necessarily intolerant people. They invade cultures not their own, and by pushing Jesus and the gospel, they announce that they think their religion and culture are superior to the local one—and that, surely, is the very essence of intolerance. As one recent critical missionary biographer puts it, missionary work is "inherently patronizing to the host culture. That's what a mission is—a bunch of strangers showing up somewhere uninvited to inform the locals they are wrong."[2]

So what are we doing in 2011 in Solihull, celebrating the 150th anniversary of Grace Baptist Mission? Instead of celebrating, wouldn't it be more admirable to hold a service of public contrition and tell the world we're sorry and will not send any more missionaries?

---

1 This chapter was originally published as D. A. Carson, "Take up Your Cross and Follow Me," *Themelios* 37, no. 1 (2012): 1–3. It is a lightly updated transcript of one of Carson's addresses at the 150th anniversary of Grace Baptist Mission in the United Kingdom. This one was broadcast over BBC Radio 4 on October 30, 2011. It is a brief apologia for mission in a world that regularly despises mission.

2 Sarah Vowell, *Unfamiliar Fishes* (New York: Riverhead, 2011), 55.

Christians, of course, cannot forget that during his lifetime Jesus himself trained people to go and herald the good news. Christians remember that Jesus was sent by his Father, he insisted, to seek and save those who are lost. So it is not too surprising that he in turn sends his followers. That's what our word "mission" means: it derives from the verb "to send." "As the Father has sent me," Jesus once said, "I am sending you" (John 20:21). Among his last recorded words are these:

> All authority in heaven and on earth has been given to me. Therefore go and make disciples of all nations, baptizing them in the name of the Father and of the Son and of the Holy Spirit, and teaching them to obey everything I have commanded you. And surely I am with you always, to the very end of the age. (Matt. 28:19–20)

So Christians, understandably, will entertain a high view of those who actively seek to discharge Jesus's mission.

There are two common objections raised against this Christian view of missionary endeavor. It's worth reflecting on them before we contemplate the most convincing reason that missionary work is essential.

First, Jesus himself insists, "Do not judge, or you too will be judged" (Matt. 7:1). Doesn't this mean that if we follow Jesus's teaching we should refuse to make moral and religious evaluations? Certainly that view is common on the street. "I don't mind Jesus," we hear; "it's Christians I can't stand. Christians run around self-righteously telling people how to live, condemning other religions, sending missionaries off to meddle in other cultures. Why don't they follow the instruction of the Jesus they claim to serve? After all, he said, 'Do not judge, or you too will be judged.'"

When I was a boy I learned a few of the first principles of interpreting texts. I learned, "A text without a context becomes a pretext for a proof text." So I suppose we better remind ourselves of the context where Jesus says, "Do not judge, or you too will be judged." It's found in the Sermon on the Mount. That sermon contains quite a few teachings of Jesus. Here, for example, Jesus criticizes the man who looks at a woman lustfully, on the ground that such a man has already committed adultery in his heart (Matt. 5:28). Here he teaches us not to store up treasures on earth, where moths and vermin destroy and where thieves break in and steal; rather, we must store up for ourselves treasures in heaven, knowing that where our treasure is, there our hearts will be too (6:19–21). Here he tells us to watch out for false prophets, which presupposes we must make distinctions between the true and the false (7:15–20). Here he insists that on the last day not everyone who says to him "Lord, Lord" will enter the kingdom of heaven, but only the one who does the will of his Father who is in heaven (7:21–23). In all these utterances, Jesus is making moral, religious, and cultural evaluations. He is, in short, making judgments. So after making all these judgments, what does he mean by saying "Do not judge, or you too will be judged"? The context shows that he means something like "Do not be cheaply critical, or you will be subjected to the same criticism." In other words, there is no way on God's green earth that this command prohibits his followers from making moral judgements, when making moral judgements is precisely what the sweep of his teaching demands that they do. But he does insist that when they follow his instruction and make evaluations and judgments they must do so without cheap criticism of others—a notoriously difficult requirement. There must be no condescension, no double standard, no sense of superiority, no patronizing sentimentality. Christians are never more than poor beggars telling other poor beggars where there is bread. This humble tone ought to characterize all Christian witness, all Christian missionary endeavor. But to argue that Jesus wants his followers to make no judgments at all merely betrays biblical illiteracy.

Second, people often protest, "Yes, but isn't missionary work, indeed all attempts at trying to win another to your faith, terribly intolerant?" Well, no—not if one operates with older definitions of tolerance. Tolerance used to be understood to be the stance that, while disagreeing with another's views, guarded the right of those views to be heard. The new tolerance insists that disagreeing with another's views, saying they are wrong, is intrinsically intolerant. But frankly, that notion of intolerance is incoherent. The Labour Party doesn't agree with the Conservatives; Marxists don't agree with capitalists; Muslims don't agree with Christians. Each pair may acknowledge some commonalities, but on many fronts, they differ. Yet each tolerates the other if each insists that the other has equal right to speak and convince others of their position. Intolerance is introduced not when one says another party is wrong, but only when the views of others are quelled by force or corruption. If missionaries try to impose their views on others by force of any kind, they have lost the richest Christian heritage; where they seek to teach and put their case, all the while loving others sacrificially, they are upholding the highest standards of both intellectual integrity and tolerance.

But the best warrant for Christian mission is Jesus himself. He claims all authority is his, yet he speaks not as a cosmic bully but as the crucified Lord. He insists that men and women have rebelled against his heavenly Father, but he joins himself to the human rebels so as to identify with them. He declares they deserve punishment, then bears the punishment himself. He claims to be the Judge they will meet on the last day, and meanwhile entreats them to turn to him, to trust him, and live. If one is going to follow a leader, what better leader than the one who demonstrates his love for his followers by dying on a cross to win them to himself? What political leader does that? What religious leader does that? Only God does that!

And then, in a small piece of mimicry, his followers are challenged to take up their cross and follow him. If one of the results is a worldwide missionary movement, I for one will pray for it to thrive.

PART 5

REFLECTIONS ON
CHURCH LEADERSHIP

24

Some Reflections on
Pastoral Leadership

SOME CHRISTIAN TRADITIONS—for example, Roman Catholics, Anglicans—hold that there are three biblically mandated offices in the church: bishop (overseer), pastor/priest/elder, and deacon.[1] In the "high" church tradition, it is the unbroken line of duly consecrated bishops that actually *defines* the true church. The ground of this view is often found in the famous dictum of Ignatius toward the beginning of the second century: "Where the bishop is, there is the church." Most recognize today that a more faithful rendering might be, "Where the bishop shall appear, there let the multitude [of the people] also be"—which sounds a tad less definitional.[2] In any case, the argument that the New Testament documents recognize only two church offices, namely, the bishop/elder/pastor and the deacon, is by far the more common view among "low" churches and, as everyone in the field knows, was nowhere better defended than by the Anglican J. B. Lightfoot in his commentary on Philippians.[3]

Although the question—two offices or three—continues to be discussed from time to time, it rarely occupies center stage in contemporary

---

1 This chapter was originally published as D. A. Carson, "Some Reflections on Pastoral Leadership," *Themelios* 40, no. 2 (2015): 195–97.

2 *Epistle to the Smyrnaeans* 8.2, Loeb Classical Library. Alternatively, Ehrman translates this, "Let the congregation be wherever the bishop is; just as wherever Jesus Christ is, there also is the universal church."

3 J. B. Lightfoot, *Saint Paul's Epistle to the Philippians*, 8th ed., Classic Commentaries on the Greek New Testament (London: Macmillan, 1913), 95–99.

ecclesiastical discussion. The primary New Testament passages that tie together bishop, elder, and pastor are Titus 1:5–9, which unambiguously connects elder and bishop, and 1 Peter 5:1–4, which links all three descriptors (clear in the Greek text, not in all our translations). Because διάκονος ("deacon") is commonly used to describe how all Christians must serve, a handful of scholars do not see "deacon" as a second office. But the context of passages such as 1 Timothy 3:8–10 suggests that the word "deacon" is not a *terminus technicus* but can in the right context refer to a church-recognized office, even if in other passages it serves as a generic term for Christians.

My interest at the moment is not whether there is one office (as Benjamin J. Merkle maintains)[4] or two, but in the office that in the New Testament is covered by all three terms: bishop/overseer, elder/priest, and pastor. To simplify the discussion a little, I shall choose overseer over bishop because the latter has become, in English, a technical term that refers to an ecclesiastical officer with jurisdiction that reaches over more than one local church (at least in White American circles; this is less commonly the case in African-American circles). I shall choose elder over priest because, despite the persistent efforts of some of my "low" Anglican friends to remind me that the word "priest" comes from the Greek πρεσβύτερος via the Latin *presbyter*, in modern usage, at least in most circles, "priest" translates ἱερεύς and conjures up images of mediation that belong, under the new covenant, exclusively to Jesus Christ or, paradoxically, to all believers, but not to restricted office holders.

So we are focusing on the person rightly designated overseer/elder/pastor—and the order in which I mention the three terms is not significant. Moreover, the three terms do not denote separable spheres of responsibility; rather, they overlap considerably. "Pastor," of course, simply means shepherd and derives from the agricultural world of biblical times in which shepherds led, fed, healed, protected, and disciplined their flocks. "Elder" springs from village and synagogue life and carries an overtone of seniority, or at least maturity, that qualifies a person, ideally, for respect and for leadership responsibilities. "Overseer" conjures up administrative and ruling functions—functions that are not entirely absent from the other two labels.

---

4   Benjamin J. Merkle, *The Elder and Overseer: One Office in the Early Church*, Studies in Biblical Literature 57 (New York: Peter Lang, 2003).

Contemporary books and essays have tended to focus on four things about the pastor/elder/overseer. (a) The biblical lists of qualifications for elders (e.g., 1 Tim. 3:1–7) are mostly made up of virtues and attributes that are elsewhere demanded of all Christians. The one exception is that he be able to teach. Other individuals than pastors teach in the New Testament, but it is a requirement of all pastors/elders/overseers that they be able to teach, whether to large groups, in small groups, or one-on-one. A lot of discussion revolves around the preaching and teaching responsibilities of this office. (b) Recent years have witnessed a plethora of books and articles dealing with the plurality of elders. The shape of that discussion in Presbyterian circles is a bit different from what it is in, say, Baptist circles, but the discussion continues. (c) An extraordinary amount of energy has been devoted to ongoing debates about whether women may be pastors/elders/overseers—and if not, why not. (d) A number of helpful books and articles have been written of the "how-to" variety: how to find and train elders, the importance of seeking out potential elders (e.g., 2 Tim. 2:2), and the like.

Almost no attention, however, has been paid to the particular overtones cast up by the word "overseer." Of course, something of oversight is taking place if one is actively attempting to find and train new elders, or if one is leading the other elders and the congregation itself in a difficult instance of church discipline, or if one is laying out a long-term preaching/teaching program. But it is worth pausing to reflect on why, when the chief ecclesiastical office is mentioned, "overseer" is one of the three terms used to describe it.

I know a pastor who, both in his teaching and pastoral care, is a good and godly man, and more skilled than most at those tasks. He became pastor of a small church, and under his ministry it grew to almost 600 people. Then, gradually, it began to decline. There were no splits, but people drifted away. When it shrank to about 250, he decided he should resign and move on. And if I had to put my finger on one big factor, perhaps the biggest, that contributed to this decline, it was that the man, though an able preacher, was a poor leader—that is, he almost entirely ignored his episcopal responsibilities.

Another way to look at this is to consider the overlapping ministries of Ezra and Nehemiah. Nehemiah was clearly a gifted leader and administrator, but when it came time for the Bible conference, Ezra was the man who was called in—and he was a gifted leader and teacher, training the Levites in the massive work of teaching the people of God the word of God. Both men were leaders; both appealed to the word of God (Ezra to teach it and to arrange for others to teach it, Nehemiah to call the covenant people of God back to it and to live out its precepts), but it was Nehemiah who was (if I may use anachronistic terms) more overseer than preacher.

Some make a sharp distinction between teaching elder and ruling elder, based not least on 1 Timothy 5:17. As far as I can see, however, an elder is an elder/pastor/overseer, never less, and every elder/pastor/overseer must be able to teach (1 Tim. 3:2). In other words, it is difficult to warrant an absolute division of labor. But if all one means by the difference between a teaching elder and a ruling elder is a division of emphasis, one simultaneously does justice to 1 Timothy 5:17 and reflects the fact that one of the distinct labels for this office is overseer.

A substantial part of the ruling/oversight function is discharged through the preaching and teaching of the word of God. This is where a great deal of the best leadership is exercised: "What does Scripture say?" means "What does God say?" (cf. Gal. 3:8). Therefore those whose peculiar responsibility it is to teach the Scriptures are helping the church hear what God says. In substantial measure, this is how the head of the church exercises his leadership of the church.

But oversight of the church is more than simply teaching and preaching. Occasionally one observes a church where the senior pastor does most of the preaching to the entire congregation, while the "executive pastor" (overseer?) becomes responsible for everything else, including leading the other pastors, maintaining accountability, casting a vision for the next stage of growth and outreach, running the internship program, and much more. Nominally this frees the senior minister up for study, prayer, and preaching—what Acts 6:4 calls "prayer and the ministry of the word." In reality, this fails to grasp that a comprehensive vision of the ministry of the word demands oversight—not necessarily of the distribution of food to the needy, for which the seven servants (deacons?) were appointed, but of the entire direction and priorities of the church. Failure to see this as part of the responsibility of all pastors/elders/overseers (even though some may contribute more administrative gifts than others, while others will do more teaching/preaching) will result either in a church that is drifting or in a church where the executive pastor actually steals the church away from the senior pastor (intentionally or otherwise).

To put this another way: As important and central as is the ministry of the word of God, the thoughtful pastor/elder/overseer will devote time and energy to casting a vision, figuring out the steps for getting there, building the teams and structures needed for discharging ministry and training others, building others up, thinking through the various ways in which the gospel can be taught at multiple levels to multiple groups within the church, how to extend faithful evangelism and church planting, how to engage the surrounding world as faithful believers, and much more. Just because a person is an able preacher does not necessarily make him an able pastor/ elder/overseer. Indeed, if he shows no propensity for godly oversight, then no matter how good a teacher he may be, he is not qualified to be a pastor/ teacher/overseer. It is not for nothing that Scripture applies all three labels to the one office.

25

Generational Conflict in Ministry

ABOUT FIVE YEARS AFTER the Berlin wall came down and the communist regimes of Central and Eastern Europe had mostly fallen or been transmuted into something rather different, I had the privilege of speaking at a conference for pastors in one of those formerly Eastern Bloc countries. The numbers were not large. Most interesting was the way this group of men reflected a natural breakdown. They were clearly divided into two groups. The older group—say, over forty or forty-five—had served their small congregations under the former communist government. Few of them had been allowed to pursue any tertiary education, let alone formal theological training. Most of them had served in considerable poverty, learning to trust God for the food they and their families needed to survive. Some had been incarcerated for the sake of the gospel; all had been harassed. The men in the younger group—say, under forty or so—without exception were university graduates. Several had pursued formal theological education; two or three were beginning their doctorates. They were interested in ideas and in the rapidly evolving cultural developments taking place in their country now that their media were a good deal freer. Quite a number were engaged in university evangelism and wanted to talk about postmodern epistemology.[1]

The older group viewed the younger men as untested, ignorant of the lessons learned by suffering, far too cerebral, dizzyingly scattered and ill focused, cocky, impatient, even arrogant. The younger group viewed the

---

1 This chapter was originally published as D. A. Carson, "Generational Conflict in Ministry," *Themelios* 36, no. 2 (2011): 180–82.

older men as, at best, out-of-date: they had slipped past their "sell by" date as much as the communist regimes had. They were ill trained, defined too narrowly by yesterday's conflicts, unable to evangelize the new generation, vainly clutching to power, consumed rather more by tradition than by truth.

And in very large measure, both sides were right.

More recently I spoke at a denominational meeting of ministers in a Western country. Again there was a generational breakdown, cast somewhat differently. The older men had, during the decades of their ministry, combated the old-fashioned liberalism that had threatened their denomination in their youth. Many of them had been converted out of rough backgrounds and subsequently built strong fences around their churches to keep out alcohol and sleaze of every sort. Most of their congregations were aging along with their ministers; only a handful of them were growing. They loved older hymns and patterns of worship. The younger men dressed in jeans, loved corporate worship where the music was at least 95 decibels, were interested in evangelism, and loved to talk to the ecclesiastically disaffected—homosexuals, self-proclaimed atheists, mystically orientated "spiritual" artists. Some were starting Bible studies, fledgling churches, in pubs. This group thought the older men were out-of-date, too defensive, unable to communicate with people under twenty-five without sounding stuffy and even condescending, much too linear and boring in their thinking, largely unable to communicate in the digital world (except by emails, already largely dismissed as belonging to the age of dinosaurs), and mere traditionalists. The older group thought the younger men were brash, disrespectful, far too enamored with what's "in" and far too ignorant of a well-integrated theology, frenetic but not deep, energetic but not wise, and more than a little cocky.

And in very large measure, both sides were right.

Doubtless there have always been generational conflicts of one sort or another. Arguably, however, in some ways they are becoming worse. There are at least two reasons for this. First, the rate of cultural change has sped up, making it far more difficult for older people to empathize with a world so very different from the one in which they grew up three or four decades earlier, while making it far more difficult for younger people to empathize with a world in which people used typewriters and wired telephones and had never heard of Facebook or Twitter. Second, and far more important, the social dynamics of most Western cultures have been changing dramatically for decades. The sixties tore huge breaches into the fabric that had united young and old, assigning more and more authority to the young. The cult of youth and health that characterized the eighties and nineties, complete with hair transplants and liposuction, along with gated communities for the middle-class elderly and social welfare that meant families did not really have to care for or even interact much with the older generation, built a world in which integration across generational lines could be happily avoided. Even the new digital tools that facilitate interaction tend to enable people to link up with very similar people—very much *unlike* the way the church is supposed to be, bringing together very different redeemed people who have but one thing in common, Jesus Christ and his gospel.[2]

Ideally, how should both sides act so as to honor Christ and advance the gospel?

First, listen to criticism in a nondefensive way. This needs to be done on *both* sides of the divide. It is easy to label criticism as hostile or nonempathetic and write it off. Nevertheless, the path of wisdom is to try to discern what validity the criticism may have and learn from it. It may be that some older pastors do *not* know very well how to communicate with a younger generation. How, then, could they strengthen their ministry in these domains? It may be that some younger pastors *are* brash and intemperate in speech, finding it easy to build a following out of the gift of the gab. How then might reflection on 1 Corinthians 2 modify their speech? Even well-intentioned criticism hurts enough that we are sometimes seduced into a defensive posture because we have forgotten that the wounds inflicted by a friend are faithful and helpful, but wisdom also listens carefully and respectfully even to disrespectful speech in order to learn lessons not otherwise picked up.

Second, be prepared to ask the question, "What are we doing in our church, especially in our public meetings, that is not mandated by Scripture and that may, however unwittingly, be functioning as a barrier to getting the gospel out?" That question is of course merely another way of probing the extent to which tradition has trumped Scripture. There is no value in

---

2   On the changing social dynamics, it is worth reading Matthew Shaffer, "Ages Apart," *National Review* 68 (June 2011): 35–37, https://www.nationalreview.com/.

changing a tradition merely for the sake of changing a tradition. The two tests buried in my question must be rigorously observed: (a) Is the tradition itself mandated by Scripture, or, in all fairness, is its connection with Scripture highly dubious? (b) Is the tradition helpful only to the traditionalists, while getting in the way of outreach?

Even when the question is asked, the answers are rarely easy or clear-cut. The answers may bear on, say, what we wear, styles of music, the order of service, what we do with our massive pulpit. In each case, the bearing of Scripture and tradition can lead to conflicting inferences. Obviously there is no specific biblical mandate for a large pulpit front and center in the sanctuary, preferably elevated to ensure the minister is six feet above contradiction. Knowledge of historic disputes reminds us of the way this arrangement has functioned in the past: the Reformation taught us that it was not the "altar"[3] that was to be central but the word of God—so the large pulpits were installed in the center. In today's climate, however, the very same furniture may signal something else to casual visitors—not the centrality of the word, but the lecture hall, or talking down to others. How can one rightly emphasize the authority of the word of God without, on the one hand, erecting unnecessary barriers, and without, on the other hand, turning the front of the building into a "stage" associated with entertainment and performance arts? Fine pastors may disagree on the prudential outworking of such reflections in their specific contexts. Unless the questions are addressed with ruthless rigor, however, unbending lines will be drawn and positions staked out that serve only to foster division, not thought.

Third, always focus most attention on the most important things, what Paul calls the matters of first importance—and that means the gospel, with all its rich intertwinings, its focus on Christ and his death and resurrection, its setting people right with God, and its power to transform. So when we take a dislike of another's ministry primarily because he belongs to that *other* generation, must we not first of all ask whether the man in question heralds the gospel? If so, the most precious kinship already exists and should be nurtured. This is not to say that every other consideration can be ignored. Some ministers *are* pretty poor at addressing homosexuals in a faithful and winsome way, at speaking the truth in love, at coping with the rising

---

3   "Altar"? What new covenant warrant is there for such terminology?

relativism without sounding angry all the time, at avoiding the unpretty habit of nurturing a smart mouth. But Paul in Philippians 1 understands that whatever the shortcomings and confused motives of some ministers, if they preach Christ faithfully, he will cheer them on and be grateful.

Fourth, work hard at developing and fostering good relations with those from the other generation. This means meeting with them, even if, initially at least, you don't like them. It means listening patiently, explaining a different point of view with gentleness. It means that the new generation of ministers should be publicly thanking God for the older ministers, praying for them with respect and gratitude; it means that the older generations of ministers should be publicly thanking God for the new generation, seeking to encourage them while publicly praying for them. It means that ideally, disputes should be negotiated in person, winsomely, not by blog posts that are ill-tempered and capable of doing nothing more than ensuring deeper divisions by cheering on one's supporters. It means shared meals, shared prayer meetings, shared discussions. It means younger men will seek out older men for their wisdom in a plethora of pastorally challenging situations; it means older men will be trying to find out what these younger men are doing effectively and well, and how they see the world and understand their culture in the light of Scripture. It means that younger men will listen carefully in order better to understand the past; it means that older men will listen carefully in order better to understand the present. It means humility of mind and heart and a passion for the glory of God and the good of others.

26

Seekest Thou Great Things for Thyself?

PROBABLY IT'S A SIGN of my advancing years, but not infrequently a young pastor or a theological student asks me the question, "What choices did you make to get to where you are today?" I fear I always have to disabuse the questioner. No one is more surprised than I am at the turns my life has taken.[1]

Not as frequently, but far from rarely, I hear a variation on that question. In the following quote, I consolidate several different questions that have come to me recently, questions that can usefully flock together. Some of them spring from zealous young Christians who spring from a somewhat charismatic background. Nevertheless, similar questions, with variations, are posed by zealous young Christians with cessationist commitments. If I had to make a composite of these questions, they'd run something like this:

> Several times during the last few years, brothers and sisters in Christ have prayed over me or prophesied over me, saying that they see me one day ministering to "masses" or "vast crowds" or "preaching to the nations" or the like. Some have told me that I have the potential to be the next Spurgeon [or Whitefield or Billy Graham or whoever]. One person simply prayed the word "fame" over me. Frankly, I find these voices both exciting and unsettling—exciting because I would like to minister to large numbers of people, and, if I am honest, I would enjoy their approbation,

---

1 This chapter was originally published as D. A. Carson, "Seekest Thou Great Things for Thyself?," *Themelios* 41, no. 3 (2016): 407–9.

yet unsettling because I know I am vain, and could easily pursue public recognition for sinful reasons—less to serve and more to win adulation. Yet it has to be said that I know of men and women of God who have unabashedly leveraged their means, gifts, and reputations to gain "spotlight" roles in history that wonderfully glorify God. So now I find myself wrestling with God, afraid of my pride, but wondering if I should redouble my efforts to be as useful as I can be. So one part of me wants to hide and serve in as small and secret a place as possible, avoiding the temptations associated with the spotlight. But on the other hand, if I am to take seriously what some have told me, should I be trying to network, study certain things, ask advice from people who have been around power without, apparently, being corrupted by it? I fear that pride could drive me to avoid a more visible ministry; I fear that pride could ruin me in a very public ministry. Please direct me if you can, and pray that I may gain clarity and increased humility.

The questions these folk are asking are important and multifaceted. Any response, even an inadequate response like this one, will necessarily require a bit of nuance. I might respond along the following lines, enumerating several points, in no particular order of importance.

1. Let's begin with your words, "I know of men and women of God who have unabashedly leveraged their means, gifts, and reputations to gain 'spotlight' roles in history that wonderfully glorify God." It's the word "leveraged" that troubles me, for it implies that these believers have cleverly worked things out, played their cards, chosen their courses, made their decisions—in short, "leveraged their means, gifts, and reputations"—so as to play "spotlight" roles in history, roles "that wonderfully glorify God." Obviously the motives of Christians can be embarrassingly mixed, but that doesn't make the mixture a good thing! Those who are truly godly will be very hesitant to "leverage" their gifts and means to play "spotlight" roles: they will be too afraid of their own motives. By contrast, their greatest desire will be to be found faithful.

2. Moreover, not a few leaders who have transparently sought out spotlight roles have ended up in moral and spiritual shipwreck. God does not give his glory to another. We do not need to mention names: it is easy to think of some of them. By contrast, John Calvin did not set out to make a

name for himself in Geneva. Guillaume Farel had to persuade him to stay there in 1536. After they were both expelled, Farel had to badger him to return in 1541. So be very careful about using verbs like "leverage."

3. Pragmatically, if the Lord does lay a large vision on your heart, feel free to think big, but start small: small assignments, small crowds, faithful relationships. Tim Keller spent the first dozen years of his pastoral ministry in the blue-collar town of Hopewell, Virginia. That, Tim says, is where he learned to preach and to give simple, straightforward answers. Lloyd-Jones spent eleven years as pastor in Sandfields, in the working-class town of Aberavon in Wales, and frankly expected to be there all his life until he was called to London. At one crucial point in Spurgeon's life, he was tempted to turn aside from his ministry to gain more education. Education can be a very good thing, of course, but it can also be a stimulus to arrogance. Spurgeon records how, while walking slowly one afternoon through Midsummer Common in Cambridge, "I was startled by what seemed a loud voice. . . . I seemed very distinctly to hear the words, 'Seekest thou great things for thyself? seek them not!'" (referring, of course, to Jeremiah 45:5 in the King James Version).[2] If God is in fact going to thrust you into spotlight ministry, do your best to ensure it is clearly God's doing, not your machination. You will then be much more likely to respond with gratitude than with pride.

4. For what it is worth, and at a much smaller scale, I made a vow a long time ago never to accept or reject an invitation on the basis of either numbers or money. When students ask me how I "planned" to be in this position at this time of life, I simply have to laugh. Again and again, the Lord surprised me and plunked me into situations that, in time, were rich in blessing. True, I sometimes asked what would be most "strategic," but I tried to avoid measuring "most strategic" in terms of numbers and money and fame and rather in terms of need. I did not plan to be a pastor; I did not plan to get a PhD; I did not plan to move to the United States; I did not seek out a spot on the Trinity Evangelical Divinity School faculty; when Tim Keller and I first started talking about what would become the Gospel Coalition, we had no idea it would have anything like the present configuration; and so on and so on. I'm not saying that any one of these

---

2 C. H. Spurgeon, *C. H. Spurgeon's Autobiography*, ed. Joseph Harrald and Susannah Spurgeon (London: Passmore and Alabaster, 1897), 1:242.

plans would have been evil, but I am saying that the arc of my life testifies to God's surprising grace rather than to my planning!

5. While most of us go through life afraid that people will think too little of us, one cannot help but notice that Paul goes through life afraid that people that will think too much of him (2 Cor. 12:6). If you grow in your knowledge of sin and of your own heart, and of the matchless grace in the cross, your fear will increasingly run in the same direction as Paul's—and then so-called "spotlight" ministry will increasingly become something you fear more than lust after.

6. To be frank, I am slightly suspicious of people who utter prophecies pronouncing fame and success on certain people. I'm not saying such prophecies cannot possibly be valid, but I worry that they sound suspiciously like a spiritualized version of the health, wealth, and prosperity gospel. After the Damascus road experience, God tells Paul not how influential he will be, but how much he must suffer for Jesus's sake. Paul tells the Philippians that it has been granted to them (!) on behalf of Christ not only to believe on him, but also to suffer for his sake (Phil. 1:29). Why is it that so few ostensible prophecies tell people today how much they must suffer for Jesus's sake?

7. In the relatively few instances in the Bible where God promises greatness to an individual, invariably there are constraints or tough entailments. Yes, Abraham is told that he will become the father of a great multitude, of many nations. But that is a promise he must grasp in faith, for the promise is certainly not fulfilled in his lifetime. God tells David that he will establish through David's heirs a dynasty that will never pass away. David rightly responds with grateful awe (2 Sam. 7:18–29)—but one must also remember that his position of leadership did not prevent him from committing grievous, horrible sins. Yes, God told Paul that he would become the apostle to the Gentiles, but that crucial ministry was accompanied by the life-sapping batterings he lists in 2 Corinthians 11:23–33. Read that list slowly, and ask how much you want a "spotlight" ministry. In most cases, large public ministries paint you as large public targets.

8. God's calculations of what is "important" ministry is rarely ours. When the saints go marching in, the widow who gave her mite will doubtless stand closer to the head of the queue than many a multimillionaire Christian philanthropist. And (dare I say it?) pastors of some tiny churches, pastors

like my dad,[3] I am certain, may well be preferred above names that are better known in merely human courts. God's gifts and graces are his to distribute as he wills: some workers put in twelve hours and seem to be mighty in the land, others work for one hour, and if the master decides to give both the same "reward," it is a salutary reminder that the "rewards" are his to give, and all of us are debtors to grace. I am fully persuaded that on the last day, there will be countless brothers and sisters in Christ, unknown to the annals of history, many of them illiterate or semiliterate, who have been starved, maligned, beaten, imprisoned, mocked, and finally killed ("the world was not worthy of them," Heb. 11:38), brothers and sisters who never enjoyed one day of spotlight ministry, who will be given the crown of martyrs never earned in spotlight ministries.

Seekest thou great things for thyself? Seek them not; seek them not.

---

3 See D. A. Carson, *Memoirs of an Ordinary Pastor: The Life and Reflections of Tom Carson* (Wheaton, IL: Crossway, 2008).

27

The Underbelly of Revival? Five Reflections on Various Failures in the Young, Restless, and Reformed Movement

NOT LONG AGO, a friend wrote me asking questions about what he called "the underbelly of revival."[1] Here in the US, and to some extent elsewhere, we have witnessed a significant movement of (mostly young) Christians who have sometimes been tagged "the young, restless, and Reformed."[2] In part, this movement is embodied in such organizations as Together for the Gospel, Desiring God, the Gospel Coalition, 9Marks, and Acts 29; in part, it surfaces in many local churches in many countries. My friend, however, drew attention to the sad litany of the last few years: squabbles, accusations of inappropriate behavior, adultery, burnout, and more. We need not attach names and events to these things; most of us know about them, and all of us can imagine them or have seen them elsewhere. So my friend posed the questions:

---

1 This chapter was originally published as D. A. Carson, "The Underbelly of Revival? Five Reflections on Various Failures in the Young, Restless, and Reformed Movement," *Themelios* 39, no. 3 (2014): 405–10. The quotations in this article without specific cited sources are from the author's personal experience.

2 This phrase comes from Collin Hansen's essay, "Young, Restless, Reformed," *Christianity Today*, September 22, 2006, https://www.christianitytoday.com/, and his book *Young, Restless, Reformed: A Journalist's Journey with the New Calvinists* (Wheaton, IL: Crossway, 2008).

But it makes us wonder . . . whether the thrill and euphoria of being part of something that feels like revival may serve to dull the senses in some. Has the "success" of this movement some call "young, restless, Reformed" blinded many of us to ministry's true nature? Has the perceived fruitfulness clouded the vision of some (many?) to some of the things that matter most? Have some of us grown lax and flabby? Are we making silly presumptions based on perceived "success" in ministry in recent years?

Two prefatory things must be said. First, the word "revival" embedded in these questions is used a bit loosely. Mercifully, it is not used in the sense common in some Southern states where it often serves as the near equivalent of "evangelistic meetings" (as in, "Last month we held a revival"). It is closer to the more historic sense of a special movement of God's Spirit that brings with it deep conviction of sin, fresh contrition and fresh holiness, and concomitant zeal for God's word and God's glory—a special movement that may be as short as a few hours, or as long as many years, and may result in thousands being renewed and more thousands being converted. Some of the characteristics of revivals have not been particularly strong in this "young, restless, and Reformed" movement.

Second, it must be said that some observers would be very happy to see the movement sputter out, especially if it could die in shame. There is no glee quite so mean as that which harbors an "I told you so" delight at the failures of a movement that God has blessed. But my interlocutor does not belong to these critics; he is not among the heirs of the critics of the New England awakening that took place at the time of Jonathan Edwards, critics who could find only things to criticize but who could not see the glory. Rather, he belongs to the movement itself and wants to learn the hard lessons as well as the happy ones.

In what follows, I offer five brief reflections called forth by my correspondent's questions.

1. The failures that have taken place during the past few years were not the sorts of things that could happen only when a movement is flourishing. Flawed leadership, immorality, bullying, and dissensions are frequently found in churches and organizations with no history of remarkable growth, with no sign of extraordinary blessing from God. Long before the young, restless, and Reformed movement started, I witnessed churches that had

to dismiss their senior minister because he had committed adultery. I saw a dear friend abandon his wife of twenty-nine years and his highly influential expository ministry because he chose to "come out" and declare himself a homosexual. Certainly I observed some remarkably sad and barren church splits.

During the lean years in Québec before 1972, before the Lord began to pour out remarkable blessings on the church, it would not have been true to say that although the churches were small and struggling they were all mature, sanctified, and passionate about the gospel. We did not have to wait until the period of growth and vitality (growing from about thirty-five churches to just under five hundred in eight years) before we witnessed moral failures.

In at least some cases, it may be that the growth in numbers of serious Christians brings with it a corresponding growth in the number of moral failures without the proportion of failures being any higher. We do well not to talk ourselves into an assumption that revival must have an ugly underbelly that would not exist if the revival were not there.

2. The scope and intensity of the blessings of a fruitful movement nevertheless do frequently have a bearing on this ugly underbelly, whether in perception or in reality, in at least four ways.

First, when many good things are happening, a calamitous failure stands out and draws attention to itself. In a time of spiritual declension and no growth, should a minister embezzle funds or sleep with someone other than his spouse, he will draw local attention to his failure, but the failure will not attract national comment. Yet if the minister is publicly identified with an expanding and vital ministry, not only will his failure draw much more widespread attention, but inevitably some pundits will start speculating (or pontificating!) on the intrinsic weaknesses of the movement.

In South Korea, the church saw spectacular growth during much of the twentieth century, attended by such things as the "prayer mountain movement." Many, many leaders had suffered for Jesus, and their constancy and faithfulness won a great deal of admiration. Twenty-five years ago, when citizens were asked to rate the three principal religions—Buddhism, Catholicism, and Protestantism (a large majority of the latter being Reformed evangelicals)—the preference, in order, was Protestantism, Catholicism, and Buddhism. Nevertheless, the very success of the movement led not a few to substantial triumphalism. All it took was a handful of public scandals, and the damage was done. Today church attendance has shrunk by about fifteen percent, and in recent polls Buddhism comes first, then Catholicism, and Protestantism ranks last.

Second, once fruitful movements and even revivals are well established, they frequently breed a naive optimism. It's not as if anyone would come right out and say, "God is transparently at work here; what can go wrong?"— yet something of that optimism prevails and overlooks the reality that the flesh still wars against the Spirit and that the devil still prowls around as a warring lion and as a messenger of deceit. In other words, the very revival that brings a renewed consciousness of sin and therefore a better grasp of the cross also breeds in some people a blissful assumption that things are going very well, and therefore they let their guard down in a way they would not do if ministry were perennially discouraging.

Third, a movement that is genuinely from God may display such blessing that at least some people are attracted to the blessing who are not really drawn to God. When the church suffers under persecution, there are relatively few spurious conversions or nominal Christians. But when things seem to be going swimmingly, the church is likely to attract more people who want to go along for the ride. In this sinful world, any church can become infested with a few hypocrites; in times of blessing, the attractiveness of hypocrisy becomes proportionately stronger. Hence an Ananias and Sapphira want a reputation for holiness and generosity more than they want to be holy and generous (Acts 5:1–11). I have read scholarly studies that have shown that nine months after the height of the revivals in Kentucky in the nineteenth century, there was a statistically significant uptick in the number of illegitimate children who were born. It is not hard to imagine. The intimacy bred by people who were getting right with God spilled over into more general intimacy, and intimacy often breeds intimacy, including sexual intimacy.

Fourth, matters may become worse if the blessings of a genuine movement from God tempt ministers and other Christian leaders to become less careful, less discerning. When people are eager to join the people of God and identify with them is precisely when more discernment is needed, not less. When the power of the Spirit is evident, there will always be some folk who want to throw money around and take the part of Simon in Acts 8, and therefore there will be a need for a Peter to tell him, "May your money perish with you" (Acts 8:20).

Of course, some observers treat these dangers as so sweeping and unavoidable that they think we should be suspicious of revivals and other movements with ostensible blessings beyond the ordinary. Bigness is intrinsically suspicious; in Schumacher's phrase (though he applied it to another realm), "Small is beautiful."[3] Shall we be similarly suspicious of the astonishingly rapid growth of the church in Jerusalem? The abuses that called forth the discernment of Jonathan Edwards did not tempt this prince of a theologian to deny the powerful transforming work of the Spirit of God.[4] Revival blessings demand not cynicism, but discernment.

3. Usually great movements of God call forth remarkable leaders. The Reformation was led by Reformers with great and diverse gifts; the early British missionary movement called up William Carey and others; the Evangelical Awakening was largely led by Howell Harris, George Whitefield, John and Charles Wesley, and the many others they trained.

Shall we conclude that in each case what triumphed was a rather nauseous celebrity culture?

Clearly the dangers of celebrity culture must not be ignored or minimized. Some preachers and other leaders seem to feed on approval and fame. This can happen at any level, of course, including the local church, but the scale of applause (and criticism!) in a large movement makes the temptations more blatant. Worse, such leaders and movements may, wittingly or unwittingly, seduce countless numbers of Christians into thinking that "real" or "vital" or "powerful" or "truly spiritual" Christian life is all about the big event, the larger-than-life leader. The result is such a massive distortion of Christian life that we turn with gratitude to the insight and wisdom of Michael Horton's recent book, *Ordinary*.[5] So when some celebrity ministries implode, this is no more than what we should expect: "they will not get very far because . . . their folly will be clear to everyone" (2 Tim. 3:9).

---

3   E. F. Schumacher, *Small Is Beautiful: Economics as if People Mattered* (London: Blond and Briggs, 1973).

4   See Jonathan Edwards, *The Religious Affections*, reprint ed. (Edinburgh: Banner of Truth, 2004).

5   Michael Horton, *Ordinary: Sustainable Faith in a Radical, Restless World* (Grand Rapids, MI: Zondervan, 2014).

Even here, however, we should be careful in our analysis and with our labels. Celebrity culture is nothing new. In his day, Paul had to oppose certain celebrity preachers: he called them "super-apostles" (2 Cor. 11:5; 12:11). But what made them superapostles (and, equally, "false apostles," 2 Cor. 11:13) was not the size of their ministries or the reach of their influence (for on that ground, Peter and Paul would both stand condemned), but their lust for power and not service, their preaching of a triumphalist Jesus and not the Jesus of the cross, their blatantly boastful accounts of their spiritual experiences in order to enhance their reputations over against Paul's fear that people would think too highly of him (2 Cor. 12:6). Paul treats such people with severity, demanding that the church in Corinth remove them from leadership and influence. One must not forget, however, that this same Paul treats very differently those who preach the truth faithfully, even if their motives leave something to be desired: "But what does it matter? The important thing is that in every way, whether from false motives or true, Christ is preached. And because of this I rejoice" (Phil. 1:18). And even here we are doubtless dealing with a spectrum. Paul is convinced he must correct Peter, but shall Peter be written off for pastoral and theological mistakes (Gal. 2:11–14)? May not Christian leaders disagree sharply on how to handle a John Mark (Acts 15:39)?

In other words, while we rightly identify the dangers in celebrity culture and grapple with the negative effects they have on a God-given revival, our analysis must not prove so shallow and sweeping that we happily condemn faithful preachers who happen to be more fruitful than we are. There is a kind of condemnation of celebrity culture that seems to be seeking a kind of celebrity over its own insight.

4. Yet although the evils of celebrity culture surface in just about every generation, there is one element in revivals and other movements of God that probably accelerates them. When rapid growth takes place, it is easy to promote people too rapidly. In his provocative book *Indispensable*, Gautaum Mukunda establishes what he calls his "leader filtration theory."[6] In most industries and organizations, he argues, leaders are "filtered": they are tested, scrutinized, battered a little, and they learn a great deal as they slowly rise

---

6 Gautaum Mukunda, *When Leaders Really Matter* (Boston: Harvard Business Review Press, 2012), 21.

through the system. A few leaders make it through "unfiltered," and these "extreme leaders" tend to be either geniuses or wackos.[7] I'm not sure this analysis is always accurate, but what is obvious is that when a movement is expanding rapidly there is more opportunity for leaders to rise into positions of real power without ever having been "filtered."

The apostle sees the danger: an elder "must not be a recent convert, or he may become conceited and fall under the same judgment as the devil" (1 Tim. 3:6). Transparently the question of who is a "recent convert" will vary with the context. The prophet Jeremiah was a very young man when he began his ministry; so also was the apostle John. On the return leg of his first recorded missionary journey, Paul, along with his coworker Barnabas, appointed elders in each place where they had planted a church a few months earlier (Acts 14:23), so they were appointing men who had been Christians for a few months or a year at most. But clearly it would not do, at this juncture, to appoint such recently converted men as elders in, say, Jerusalem or Antioch. When there is rapid growth, however, that is precisely what happens, as it did in Québec in the mid-70s. One tries to compensate by putting in place various accountability structures and by ensuring there are some older, wiser heads around to ward off the worst mistakes. The same Paul who warns against the appointment of recent converts also knows that youth can be faithful and effective (1 Tim. 4:12). But the dangers are transparent.

Perhaps they are exacerbated in our generation because of the rampant individualism that shapes so much of the culture. In their zeal, some plunge into evangelism and the gathering of a church without the advantages of structure, accountability, and of voices of wisdom, authority, and experience. Either they learn quickly and painfully, and begin to seek out wise counsel, or many of them burn out and even make shipwreck of their lives and of the lives of others. In other words, Western devotion to individualism tends to draw entrepreneurs away from the church structures that often serve as an ecclesiastical filtration system. (But let us also acknowledge that sometimes what is supposed to be a system that builds leaders up and teaches them accountability merely knocks people down and discourages them, which they then use as an excuse for independence and individualism.)

---

7 Mukunda, *When Leaders Really Matter*.

In short, what begins as zealous vision sometimes slips into unaccountable and incorrigible "leadership" characterized by massive egos and substantial bullying, driven in part by painful immaturity.

5. The astonishing range and power of the media have become so ubiquitous that it is difficult to grasp both their promise and their danger. Which of us can do anything but thank God for the ways in which gospel truth is circulating, often without expense to the end user, more rapidly and more cheaply than at any time in history, and often behind borders and barriers that cannot be breached any other way? The realities in some parts of the world are so politically sensitive that I cannot share with you distribution figures that are frankly staggering.

Nevertheless, all of us are becoming aware of some of the darker sides of the digital world. Quite apart from obvious things, like readily available violence, porn, and entertainment for couch potatoes, we are beginning to reflect on friendships that hide behind digital keypads but never deal with real people face-to-face, ways of manipulating people and sales and movements by the convenient arrangement of billions of pixels, and the insidious temptation to count "friends" and "followers" and "hits" as a measure of one's significance. Moreover, the scale and speed of the media can turn a relatively minor matter into national outrage. The media can puff people up for no substantive reason and utterly destroy them on grounds equally insignificant. So there is the challenge: how can we wisely and faithfully use the media without allowing them to destroy us?

At one level, this is nothing new; it is the scale that is new. In 1970 I was serving a church in Vancouver when what came to be called "the Canadian revival" broke out in a small town in Saskatchewan. For one reason or another I hopped across the country several times that year and had opportunity to watch the revival spread. But by the time it reached Vancouver, though it was still attracting substantial numbers, it felt phony, forced, spiritually insubstantial. I recall hearing an utterly authentic, moving, gospel-saturated testimony in the Prairies, a testimony that brought many to tears and contrition. Sadly, someone thought it was so good that he promptly talked the person who had given the testimony into flying around the country to repeat his story so that people could "catch" the revival. Pretty soon it sounded as canned as the marketing that drove it.

From this experience, and from reading of many other movements with their origin in God's good hand of grace, I've come to some resolutions should God in his mercy ever place me in such circumstances again. The first and foremost is this: Don't trust the media, and trust your own heart with respect to the temptations of the media even less. Don't "puff" the movement; God will not share his glory with another. The second is this: Use all the spiritual and emotional energy that such a movement stirs up to train the next generation of leaders. The alternative is to focus on certain experiences, experiences that are frequently puffed by the media but that serve as a distraction from the message of the cross. That does not mean that we must not use the media to get the message across. Far from it; Paul's "so that by all possible means I might save some" (1 Cor. 9:22) calls to us still. But it is one thing to use the digital world to circulate truth; it is another to seek our own glory through it; it is yet another to play to the media experts whose agenda is rarely that of God's; and it is yet another to forget that, like death, the media often have insatiable appetites, a huge maw that devours people and movements with little care and less respect. If we play to the media, the chances are, humanly speaking, that they will eventually turn around and eat us.

"The underbelly of revival?" We must not think in deterministic categories but reflect on the biblical narratives of times of great blessing, even though great evils attend them, and learn, too, from the history of the church. On each of the topics on which I have briefly reflected, there is a sort of "yes, but" element in the argument: yes, let us beware of the elixir of celebrity status, but let us thank God for gifted leaders; yes, let us not become snookered by ratings and digital reach, but let us use all lawful means to spread the gospel; and so forth. So we beg God for grace to persevere, to serve joyfully and faithfully, and to learn from any "underbelly" we stumble across that apart from the grace of God we are all undone. And we pray for one another in biblical terms:

Now may the God of peace, who through the blood of the eternal covenant brought back from the dead our Lord Jesus, that great Shepherd of the sheep, equip you with everything good for doing his will, and may he work in us what is pleasing to him, through Jesus Christ, to whom be glory for ever and ever. Amen. (Heb. 13:20–21)

28

When Revival Comes

RECENTLY I WAS SPEAKING in a part of the country known for its antagonism to the gospel. Church planting in that area is very hard work. The small number of confessionally strong churches are making headway, but slowly. I admire these pastors, evangelists, and church planters more than I can say; it is a pleasure and a privilege to spend time with them.[1]

In the course of a meal with several of them, one pastor said, "I know full well that I may serve all my years working in the teeth of strenuous opposition that may get worse before it gets better. But suppose that genuine revival breaks out, whether in one church or in a larger region. What should my priorities be?"

Great question—not least because this brother was not awash in pessimism. While working faithfully in a day of small things, he retained confidence that the Lord's arm is not shortened, such that he could not save. By this time, the pastor in question has a pretty good idea of what godly ministry looks like when the opposition is pretty intense, but he wondered how his priorities should change if the Lord in his mercy visited him with the blessings of reformation and revival.

As it happens, I've been on the edge of such visitations a couple of times. In 1970 and 1971, when the so-called Canadian Revival swept through parts of Western Canada, sparked by ministry led by the Sutera twins, I was serving as pastor of a church in British Columbia. And then, brought up

---

1 This chapter was originally published as D. A. Carson, "When Revival Comes," *Themelios* 43, no. 2 (2018): 169–71.

as I was in French Canada, I witnessed the unprecedented (for Québec) multiplication of about 35 French-speaking churches to just under 500 in 8 years (1972–1980). More importantly, I've tried to read some of the histories of revivals in various corners of the world, partly to think through what is genuinely of God and what is not. As a result of my own experience and of my reading, filtered by what I understand Scripture to say, my list of dos and don'ts when revival comes, in no particular order of importance, would look something like this:

1. Reread some serious literature about what is real and what is most likely fraudulent in revival. You cannot do better than to begin with *A Faithful Narrative of the Surprising Work of God* and *The Religious Affections*, both, of course, by Jonathan Edwards. Edwards is remarkably open to various displays, yet the real test is never the display but God-centered righteousness, gospel-fueled integrity. About a century after Edwards, some "revivals" in Kentucky and elsewhere produced a disproportionate number of illegitimate births—emotional intensity often combines with human intimacy which, if it is not of God, is more likely to produce babies than righteousness. Knowledge of abuses easily breeds a slightly supercilious cynicism, while infatuation with revival easily breeds naivete. Don't be cynical; don't be gullible; be discerning.

2. Examine your own heart; fan the flames of personal devotion to Christ. Abundantly use the ordinary means of grace: that is, instead of relying on the intensity of the revival, turn again and again to Bible reading, prayer, self-examination and confession, death to self-interest, a joyful focus on the cross, faithful evangelism, service, and eager anticipation of the glories yet to come. If instead you rely for your sustenance on the sweeping movement of the revival, ignoring the ordinary means of grace, you are likely to burn out in a frenzied pursuit of what is instantly gratifying but not very nourishing.

3. When revival comes, large numbers of people display boundless energy for the things of God. In your role as a minister of the gospel, direct that overflowing energy toward Bible study and prayer, toward corporate worship that is full of the word, not toward revival experiences but toward Jesus himself. Times of revival are clarion calls for increased commitment to anointed expository preaching, not an excuse for informal chats studded with pious clichés. One of the great things that happened in connection with the Québec movement was the farsighted establishment of Séminaire

Baptiste Évangélique du Québec, which became a conduit for the theological and pastoral training of that generation and the next. It is easy to think of genuine movements of God that petered out in silliness and warm nostalgia because the energy released in the movement was never directed toward training.

4. Keep out of the press. Transparently, that's not possible, not even strictly advisable—but work toward that end. More precisely, if in God's mercy you find yourself serving in a time of great blessing, do not announce it, do not "puff" it, do not promote it. By all means work to expand the ministry, but by service and teaching and preaching, not by gimmicks. Eventually, of course, the press will find you. Then you must answer questions with self-deprecation, with lots of emphasis on the matchless grace of God, with a steadfast refusal to promote "stars" and "celebrities." Do everything you can to avoid the "experts" who arrive en masse, trying to analyze the revival and "catch" the revival to carry it somewhere else. One of the great advantages enjoyed by those involved in the work in Québec between 1972 and 1980 was the language barrier: most American press voices didn't know enough French to find out what was going on. Today, of course, the quickest forms of distribution of information (and of vicious attacks, too) are not tied to the organs traditionally labeled "the press," but to social media—and they are much more difficult to avoid. But among the leaders where you have influence, foster restraint, a refusal to get caught up in every outraged blog, a quiet perseverance in faithful ministry while remaining highly suspicious of the siren call of renown, especially your own.

5. Eschew manipulation. During the Canadian revival, I recall the spontaneous testimony of a man who had been minding his own business, a happy secularist who was oblivious to the rising movement, when suddenly he felt compelled to enter the church building in Saskatchewan where the revival began, where he was crushed by the convicting work of the Spirit, heard the gospel, and was dramatically saved and transformed. His testimony was captivating, compelling, powerful—a tool God used to bring others to repentance and faith. Sadly, a pastor (not from that church) caught up with the man and persuaded him to embark on a speaking tour in which he would "share his testimony" at major venues across Canada. I heard it in Vancouver. The words were the same, the story was the same, but the whole thing had become canned. What was a spontaneous and Spirit-anointed

testimony became a bit of manipulation in an effort to spread the revival elsewhere. Christian leaders who should have known better were relying on moving testimonies that were no longer spontaneous and irrepressible outpourings of God's grace, but were substitutes for preaching Christ and the cross. It would be easy to provide many examples where the line between zeal and manipulation was breached.

6. Never imagine, not for a moment, that this movement from the Spirit of God depends on you. Why is it that during the twentieth century South Korea witnessed spectacular growth in converts and theological maturity while Japan struggled with minimal numbers? Are we to conclude that the leaders in South Korea were much more capable or gifted than those in Japan? Why is it that a Josiah presides over national revival, while a Jeremiah devotes his life to tears, discouragement, and judgment? If God gives you the privilege to participate in a time of great renewal, thank him for the opportunity, give yourself to being a faithful conduit of God's blessings, but do not presume that God is rather lucky to have you. Cultivate humility.

Beware the dangers that attend a movement's popularity. Many pundits have observed that today in many parts of North America, the number of nominal Christians is falling off rather rapidly. This development is fueled by the fact that there are rising social and cultural forces that are marginalizing and opposing Christians and Christianity. Where opposition abounds, numbers of nominal Christians decline. The result is that it is getting easier and easier to discern who is a genuine Christian. Conversely, however, a movement faces a new set of dangers when it becomes popular. Not infrequently, when a reforming and revivifying movement breaks out, it is initially opposed, but once it becomes popular, a lot of people want to clamber on board. And that means leaders need to ask God for discernment.

7. Restrain yourself from offering purely naturalistic explanations. During a movement of genuine revival, and certainly in its aftermath, many people will ask what the circumstances were that precipitated it. Usually it is easy enough to make a list: a praying circle of brothers and sisters, a time of spiritual declension that made some people really eager for renewal, cultural unrest and upheaval (in Québec, it was "the Quiet Revolution"), and much more of the same. Usually it is entirely reasonable to look at such phenomena and see God's providential hand in them. Nevertheless, there is an unhealthy way of reporting these phenomena—a way that gives the

impression that these things were sufficient in themselves to bring about revival, a way that implies if you could duplicate these phenomena elsewhere you could bring in revival there, too. A little reflection, however, suggests that all of those accompanying cultural phenomena could take place without revival, that no one predicted the onset of revival on the basis of such phenomena. God will not be tamed. Detailed analyses may serve no end other than our own self-promotion. The analyses tend to give the impression that we control the movement, though of course we'd never be so crass as to say so. By all means ponder the enormously complex intertwinings of history and culture, by all means discern the providential hand of God in them, but leave plenty of space for simply confessing, "This is the Lord's doing, and it is marvelous in our eyes" (Ps. 118:23 ESV).

29

On Knowing When to Resign

CERTAIN KINDS OF QUESTIONS come my way by email fairly regularly—every few weeks, every couple of months. One of these regulars runs something like this: "How do I know when it is time to resign?" If this is being asked by a pastor who is still young, it is usually prompted by a difficult situation that he longs to flee. Circumstances of that sort are so diverse that I won't attempt to address them here. What I have in mind is the pastor who poses this question at the age of 55, or 60, or 65, or 70. This pastor is wondering when it is time to lay down the burden of local church ministry and consider something else—itinerant ministry, perhaps, or teaching overseas for a while, or working with a mission agency, or half-time pastoral work, perhaps as someone else's associate. Are there any biblical and theological principles that should shape our reflection on these matters?[1]

1. In one sense, this is the right question to ask. Here is not someone who has reached some long-awaited ideal retirement age and is looking for an excuse to withdraw from ministry in favor of buying an RV to spend the next couple of decades alternating between fishing lakes and visiting grandchildren. After all, there is no well-articulated theology of retirement in Scripture. Rather, this is a serious question from someone who has borne the heat of the day, and who, for various reasons, wonders if it is not only permitted but right to ask if it is time to move on.

1 This chapter was originally published as D. A. Carson, "On Knowing When to Resign," *Themelios* 42, no. 2 (2017): 255–58.

2. In recent years, I've been passing on what I've picked up from a few senior saints who have thought these things through. The most important lesson is this: Provided one does not succumb to cancer, Alzheimer's, or any other seriously debilitating disease, the first thing we have to confront as we get older is declining energy levels. Moreover, by "declining energy levels" I am referring not only to the kind of declining physical reserves that demand more rest and fewer hours of labor each week but also to declining emotional energy, which makes it difficult to cope with a full panoply of pastoral pressures. *When* those energy levels begin to fall is hugely variable (at age 45? 65? 75?), as is also *how fast* they fall. But fall they will! It follows that if one attempts at age 85 to do what one managed to accomplish at age 45, a lot of it will be done badly. Frustrations commonly follow: old-man crankiness, rising resentments against the younger generation, a tendency to look backward and become defensive, even an unwitting destruction of what one has spent a lifetime building up.

Three things follow.

a. As long as God provides stable energy levels, one should resist the glitter of common secular assumptions about retirement—for example, that there is (or should be) a universal retirement age, that somehow your work entitles you to a retirement free from all service, that the end of life should be dominated by pleasurable pastimes emptied of self-sacrifice and service. This is not to argue there is no place for, say, time devoted to creative tasks of one sort or another; it is to argue that it is sub-Christian to imagine that our service across the decades *entitles* us to a carefree retirement.

b. Once energy levels start to decline (whenever that might be), then, assuming that neither senility nor some other chronic disease is taking its toll, the part of wisdom is to stop doing some things so that with one's remaining energy one can tackle the remaining things with enthusiasm and gusto. I can think of two or three senior saints who have become wholly admirable models in this regard. In their late 60s, they slowly started to put aside one task after another, with the result that now, in their early 90s, they can still do the one or two remaining things exceptionally well. One of them, for instance, will still preach, but never more than once a week. And he won't fly anywhere: travel to the place he is to preach is either by car (with someone driving him), or by train. But when he does preach, you can close your eyes and listen to a man thirty or forty years younger.

c. There is another element in such decisions that is partly subjective, partly temperamental, partly a reflection of one's sense of call—factors that interact with one another in various ways. John Calvin died on May 27, 1564, at the age of 54. All his life he held himself to the most rigorous, punishing schedule. That stunning self-discipline, a reflection of his passion for the glory of God and for the promotion of the gospel, was used by God to make the man astonishingly productive. On the other hand, all the biographies I have read of him speculate that if in his latter years he had slowed down a little, he might have lived a good deal longer—and had he lived another decade or two, still with stable health, he may well have produced a great deal more. But who are we to tell John Calvin what he should have done? Human motives are usually mixed. On the one hand, there is something hauntingly exemplary about a person who wants to burn out for Christ, to waste no time, to serve others, "fill the unforgiving minute / With sixty seconds' worth of distance run";[2] on the other hand, there may be a wee touch of workaholism in such a stance, in which our very self-identity is tied to the number of hours we put in or the number of things we produce. On the one hand, it might be a careful and thoughtful stewarding of our declining energies to make a wise calculation about dropping certain responsibilities so as to maintain more important priorities; on the other hand, who is to deny that there may also be a touch of entitlement, or a cooling of youthful ardor, a dangerous love of mere ease? Each of us will have to give an answer to our own beloved Master, who knows us better than we do. It is probably not too much to suggest that if we are temperamentally drawn to one or the other of these extremes, we should be especially diligent to explore our motives most carefully.

3. All things being equal (and of course, they never are), one should not leave one's ministry until one or more of the following conditions is met.

a. One has to leave for moral reasons. Sadly, such failures are not restricted to young pastors. The older one gets, the more one should pray for grace to finish well.

---

b. Serious health issues mean that one can no longer discharge one's pastoral duties fruitfully, with no realistic hope of returning to full strength (e.g., What is the prognosis after a serious stroke?).

c. One is clearly called by God to some other ministry. All of the usual complex factors have to be borne in mind.

d. One judges that it would be a good thing for this ministry if the baton were passed to a younger leader in an orderly way. There is no absolute rule, but the rule of thumb is that the longer a person has stayed in one ministry and the more fruitful that person has been, the wiser it is for that pastor to help arrange the transition to a successor before bowing out. It is not hard to think of exceptions, of course: for example, an old man merely trying to deploy a bit of nepotism or control the future while neither consulting anyone nor using the transition to train church leaders. Generally, however, the rule of thumb proves valuable.

e. One senses one's energy levels are declining, and it seems wise to let go of some responsibilities so that one can more faithfully discharge remaining responsibilities. In some cases that can most easily and fruitfully be worked out by taking on a reduced load in the church while someone else steps up to the primary leadership; in other cases, the only way to opt for reduced responsibilities is by resigning from that charge and taking on a smaller and different assignment.

f. Sometimes one must relinquish one's position and work because of the declining health of a spouse. I have known several pastors who reduced their work dramatically, and finally resigned, to look after a spouse suffering from advanced dementia.

g. The final condition that may justify leaving one's ministry is precipitated by a developing crisis. In some instances pressures build up among the elders that reflect differences in vision and priorities. These disparate visions may harden into deeply opposed camps. One may argue that the situation should not have been allowed to develop so far—but there it is. At their worst, such situations are extraordinarily difficult for outsiders to analyze accurately. Has the problem arisen primarily because one or two elders are power hungry and are wanting to become ecclesiastical bosses—people who, quite frankly, need to face discipline? Or because a senior pastor has become entrenched in the conviction that he is always right and has nothing to learn from anyone? Or is it a case of a Barnabas and a Paul unable to reach an amicable agreement on a pastoral issue where both sides feel strongly and can marshal compelling arguments? In some instances of this sort, one should *not* leave but try and sort it out before stepping down and leaving a potential mess to a successor; but in other instances, one *should* step down, conscious of the fact that the differences of opinion, while deep, are not about orthodoxy or morality, and the strong action that would be necessary to restore unanimity among the elders is likely to split the church for little if any gospel gain. It may be best simply to step aside with humility and grace, committing the elders and the church to the grace of God.

4. Finally, the frequency with which pastors move from local church ministry to itinerant ministry is a topic that deserves more study than it has received. Clearly this can be a wise move. I know former pastors and professors who "retire" into carefully selected teaching ministries in the Two-Thirds World, where their years of accumulated experience benefit many people who do not otherwise have ready access to excellent teaching. Others very fruitfully take on a series of interim ministries where the fixed end of the interim period greatly reduces the stress but provides an opportunity to provide strategic help. Many others set up independent nonprofit organizations that specialize in niche ministries—on the family, for instance, or on repentance and holiness. Many of these nonprofits solicit funds to support the ministry. The former pastor becomes a niche guru on the selected topic.

It would be both uncharitable and mischievous to suggest that all of this is intrinsically bad. But it would be naive not to perceive that there are some dangers to these developments. Some forms of itinerant ministry generate indolence: you preach the same "package" wherever you go with the result that you quit studying and growing in your knowledge of Holy Scripture and in your ability to teach parts of it you've never taught before. Being a guest preacher tends to garner thanks and commendations without the criticism and rebukes that regular ministry in a local church or seminary tend to provide as a counterbalance—and an exclusive diet of praise is not good for anyone. In short, sometimes itinerant ministry appears to be green grass on the other side of the fence, with too little awareness of the rattlers lurking in the undergrowth. As always, there is great value in testing our motives.

What all of this boils down to is that there is no formulaic answer for pastors who pose the question, "How do I know when it is time to resign?"

Nevertheless, there are some guidelines that many find helpful, guidelines bound up with the glory of the gospel, the primacy of the local church, the honesty to admit when we are aging, the urgency of training up the next generation, the passion to glorify Christ in our senior years, and the hunger to teach the whole counsel of God.

30

Motivations to Appeal to in Our Hearers When We Preach for Conversion

MOST OF US, I SUSPECT, develop fairly standard ways, one might even say repetitive ways, to appeal to the motivations of our hearers when we preach the gospel. Recently, however, I have wondered if I have erred in this respect—not so much in what I say as in what I never or almost never say. What follows is in some ways a mea culpa, plus some indication of why I think the topic should be important for all of us.[1]

Before I survey the motivations themselves, I should specify that because the gospel is to be preached to both unbelievers and believers, the motivations that here interest me may be found among both parties. Nevertheless, I shall tilt the discussion toward those motivations of *unbelievers* to which we should appeal when we preach the gospel to them, aiming, in God's mercy, at their conversion.

A Survey of Possible Motivations

The eight motivations I am about to list are not necessarily mutually exclusive. Several may, and often do, coexist at one time and in one person. In no particular order of importance:

---

[1] This chapter was originally published as D. A. Carson, "Pastoral Pensées: Motivations to Appeal to in Our Hearers When We Preach for Conversion," *Themelios* 35, no. 2 (2010): 258–64. It is based on a paper presented at the Gospel Coalition's Pastors' Colloquium in Deerfield, Illinois, on May 19, 2010.

Fear

The letter to the Hebrews insists that people are kept all their lives in fear of death but that the coming of the Son of God as a human being, a son of Abraham, set in train the destruction of him who has the power of death, namely, the devil himself (Heb. 2:14–18). With respect to this particular fear, then, the preaching of the gospel promises a *reduction* in fear. On the other hand, in various ways Jesus tells his hearers to fear him who has power to destroy body and soul in hell (Matt. 10:28). Not a few of the parables end in a simple polarity: gathered into barns or burned (Matt. 13:30), entering the home of the wedding feast or being shut outside where there is weeping and gnashing of teeth (Matt. 22:10–13), and so forth. Some apocalyptic images depict people calling for the rocks and mountains to fall on them and hide them from the wrath of the Lamb (Luke 23:30; Rev. 6:15–17). Belonging to the same theme are texts asking us, rhetorically, where the profit lies if we gain the whole world but lose our own souls (Matt. 16:26), or insisting that it is a dreadful thing to fall into the hands of the living God (Heb. 10:31).

Obviously it is possible to preach the wrath of God in such an angry and self-righteous fashion that we bear a much closer resemblance to Elmer Gantry than to Jesus Christ. On the other hand, in addition to the example of Jesus and the apostles, we have occasional examples from church history where God has used the appeal to the fear of judgment in powerful ways. The best-known witness is doubtless Jonathan Edwards's "Sinners in the Hands of an Angry God," which I reread some weeks ago to remind myself how biblical most of it is.

The Burden of Guilt

I specify "the burden of guilt" instead of "guilt" because I prefer to use the latter for one's moral and legal status before the Holy God. In other words, one may *be* very guilty and not feel guilty, that is, not labor under any burden of guilt. If one is in fact guilty but feels nothing of the burden of guilt, the objective guilt is not a motivation for conversion. Until one cries, in these words or something similar, "Against you, you only, have I sinned and done what is evil in your sight" (Ps. 51:4), one is not strongly motivated by the burden of guilt. On the other hand, that guilt, rightly perceived, can be a crushing burden and thus a powerful and desperate motivation for relief.

It is a truism of much Reformed theology, not least Puritan theology, that the law must do its work before grace can do its work. Without an adequate dose of the former, the latter is likely merely to heal the wounds of the people slightly (to use King James English; see Jer. 6:14). That Puritan heritage influenced many who were, strictly speaking, outside that heritage. For example, John Wesley's advice to a young minister on how to preach the gospel in any new situation is replete with this perspective.[2] The text to which many in this tradition appealed was Galatians 3: the law is our παιδαγωγός to bring us to Christ, for the law was added to turn sin into transgression, to make us see our fault, to shut us up under condemnation (Gal. 3:19–25). Careful exegesis has often shown, of course, that this interpretation is substantially mistaken: Galatians 3 is less interested in the psychological and moral profile of the person transitioning from guilt to grace than in unpacking the place of the Mosaic law in redemptive history. Nevertheless, the Puritan vision of the place of the law is not as off base as some think. For even if Paul's primary point in Galatians 3 is to locate the law's rightful place in redemptive history, over against the place that many Palestinian first-century Jews thought it should have, the conclusion one must inevitably draw is that God took extraordinary pains to establish and nurture the law covenant across a millennium and a half as *preparatio Christi*. Total ignorance of this Old Testament background is one of the reasons that so many in contemporary culture feel almost no burden of guilt when they are first confronted with the Bible, with Jesus, with the gospel. In fact, nurtured on a spongy epistemology, many hear the law's demands and conclude, at least initially, that the God who thought this lot up is not worth respecting, for he must be a manipulative and power-hungry despot. Still, at some point the burden of guilt catches up with many people, and it can become a powerful motivation in their conversion.

Shame

A glance at the literature shows how difficult it is to distinguish absolutely between guilt and shame.[3] Some cultural anthropologists speak of "shame cultures" as if such cultures know little of guilt, and of some traditional Western cultures as if they are guilt ridden but know little of shame: the two

2   John Wesley, "To an Evangelical Layman," in *The Works of John Wesley: Volume 26: Letters II: 1740–1755*, ed. Frank Baker (Oxford: Clarendon, 1982), 482–89.

3   On guilt and shame, see chapter 14, "The Changing Face of Words," originally published in *Themelios* 43, no. 3 (2018): 339–42.

kinds of cultures are sometimes treated as if they are categorically disjunctive. Some in the field of psychiatry assert that guilt arises from what we do, while shame arises from what we are, but that is certainly not a biblical distinction. In the Bible we may be guilty and feel guilty for what we are, and equally we may be ashamed of what we do.

In popular parlance, I suspect that shame has more to do with losing face, primarily (though not exclusively) in horizontal relationships. Nevertheless, if one loses face before one's family or peers, it is usually because one has done something "wrong" as judged by those peers, so it is hard to see why guilt feelings do not also intrude. Similarly, one may be genuinely guilty of some sort of moral breach and be ashamed of what one has done. Initially Adam and Eve are naked and unashamed: they have nothing to hide. But when sin changes everything, does Adam hide from God because he feels guilty or because he feels ashamed? Must one choose? Nevertheless, there does appear to be a slight difference in focus between the two: shame has to do with losing face, often objectively, and hence feeling shamed. Such loss of face commonly springs from one's own faults, but of course it may spring from something one has endured—like David's envoys who are ashamed of losing half their beards at the hands of the Ammonites and whom David therefore consoles by instructing them to remain at Jericho until their beards grow back (2 Sam. 10:1–5). They have lost face, but of course in this instance they are not guilty of anything.

Many have argued that in a culture like ours, which protests that it is unmoved by the law's demands and refuses to admit to guilt feelings because it refuses to admit to guilt, a better way to unpack the nature of sin is to unfold the nature of idolatry rather than the nature of law. Idolatry is bound up with corrosive relationships, with de-godding God, with shameful distortions and substitutions; and, it is argued, these evils are more easily admitted among yuppie postmoderns than are the evils of transgressing law. In other words, shame is more readily acknowledged than guilt.

The Need for "Future Grace"

When John Piper unpacks this category, he primarily has Christians in view.[4] Historically, however, a great deal of evangelism has been carried

---

4   John Piper, *Future Grace: The Purifying Power of the Promises of God*, revised ed. (Colorado Springs: Multnomah), 2012.

out by urging people to prepare to meet God, to receive the grace now that alone prepares a sinner for resurrection existence in the new heaven and the new earth. Where is the profit in gaining the world and losing one's soul? Where there is widespread belief that one must finally give an account to a holy God who does not grade on the curve, this sort of appeal carries quite a lot of weight. The motivations to which one appeals are a mixture of fear (which I have already mentioned) and the desire to be found right or just before this God, acceptable to him.

The Attractiveness of Truth

Frequently the apostles declare that they bear witness to the truth, that they declare the truth, that they do not peddle the truth, that they cannot do other than speak the truth, that they speak the truth plainly in the eyes of all, and so forth (e.g., John 19:35; Rom. 9:1; 2 Cor. 4:2; 11:10; 13:8). The assumption, of course, is that by the grace of God, the truth itself is attractive to some. Cornelius was such a man. He was a good deal more eager to hear the truth, at least initially, than Peter was to declare it. For those with eyes to see and ears to hear, the truth can be self-attesting; for others, like some of Jesus's opponents in John 8, the truth is precisely what is detested: "Because I tell you the truth, you do not believe me" (John 8:45; cf. Isa. 6:9–10, cited in Matt. 13:14–15 and elsewhere). To draw an analogy: the one gospel can be a wonderful aroma to those who are being saved and a disgusting stench to those who are perishing (1 Cor. 1:18). So also the truth can appear wonderful to those who by grace begin to see its beauty and compelling nature, while actually causing offense and unbelief in those who are perishing.

When I was a young man, many university missions spent a lot of time defending, say, the deity of Christ or his resurrection from the dead. The widespread assumption, both among the evangelists and among many of the student hearers, was that if one accepted the truth of these claims, one was already on the path toward becoming a Christian. This assumption sustained quite a lot of evidentialist apologetics. The approach is flawed in several ways, of course. James reminds us that the devil knows and believes such truths, but such "faith" does not save him (James 2:19). Granted, however, the need for grace to enable the "natural" person to perceive the truth, one cannot deny that one of the motivations in people as they begin to "close" with Christ (to use an old Puritan expression) is the attractiveness of the truth. While some in Athens sneered, others, in some ways already hooked by what the apostle Paul was saying, wanted to hear him again on these matters (Acts 17:32). They were drawn to the truth.

A General, Despairing Sense of Need

It is pretty clear from the Gospel accounts that many who pursued Jesus did not do so out of a well-thought-out theology (as law precedes gospel, and they were under deep conviction of sin), but out of desperation fed by their most acutely perceived need. Witness the woman with the history of hemorrhaging (Matt. 9:20–21), the two blind men by the side of the road calling for the Son of David to have mercy on them (Matt. 9:27), the Syrophoenician woman (Mark 7:25–28), and many others. In some cases, of course, Jesus responds to such needs yet also pushes on a little farther to deal with the sin in their lives (the Samaritan woman in John 4:10–18, the man by the pool of Bethesda in John 5:5–14). Moreover, it does not follow that everyone who is healed by Jesus is "saved" in the fullest theological sense of that word. For instance, nine of the ten healed lepers do not have the courtesy of gratitude, let alone saving faith (Luke 17:11–19). Yet where there is a wholehearted and desperate plea to Jesus, even absent much theological understanding, it is wonderful to see how embracing Jesus is.

Pastoral experience supports this assessment. Many of us have witnessed people turning to Christ with remarkably little exact theological knowledge. The knowledge comes later. Why these people come, at least initially, is that they need help, need it desperately, and turn to Jesus. This may prove to be part of a broader, whole-life turning to Jesus. Their initial motivations, however, are all bound up with desperation.

Responding to Grace and Love

Both Testaments repeatedly emphasize the matchless love and grace of God. Some are drawn to Christ when they begin to glimpse the Father's love for this damned world in sending his Son to the cross and the Son's love in accomplishing his Father's will. One suspects that the appellation Mary and Martha had for their brother Lazarus—"the one you love," they say to Jesus (John 11:3)—reflects a common experience: so many felt peculiarly loved by Jesus, even the fourth Evangelist himself (John 13:23; 19:26; 20:2; 21:7,

20). Paul cannot talk long about justification and the cross-work of Christ without breaking out with an adoring exclamation such as "who loved me and gave himself for me" (Gal. 2:20). Whether it is the love of the proverbial father for his prodigal sons (Luke 15:20–24) or the assertion that Christ loved the church and gave himself for her (Eph. 5:25, 29), whether it is the gut-wrenching portrayal of the love of God in Hosea or Paul's prayer that believers might have the power, together with all the saints, to grasp the limitless dimensions of that love (Eph. 3:17–19), the response to the love of God is one of the most powerful motivations people experience, not only when they first close with Christ but also when they mature in Christ.

A Rather Vague Desire to Be on the Side of What Is Right

I know that sounds terribly vague. If I had to attach one word to what I am talking about, it would probably be the motivation of hope. Consider the encounters with Jesus in John 1:19–51. John the Baptist's disciples begin to follow Jesus because their master had pointed to him. They clearly hope he is the one to come. The Christological confession at Caesarea Philippi ("You are the Messiah, the Son of the living God," Matt. 16:16) is part of this hope, of course—even though the context shows the apostles at this point have no category for a crucified Messiah. The same sort of longing, with even less theological understanding, is reflected in the desire of Zacchaeus to entertain Jesus in his home (Luke 19:6). I am not trying to specify exactly when the apostles or Zacchaeus were converted. I am pointing out merely that at least part of their motivations in pursuing Jesus, at least initially, lay in their desire to see if he really would fulfill Scripture, if a good and powerful man would come to the home of a corrupt civil servant. They hoped so. Transparently, such hope can merge with other motivations already listed: people may hope for release from the burden of guilt, hope to be justified by God on the last day, hope that things will turn out well both short-term and in eternity.

So I turn now from this survey of possible motivations that people display when they turn to Jesus and offer four theological and pastoral reflections.

Four Theological and Pastoral Reflections on This Survey

First, we do not have the right to choose only one of these motivations in people and to appeal to it restrictively.

Consider an analogy. It has become common to speak of half a dozen distinguishable models of the atonement. I do not much like the rubric, but I shall use it for the sake of convenience. Many are the recent books that argue that since all these "models" are grounded in Scripture, we are free to choose the one we prefer. But that is precisely what we are not free to do, unless we conceive of Scripture as little more than a casebook, an inspired volume of cases, warranting readers to glom onto those few cases, and only those cases, that seem to fit their own situations or preferences most closely. If we hold to a more traditional and faithful understanding of Scripture, then to the extent that the various models of the atonement are warranted by Scripture, we must hold to all of them—and then work out how each is related to the others, what holds them together, where there is a priority among them that is established by Scripture itself, and so forth. But we dare not choose merely one or two of them.

So also here. Insofar as these diverse motivations enjoy biblical precedent or even biblical warrant, preachers do not have the right to appeal to only one or two motivations as if they were the only legitimate ones. We ought to appeal, at various times, to all these motivations—and, again, work out how each is related to the others, what holds them together, and where there is a priority among them that is established by Scripture itself. But we do not have the right to appeal constantly to, say, fear before God, without also on occasion appealing to other biblically illustrated and sanctioned motivations.

Second, on the other hand, we may have the right to emphasize one motivation more than others.

In the same way that the structure and emphases of Paul's evangelistic addresses could change, depending on whether he was addressing biblically literate Jews and proselytes (Acts 13) or completely biblically illiterate pagans (Acts 17), so the particular motivations to which we appeal may vary according to our knowledge of our audience. In a somewhat similar vein, if we are addressing biblically literate but unregenerate people, some of our appeal will presuppose that they know the Scriptures at some level, that many of them, say, will be convinced that there is a judgment to be faced, a heaven to be gained, a hell to be shunned and feared. By contrast, if we are addressing biblically illiterate people, then although all those themes will at some point have to be introduced, our initial appeals may sound quite different. Some motivations are of course unworthy, and we should never appeal to them. For example, "Come to Jesus, and you will receive a lot of cargo,"[5] or "Turn to Jesus, and you will always be free of trouble." Where motivations are not unworthy, however, and especially where they are biblically sanctioned, we may find it particularly appropriate to appeal to certain motivations rather more than others.

It would be easy to go through the list I laid out and conjure up situations where it is the part of prudential wisdom to appeal to one or two motivations rather more often than to all the rest. Had we time, it would be an excellent exercise to envisage the kind of audience that ought to find us appealing to primarily this or that motivation in our hearers.

Third, the comprehensiveness of our appeal to diverse motivations will nevertheless reflect the comprehensiveness of our grasp of the gospel.

Once again, let me draw an analogy first before establishing my point. For the last few decades, many of us have wrestled long and hard with the doctrine of justification, judging that something essential to the gospel is at stake in the current discussions. The result, however, is that we have sometimes so tied the gospel and conversion to the question of our right standing before God that we have downplayed the new birth. We have emphasized Christ's bearing our guilt and the nature of imputation without correspondingly emphasizing the regenerating work of the Spirit and the gospel as the power of God, the same power that raised Jesus from the dead, in transforming our lives, in our becoming part of the new creation. Suppose, then, that we managed to emphasize both of these elements of conversion appropriately (let us call them the forensic and the transformative). We might, of course, then tumble into neglect of the running biblical tension between our joy in the kingdom of God now already operating in the reign of King Jesus and the joy that awaits the consummation of that kingdom in the resurrection existence of the new heaven and the new earth. Understanding this tension will engender hope, thereby reinforcing all the motivations that spring from a godly anticipation of what God has promised that still lies ahead. In other words, while the exigencies of our pastoral location have demanded that we focus on forensic elements of the gospel and conversion, a robust biblical theology demands that part of

5 Cf. neo-Melanesian "cargo cults" or our own health, wealth, and prosperity gospels.

our ministry be taken up by the biblical exigencies, the shape of the gospel itself, the rich and complex nature of its outworking in conversion and in the spiritual maturation of the believer and of the church.

So also this matter of choosing the motivations to which we appeal— choices that largely shape our sermons. For pastoral reasons, we may decide, for instance, that our particular audience, with its endless frustrated and idolatrous relationships and its suspicion of law categories, needs a heavy emphasis on the generosity and freedom of God's grace: our God, as Tim Keller likes to put it, is an overwhelmingly prodigal God.[6] Well and good. But the Bible itself depicts Jesus inciting fear in the hearts of people with his insistence that the God with whom they have to deal "can destroy both soul and body in hell" (Matt. 10:28). Again, Jesus openly appeals to motivations that seek eternal rather than temporary and material rewards. He does not hesitate to elicit awareness of guilt and to invoke shame: Who goes home justified, the Pharisee or the publican (Luke 18:9–14)? Who gives more, the wealthy givers or the widow with her two mites (Mark 12:41–44)?

So while we may, for pastoral reasons, initially choose to appeal to certain motivations and not others, it is surely the path of biblical faithfulness so to teach and preach the word of God that we awaken new motivations in the hearts and minds of our people as we unpack the complex richness of the glorious gospel of our blessed God. If instead we find ourselves constantly appealing to the same two or three motivations while ignoring others, it is probably because our choices are too much shaped by our perceptions of local cultural needs and too little shaped by the richness of the biblical gospel. Sooner or later, our people may read their Bibles with limiting and even dangerous blinkers that we ourselves have given them.

Fourth, to put this another way, all of the biblically sanctioned motivations for pursuing God, for pursuing Christ, say complementary things about God himself, such that failure to cover the sweep of motivations ultimately results in diminishing God.

Thus, the motivations characterized by fear are bound up with the truth that God is holy, that he is rightfully our Judge, that he gathers some into his presence and casts others into outer darkness, that his knowledge of us

---

6   Timothy Keller, *The Prodigal God: Recovering the Heart of the Christian Faith* (New York: Dutton, 2008).

is perfect, extending not only to a grasp of our motives but even to a full-bore knowledge of what we would have done under different circumstances (a form of so-called "middle knowledge"). The burden of guilt reminds us that God does not grade on the curve, and unless we are justified by the one who is himself just while justifying the ungodly, there is no hope for us.

And so we could work through the list. The point to be made is simple: any failure to appeal to the full range of biblically exemplified and biblically sanctioned motivations not only means that there are some people we are not taking into account, but, more seriously, that there are elements in the character and attributes of God himself that we are almost certainly ignoring.

PART 6

REFLECTIONS ON
CHRISTIAN DISCIPLESHIP

31

On Abusing Matthew 18

SOME YEARS AGO I WROTE a fairly restrained critique of the emerging church movement as it then existed, before it morphed into its present diverse configurations.[1] That little book earned me some of the angriest, bitterness-laced emails I have ever received—to say nothing, of course, of the blog posts.[2] There were other responses, of course—some approving and grateful, some thoughtful and wanting to dialogue. But the ones that displayed the greatest intensity were those whose indignation was white-hot because I had not first privately approached those whose positions I had criticized in the book. What a hypocrite I was—criticizing my brothers on ostensible biblical grounds when I myself was not following the Bible's mandate to observe a certain procedure nicely laid out in Matthew 18:15–17.

Doubtless this sort of charge is becoming more common. It is regularly linked to the "Gotcha!" mentality that many bloggers and their respondents seem to foster. Person A writes a book criticizing some element or other of historic Christian confessionalism. A few bloggers respond with more heat than light. Person B writes a post with some substance, responding to Person A. The internet lights up with attacks on Person B, many of them asking Person B rather accusingly, "Did you communicate with Person A in private first? If not, aren't you guilty of violating what Jesus taught us

---

1 D. A. Carson, *Becoming Conversant with the Emerging Church: Understanding a Movement and Its Implications* (Grand Rapids, MI: Zondervan, 2005).

2 This chapter was originally published as D. A. Carson, "On Abusing Matthew 18," *Themelios* 36, no. 1 (2011): 1–3.

in Matthew 18?" This pattern of counterattack, with minor variations, is flourishing.

To this, at least three things must be said.

1. The sin described in the context of Matthew 18:15–17 takes place on the small scale of what transpires in a local church (which is certainly what is envisaged in the words "tell it to the church"). It is not talking about a widely circulated publication designed to turn large numbers of people in many parts of the world away from historic confessionalism. This latter sort of sin is very public and is already doing damage; it needs to be confronted and its damage must be undone in an equally public way. This is quite different from, say, the situation where a believer discovers that a brother has been breaking his marriage vows by sleeping with someone other than his wife and goes to him privately, then with one other in the hope of bringing about genuine repentance and contrition, and only then brings the matter to the church.

To put the matter differently, the impression one derives from reading Matthew 18 is that the sin in question is not, at first, publicly noticed (unlike the publication of a foolish but influential book). It is relatively private, noticed by one or two believers, yet serious enough to be brought to the attention of the church if the offender refuses to turn away from it. By contrast, when New Testament writers have to deal with false teaching, another note is struck: the godly elder "must hold firmly to the trustworthy message as it has been taught, so that he can encourage others by sound doctrine and refute those who oppose it" (Titus 1:9).

Doubtless one can think up some contemporary situations that initially might make one scratch one's head and wonder what the wise course should be—or, to frame the problem in the context of the biblical passages just cited, whether one should respond in the light of Matthew 18 or of Titus 1. For example, a local church pastor may hear that a lecturer in his denominational seminary or theological college is teaching something he judges to be outside the confessional camp of that denomination and possibly heretical. Let us make the situation more challenging by postulating that the pastor has a handful of students in his church who attend that seminary and are being influenced by the lecturer in question. Is the pastor bound by Matthew 18 to talk with the lecturer before challenging him in public?

This situation is tricky in that the putative false teaching is public in one sense and private in another. It is public in that it is not a merely private opinion, for it is certainly being promulgated; it is private in the sense that the material is not published in the public arena but is being disseminated in a closed lecture hall. It seems to me that the pastor would be wise to go to the lecturer first, not out of obedience to Matthew 18, which really does not pertain, but to determine just what the views of the lecturer really are. He may come to the conclusion that the lecturer is kosher after all; alternatively, that the lecturer has been misunderstood (and any lecturer with integrity will want to take pains not to be similarly misunderstood in the future); or again, that the lecturer is dissimulating. He may feel he has to go to the lecturer's superior, or even higher. My point, however, is that this course of action is really not tracing out Jesus's instruction in Matthew 18. The pastor is going to the lecturer, in the first instance, not to reprove him, but to find out if there really is a problem when the teaching falls in this ambiguous category of not-quite-private and not-quite-public.

2. In Matthew 18, the sin in question is, by the authority of the church, excommunicable, in at least two senses.

First, the offense may be so serious that the only responsible decision that the church can make is to thrust the offender out of the church and view him or her as an unconverted person (Matt. 18:17). In other words, the offense is excommunicable because of its seriousness. In the New Testament as a whole, there are three categories of sins that reach this level of seriousness: major doctrinal error (e.g., 1 Tim. 1:20), major moral failure (e.g., 1 Cor. 5), and persistent and schismatic divisiveness (e.g., Titus 3:10). These constitute the negative flipside of the three positive "tests" of 1 John: the truth test, the obedience test, and the love test. In any case, though we do not know what it is, the offense in Matthew 18 is excommunicable because of its seriousness.

Second, the situation is such that the offender can actually be excommunicated from the assembly. In other words, the offense is excommunicable because organizationally it is possible to excommunicate the offender. By contrast, suppose someone in, say, Philadelphia claims to be a devout Christian while writing a book that was in certain ways deeply anti-Christian. Suppose a church in, say, Toronto, Canada, decides the book is heretical. Such a church might, I suppose, declare the book misguided or even heretical, but they certainly could not excommunicate the writer. Doubtless they could declare the offender persona non grata in their own assembly, but this would be a futile gesture and probably counterproductive to boot. After all, the offender might be perfectly acceptable in his own assembly.[3] In other words, this sort of offense might be excommunicable in the first sense—that is, the false teaching might be judged so severe that the offender deserves to be excommunicated—but is not excommunicable in the second sense, for the organizational reality is such that excommunication is not practicable.

The point to observe is that whatever the offense in Matthew 18, it is excommunicable in both senses: the sin must be serious enough to warrant excommunication, and the organizational situation is such that the local church can take decisive action that actually means something. Where one or the other of these two senses does not apply, neither does Matthew 18.

One might of course argue that it is the part of prudential wisdom to write to authors before you criticize them in your own publication. I can think of situations where that may or may not be a good idea. But such reasoning forms no part of the argument of Matthew 18.

3. There is a flavor of playacting righteousness, of disproportionate indignation, behind the current round of "Gotcha!" games. If Person B charges Person A, who has written a book arguing for a revisionist understanding of the Bible, with serious error and possibly with heresy, it is no part of wisdom to "tut-tut" the narrow-mindedness of Person B and smile condescendingly and dismissively over such judgmentalism. That may play well among those who think the greatest virtue in the world is tolerance, but surely it cannot be the honorable path for a Christian. Genuine heresy is a damnable thing, a horrible thing. It dishonors God and leads people astray. It misrepresents the gospel and entices people to believe untrue things and to act in reprehensible ways. Of course, Person B may be entirely mistaken. Perhaps the charge Person B is making is entirely misguided, even perverse. In that case, one should demonstrate the fact, not hide behind a procedural matter. And where Person B is advancing serious biblical argumentation, it should be evaluated, not dismissed with a procedural sleight of hand and a wrongheaded appeal to Matthew 18.

---

3   This argument could be ratcheted up to the denominational level for those who—mistakenly, in my view—think that "church" in Matthew 18 has that sort of multiassembly organization in view.

32

On Disputable Matters

EVERY GENERATION OF Christians faces the need to decide just what beliefs and behaviors are morally mandated of all believers and what beliefs and behaviors may be left to the individual believer's conscience.[1] The distinction is rooted in Scripture—for example, the practice of certain kinds of behavior guarantees that a person will not inherit the kingdom of God (1 Cor. 6:9–10), but other kinds of behavior are left up to the individual Christian:

> One person considers one day more sacred than another; another considers every day alike. Each of them should be fully convinced in their own mind. Whoever regards one day as special does so to the Lord. Whoever eats meat does so to the Lord, for they give thanks to God; and whoever abstains does so to the Lord and gives thanks to God. (Rom. 14:5–6)

The matters where Christians may safely agree to disagree have traditionally been labeled adiaphora, "indifferent things." They are not "indifferent things" in the sense that all sides view them as unimportant, for some believers, according to Paul, view them as very important, or view their freedom from such behavior as very important: "Each of them should be fully convinced in their own mind." They are indifferent matters in the sense

---

1 This chapter was originally published as D. A. Carson, "On Disputable Matters," *Themelios* 40, no. 3 (2015): 383–88.

that believing certain things or not believing certain things, adopting certain practices or not adopting them, does not keep a person from inheriting the kingdom of God. Today there is a tendency to refer to such adiaphora as "disputable matters" rather than as "indifferent matters"—that is, theologically disputable matters. On the whole, that terminology is probably better: in contemporary linguistic usage "disputable matters" is less likely to be misunderstood than "indifferent matters."

In the easy cases, the difference between indisputable matters and disputable matters is straightforward. The resurrection of Jesus Christ is an indisputable matter: that is, this is something to be confessed as bedrock truth if the gospel makes any sense and if people are to be saved (1 Cor. 15:1–19). If Christ did not rise from the dead, our faith is futile, the witnesses who claimed they saw him are not telling the truth, we remain in our sins, and we are of all people most to be pitied because we are building our lives on a lie. By contrast, Paul allows people to differ on the matter of honoring certain days, with each side fully persuaded in its own mind.

Immediately, however, we recognize that some things that were thought theologically indisputable in the past have become disputable. Paedobaptism was at one time judged in some circles to be so indisputably right that Anabaptists could be drowned with a clear conscience: if they wanted to be immersed, let us grant them their wish. Until the last three or four decades, going to movies and drinking alcohol was prohibited in the majority of American evangelical circles: the prohibition, in such circles, was indisputable. Nowadays most evangelicals view such prohibitions as archaic at best, displaced by a neat transfer to the theologically disputable column. Indeed, such conduct may serve as a possible sign of gospel freedom. Mind you, the fact that I qualified the assertions with expressions like "most evangelicals" and "majority of American evangelical circles" shows that the line between what is theologically indisputable and what is theologically disputable may be driven by cultural and historical factors of which we are scarcely aware at the time. Moreover, some things can cross the indisputable/disputable divide the other way. For example, in the past many Christians judged smoking to fall among the adiaphora, but their number has considerably shrunk. Scientifically demonstrable health issues tied to smoking, reinforced by a well-embroidered theology of the body, has ensured that for most Christians smoking is indisputably a no-no.

Since, then, certain matters have glided from one column to the other, it cannot come as a surprise that some people today are trying to facilitate the same process again so as to effect a similar transfer. Doubtless the showcase item at the moment is homosexual marriage. Yes, such marriage was viewed as indisputably wrong in the past, but surely, it is argued, today we should move this topic to the disputable column: let each Christian be fully persuaded in their own mind and refrain from making this matter a test of fellowship, let alone the kind of matter on which salvation depends.

What follows are ten reflections on what does and does not constitute a theologically disputable matter.

1. That something is disputed does not make it theologically disputable, that is, part of the adiaphora. After all, there is no cardinal doctrine that has *not* been disputed, and not many practices either. When the troublemakers who followed in Paul's train argued that in addition to Christ and his death, it was necessary to be circumcised and take on the burden of the law if one was to be a Christian under the Jewish Messiah, Paul did not suggest that everyone was entitled to their own opinion. Rather, he pronounced an anathema, because outside the apostolic gospel, which is tied to the exclusive sufficiency of Jesus, there is no salvation (Gal. 1:8–9). When some in Corinth gave the impression that certain forms of fornication could be tolerated in the church and might even be an expression of Christian freedom, Paul insisted on the exercise of church discipline all the way to excommunication and emphatically taught that certain behavior, including fornication, inevitably means a person is excluded from the kingdom (1 Cor. 5–6). Across the centuries, people have disputed the doctrine of the Trinity, the deity of Christ, his resurrection from the dead, and much more, but that does not mean that such matters belong in the disputable column. In short, just because something is in fact disputed does not mean that it is theologically disputable. If this point were not valid, *any* doctrine or moral stance could be relativized and placed in the adiaphora column by the simple expedience of finding a few people to dispute its validity.

2. What places something in the indisputable column, then, is not whether or not it is disputed by some people or has ever been disputed, but what the Scriptures consistently say about the topic and how the Scriptures tie it to other matters. At the end of the day, that turns on sober, evenhanded, reverent exegesis—as Athanasius understood in his day on a different

topic. Athanasius won the Christological debate by the quality and credibility of his careful exegesis and theological integration. Similarly today, even if one disagrees with this or that detail in their arguments, the kind of careful exegetical work displayed at a popular level by Kevin DeYoung and at a more technical level by Robert A. J. Gagnon represents a level of detail and care simply not found by those who wish to skate around the more obvious readings of the relevant texts.[2] To put these first two points together: That some still argue that the New Testament texts sanction or even mandate an Arian Christology, disputing the point endlessly, does not mean that we should admit Jehovah's Witnesses into the Christian community today—they are exegetically and theologically mistaken, and their error is so grievous, however enthusiastically disputed, that the deity of the Word made flesh, of the eternal Son, cannot ever legitimately be transferred out of the indisputable column. Exactly the same thing must be asserted regarding the Bible's prohibition of homosexuality, however complex the pastoral issues. In short, the most fundamental tool for establishing what is or is not an indisputable is careful, faithful exegesis.

3. My third, fourth, and fifth observations about disputable matters arise from a close reading of 1 Corinthians 8:1–11:1. In 1 Corinthians 8, Paul does not assert that Christians should not eat meat that has been offered to idols. Rather, he insists that the meat has not been contaminated; there is nothing intrinsically wrong with eating such meat. Nevertheless, Christians with a "weak" conscience—that is, Christians whose connections with idolatry in the past are so recent that they think that eating such meat is sinful even though there is nothing sinful about the action itself—must *not* eat such meat, lest they do damage to their conscience.[3] Eating the meat that has been offered to idols is not intrinsically wrong, but violating one's own conscience is wrong. The conscience is such a delicate spiritual organ that it is easily damaged: to act in violation of conscience damages conscience, it hardens conscience—and surely no Christian who cares about right and wrong wants to live with a damaged conscience, an increasingly

---

2   Kevin DeYoung, *What Does the Bible Really Teach About Homosexuality?* (Wheaton, IL: Crossway, 2015); Robert A. J. Gagnon, *The Bible and Homosexual Practice: Texts and Hermeneutics* (Nashville: Abingdon, 2001).

3   On these matters, see Andrew David Naselli and J. D. Crowley, *Conscience: What It Is, How to Train It, and Loving Those Who Differ* (Wheaton, IL: Crossway, 2016).

hardened conscience. If we violate our consciences when we *think* that what we are doing is wrong (even though, according to Paul, the action itself is not wrong), then we will find it easier to violate our conscience when the envisaged action *is* wrong, with the result that our conscience will be less able to steer us clear of sin. Of course, over the long haul one hopes and prays that "weak" Christians will, by increased understanding of right and wrong derived from careful reading of Scripture, transform their "weak" consciences into robust "strong" consciences. There is no particular virtue in remaining perennially "weak," for that simply indicates that one's moral understanding has not yet been sufficiently shaped by the word of God.

4. Meanwhile, according to Paul in 1 Corinthians 8, Christians with a "strong" conscience—that is, Christians who rightly see that there is nothing intrinsically wrong with eating food that has been offered to idols and whose consciences are therefore untroubled if they do so eat—rightly perceive the intrinsic innocence of the act of eating such meat. Nevertheless, Paul insists, the demands of love require that they refrain from such eating if by going ahead and eating they wittingly or unwittingly encourage those with a weak conscience to follow suit. In short, the love of the "strong" Christian for the "weak" Christian may place the former in a position where he or she will choose not to do something that is not itself intrinsically wrong. In other words, an action that properly belongs in the disputable column, leaving the Christian free to engage in that action, may, because of the Christian's obligation to love the weaker believer, become off-limits to the stronger believer. This does not mean that the action has shifted to the indisputable column: that would mean, in this case, that the action is always wrong, intrinsically so. So we are driven to the conclusion that an action belonging in the disputable column is not necessarily one that Christians are free to take up. Rather, Christians may rule the action out of bounds either because they admit they have weak consciences or, knowing their consciences are strong, because they voluntarily put the action aside out of love for weaker believers.

Incidentally, one should not confuse the logic of 1 Corinthians 8 with the stance that finds a strong legalist saying to a believer who thinks that eating meat offered to idols is acceptable, "You may think that such action is legitimate, but every time you do it you are offending me—and since you are not permitted to offend me, therefore you must not engage in that activity." The person who utters words to that effect, however, is in no danger of being swayed by the actions of those who engage in the activity. They are using a manipulative argument to defend a misguided position in which they are convinced that the act of eating meat that has been offered to idols is invariably wrong. In other words, they operate out of the conviction that this activity lies in the indisputable column—and thus they find themselves at odds with Paul's wisdom and insight.

5. How, then, does the argument of 1 Corinthians 8 relate to the argument of 1 Corinthians 10:14–22, where it appears that the apostle Paul absolutely forbids eating the sacrifices of pagans, which is nothing other than participating in demonic worship? It is difficult to be absolutely certain, but it appears that in 1 Corinthians 8 what is permitted in principle is the eating of meat that has been offered to idols, while in 1 Corinthians 10 what is prohibited is eating meat that is part of participating in any service or worship or cult or rite that is tied to pagan deities. And this affords us another insight: actions that may belong to the adiaphora, that is, that are rightly judged disputable, may in certain cultural contexts become absolutely condemned, thus now belonging in the indisputable column. More briefly, in the right context, what belongs in the disputable column gets shifted to the indisputably bad column. On the basis of Romans 14 and what Paul says about some viewing one day above another and others viewing all days the same, Christians may disagree about whether it is appropriate for their children to play in soccer matches on the Lord's Day. At some point, however, if those soccer matches mean that neither the child nor the parents are meeting regularly with the Lord's people in corporate worship and for biblical instruction and edification, what appears as a disputable matter becomes indisputably bad (Heb. 10:25).

6. That leads us to a still broader consideration. Sometimes the theological associations of an action, in a particular context, establish whether an action is right or wrong. In one context, it may be absolutely right or wrong, thus belonging in the indisputable column; in another context, the action may belong to the adiaphora. Consider the strange fact that Paul absolutely refuses to allow Titus to be circumcised (Gal. 2:1–5) but circumcises Timothy (Acts 16:3). On a superficial reading, it is small wonder that Paul's opponents dismiss him as a people pleaser (Gal. 1:10) who sniffs the wind and adopts any position that seems convenient at the moment. But a little probing discloses Paul's

reasoning in both instances. In the context of Galatians 2, Paul's opponents seem to be saying that a Gentile must be circumcised and come under the law of Moses if he or she is to be saved by the Jewish Messiah. If Paul agreed with such reasoning, it would mean that Jesus's sacrificial death and resurrection are an insufficient ground for Gentiles to be accepted before God: they must also become Jews. That jeopardizes the absolute sufficiency of Christ and his cross-work and resurrection. The gospel is at stake. Paul and the other apostles ensure that Titus is not circumcised: the issue is nonnegotiable; the prohibition lies in the indisputable column. In the case of Timothy, however, no one is claiming that Timothy must be circumcised to be saved. Rather, because of his mixed parentage, he was never "done," and if he is circumcised at this stage it will make mobility in Jewish homes and synagogues a little easier, thus facilitating evangelism. It's not that Timothy must *not* be circumcised, and it's not that he *must* be circumcised. Rather, this is the outworking of the apostle's cultural flexibility for evangelistic purposes: he becomes a Jew to win the Jews and becomes like a person without the law to win the Gentiles (1 Cor. 9:19–23).

7. Under the new covenant, there is a deep suspicion of those who, for the sake of greater spirituality or deeper purity, elevate celibacy, or who prohibit certain foods, or who inject merely human (i.e., biblically unwarranted) commands, or who scrap over minor points (e.g., Mark 7:19; 1 Tim. 4:3–4; 1:6; 2 Tim. 2:14, 16–17; Titus 1:10–16; cf. Rom. 14). Such people try to elevate matters that should never be placed in the indisputable column to a high place in the hierarchy of virtues. Paul has no objection to celibacy, and in the right context he can extol its advantages (1 Cor. 7), but he resolutely sets his face against those who prohibit marriage, thinking, perhaps, that celibacy signals a higher spirituality. Almost always these topics that some individuals want to make indisputably mandated are at best relatively peripheral, external, or clearly presented in Scripture as optional or temporary.

8. Some have argued that since Romans 14:5–6 sets the observance of days into the disputable column, and since the days in question must include the Sabbath, and since the Sabbath is part of the Decalogue, and since the Decalogue summarizes moral law, therefore even moral law can change with time as new insights are uncovered. So perhaps it is time to say that the moral prohibition of homosexual marriage should also be revisited. If one moral law (which, one would have thought, lies in the indisputable column) is by

New Testament authority shifted to the disputable column, why should we not consider shifting other moral laws too? The subject, of course, is huge and complex, but a few reflections may clarify some of the issues. (a) Not a few scholars think that the days in Romans 14 refer to Jewish feast days that are tied to ceremonial laws but not to the Sabbath (e.g., Passover, Yom Kippur). (b) Others allow that the Sabbath is included in the days mentioned in Romans 14 but think the flexibility that Paul there allows means that the shift to Sunday is sanctioned. In that reading, the form of the Sabbath law is flexible, but not its one-in-seven mandate. (c) Although many believers hold that the Decalogue is the perfect summary of moral law,[4] others argue that the category of moral law, as useful as it is, should not be deployed a priori to establish what continues from covenant to covenant, but as an a posteriori inference.[5] In that case, of course, the argument that because the Sabbath law is included in the Decalogue it must be moral law, falls to the ground, yet the category of moral law is retained. (d) In any case, in the Bible there is no text whatsoever that hints that homosexual marriage might in some cases be acceptable. The pattern of prohibition is absolute. As for days, we *do* have a text that indicates a change of approach to their observance, even if we may dispute exactly what it means.

9. Some draw attention to the argument of William J. Webb in his influential book, *Slaves, Women & Homosexuals*.[6] Webb argues that the Bible establishes trajectories of moral positions, and it is these trajectories that ultimately lead the church to condemn slavery and ought to lead the church today to egalitarianism. Webb himself advances reasons why he would not allow the same argument to extend to blessing homosexual marriages—but of course that is the line of argument promoted in some circles today. This leads to the curious position that the morality attained centuries *after* the New Testament is complete and circulating is higher than what God himself gives in the biblical documents. The most robust critique of this position is doubtless the lengthy review article by Wayne

---

4   See Philip S. Ross, *From the Finger of God: The Biblical and Theological Basis for the Threefold Division of the Law* (Fearn: Mentor, 2010).

5   E.g., D. A. Carson, "The Tripartite Division of the Law: A Review of Philip Ross, *The Finger of God*," in *From Creation to New Creation: Biblical Theology and Exegesis: Essays in Honor of G. K. Beale*, ed. Daniel M. Gurtner and Benjamin L. Gladd (Peabody, MA: Hendrickson, 2013), 223–36.

6   William J. Webb, *Slaves, Women & Homosexuals: Exploring the Hermeneutics of Cultural Analysis* (Downers Grove, IL: InterVarsity: 2001).

Grudem.[7] In brief, considerable insight into Christian belief and Christian conduct, in particular what is mandated and what is disputable, is to be gained by following the trajectories *within* the Scriptures, but that does not justify treating the trajectories *beyond* the Scriptures as normative, the more so when such trajectories undermine what the Scriptures actually say.

10. A great deal of this discussion could be construed as a probe into what Christians are *allowed* to do—or, more cynically, what they can get away with. None of the discussion is *meant* to be taken that way (see, especially, the fourth point), but so perverse is the human heart that it would be surprising if no one took it that way. Yet surely serious Christians will be asking another series of questions: What will bring glory to God? What will sanctify me? What conduct will enable me to adorn the gospel? What does it mean to take up my cross and follow Jesus? What contributes to preparing me for the new heaven and the new earth? What will contribute to fruitful evangelism? What conduct effervesces in love, faith, joy, and peace? What beliefs and conduct nudge me back toward the cross and forward to loving God with heart, soul, mind and strength and my neighbors as myself? Again, what will bring glory to God?

So suppose a Christian is trying to decide whether to go to a movie that is not only R-rated but has a well-deserved reputation for laughing sleaze. Assessing the choice along the lines of this editorial—whether banning the film is an indisputable obligation of Christian morality or belongs to the adiaphora—is a useful exercise. One might acknowledge, for instance, that some with a "weak" conscience really shouldn't see it, that those with a "strong" conscience shouldn't see it if they might influence those with a "weak" conscience, and so forth, as we work our way through the various points. But surely Christians will want to ask a different set of questions: Will watching this film adversely affect my desire for purity, or will it fill my mind with images I don't want to retain but cannot expunge? What are alternative things that I might be doing? If Jesus were here, would I invite him along? Is there any way in which watching this film glorifies God?

---

7   Wayne A. Grudem, "Review Article: Should We Move Beyond the New Testament to a Better Ethic? An Analysis of William J. Webb, *Slaves, Women & Homosexuals: Exploring the Hermeneutics of Cultural Analysis*," *Journal of the Evangelical Theological Society* 47 (2004): 299–346. See also Benjamin Reaoch, *Women, Slaves, and the Gender Debate: A Complementarian Response to the Redemptive-Movement Hermeneutic* (Phillipsburg, NJ: P&R, 2012).

33

Perfectionisms

MOST READERS OF *THEMELIOS* will be aware that the word "perfectionism" is commonly attached in theological circles to one subset of the Wesleyan tradition. As far as I can tell, the numbers who defend such perfectionism today are rather depleted. They hold that progressive sanctification is not only desirable and attainable but, borne along by grace, can result in a life of sinlessness here and now: we do not have to wait for the glorification that all God's redeemed people will enjoy at the parousia. A century ago the movement was often an extrapolation of Keswick theology, then in its heyday—a movement distinguishable from Keswick theology by its claim to attain a rather higher "higher life" than most within the Keswick fold thought they could achieve.[1]

It is easy to imagine that everyone in the perfectionist camp is a self-righteous and pompous hypocrite, easily dismissed as a fool whose folly is all the more ludicrous for being laced with self-deception. Doubtless some self-designated perfectionists are like that, but most of the rather small number of perfectionists I have known are earnest, disciplined, focused Christians, rather more given to work and serenity than to joy. Certainly it is less discouraging to talk about Christian matters with perfectionists than with those who claim to be Christians but who rarely display any interest in holiness. In any case, the most comprehensive treatment of perfectionism, essentially unanswerable, is the large volume by B. B. Warfield, *Studies in Perfectionism.*[2]

---

1 This chapter was originally published as D. A. Carson, "Perfectionisms," *Themelios* 35, no. 1 (2010): 1–3.

2 Benjamin B. Warfield, *Studies in Perfectionism*, reprint ed. (Phillipsburg, NJ: P&R, 1974).

There were species of perfectionism before Wesley, of course. Some connect the doctrine of entire sanctification with *theosis*; some tie it to various strands of the complicated and largely Roman Catholic history of "spirituality." Moreover, there are uses of "perfectionism" in two other disciplines: philosophy (going back to the classical period of Greek thought) and, in the more recent post-Wesley—indeed post-theology—world, the discipline of psychology. During the last three centuries of Christian discourse, however, the connection of perfectionism with one strand of the Wesleyan tradition is inescapable.

Yet I suspect that there is another species of theological perfectionism (though it is never so labeled) that owes no connection to Keswick or Wesley. Perhaps I can approach it tangentially. More than ten years ago a gifted pastor I know told me that at the age of fifty or so he was contemplating leaving pastoral ministry. Perhaps he would serve as an administrator in some sort of Christian agency. When I probed, I discovered that his reasoning had little to do with typical burnout, still less with a secretly nurtured sin that was getting the best of him, and certainly not with any disillusionment with the gospel or with the primacy of the local church. His problem, rather, was that he set extraordinarily high standards for himself in sermon preparation. Each of his sermons was a hermeneutical and homiletical gem. Anyone who knows anything about preaching could imagine how much time this pastor devoted to sermon preparation. Yet as his ministry increased, as legitimate demands on his time multiplied, he found himself frustrated because he could not maintain the standards he had set himself. I told him that most of us would rather he continue for 20 more years at 80 percent of his capacity than for 6 months at 100 percent of his capacity.

One might dismiss this pastor's self-perceived problem as a species of idolatry: his ego was bound up with his work. Probably an element of self-importance had crept into his assessments, but let us, for charity's sake, suppose that in his own mind he was trying to offer up his very best to the Master. Certainly he held to a very high sense of what preaching should be, and he felt it was dishonoring to Christ to offer him shoddy work.

Now transfer the perceived burden of this pastor to a more generalized case. Occasionally one finds Christians, pastors, and theological students who are afflicted with a similar species of discouragement. They are genuinely Christ-centered. They have a great grasp of the gospel and delight to share it. They are disciplined in prayer and service. On excellent theological grounds, they know that perfection awaits final glorification; but on equally excellent theological grounds, *they know that every single sin to which a Christian falls prey is without excuse.* Precisely because their consciences are sensitive, they are often ashamed by their own failures—the secret resentment that slips in, the unguarded word, the wandering eye, the pride of life, the self-focus that really does preclude loving one's neighbor as oneself. To other believers who watch them, they are among the most intense, disciplined, and holy believers we know; to themselves, they are virulent failures, inconsistent followers, mere Peters who regularly betray their Master and weep bitterly.

Part of this pastoral dilemma can be thought of as a species of over-realized eschatology—not the over-realized eschatology Paul confronts in 1 Corinthians 4 that leads to pride nor the puerile over-realized eschatology of the health, wealth, and prosperity gurus, but a slightly different kind. It is the kind that knows glorification still lies in the future but also knows that the gospel is the power of God unto salvation, that Christians have been not only justified but powerfully regenerated, that the Spirit has been poured out upon us, and that sin no longer has dominion over us, making every sin a damnable failure, utterly without excuse. Doctrinally, therefore, these believers know that perfection still lies over the horizon; experientially, precisely because they know the kingdom has been inaugurated, they can sink into bleak despair as they confront their own sins. It is not that, objectively speaking, they are worse than other Christians. Far from it: these are among the finest Christians I know. Those who criticize them have rarely thought as long and hard about sin and how to overcome it as these brothers and sisters have. They remain so uncomfortable with their wrestlings because they know they *ought* to be better.

Perhaps it is unwise to suggest that their problem should be thought of as a kind of perfectionism. Certainly it is not the perfectionism in some strands of the Wesleyan tradition, in which entire sanctification is judged to be attainable. Rather, this unhappiness, sometimes descending to despair, is the fruit of frustration that perfection is *not* achievable. Yet it springs not from generalized aspirations for utopia, but from biblical declarations of the power of the gospel placed alongside our own shortcomings. It springs from the conviction that, granted the power of the gospel, perfection ought to be a lot more attainable than it is.

It springs, in short, from panting after perfection; it is another kind of perfectionism. Immediately one must say that pursuit of perfection is at many levels a good thing, a needed thing, plausible evidence that the gospel is at work in our lives. Many are the mature Christians who are acutely aware of the ongoing struggle with sin yet avoid the disabling despair of the few. Indeed, it has often been noted that the godliest of Christians are characteristically most aware of their sin yet equally aware of the limitless measure of God's love for them in Christ Jesus. What is it, then, that makes the pursuit of God and of holiness the characteristic mark of many disciples yet so utterly debilitating for some intense and devout followers of Jesus?

At least two factors are at play.

First, the Bible itself speaks to this issue in various ways, and some of those ways are cast as stark antitheses. In apocalyptic literature, for example, there are faithful followers of Christ, and there are diabolical opponents. People wear either the mark of the beast or the sign of Christ; there is nothing in between. Similarly in wisdom literature: one follows Dame Folly or Lady Wisdom, but not both. That is why a wisdom psalm like Psalm 1 casts the choice in absolute antithesis: *either* one does *not* walk in the counsel of the ungodly, stand in the path of sinners, and sit in the seat of mockers, while delighting in the law of the Lord day and night and meditating on it, finding one's life before God is like a well-watered, fruit-bearing tree, *or* the wicked are simply "not so." The Lord recognizes and owns one path, while the other perishes. There is nothing in between. The Lord Jesus can preach in many different styles, but included among them is wisdom polarity: reflect on the antitheses at the end of the Sermon on the Mount. On the other hand, over against such antithetical presentations of holiness and sin, of faithfulness and unbelief, are the many narrative portions of the Bible where God's people are depicted with all their inconsistencies, their times of spectacular faithfulness, and their ugliest warts. Abraham the friend of God repeatedly tells half-truths; Moses the meekest man loses his temper and consequently does not get into the promised land; David the man after God's own heart commits adultery and murder; Peter the primus inter pares, the confessor of Caesarea Philippi and the preacher of Pentecost, acts and speaks with such little understanding that he earns a rebuke from Jesus and another from Paul. In such narratives there is no trace of the moral polarities of apocalyptic and wisdom literature. There is instead an utterly frank depiction of the moral compromises that make up the lives of even the "heroes" of Scripture. In short, *the Bible itself* includes genres and passages that foster absolutist thinking and others that warn us to recognize how flawed and inconsistent even those we recognize as the fathers of the faithful are. Certainly we need both species of biblical literature, and most Christians see a sign of God's kindness in the Bible that provides us with both. The narratives without the absolutes might seem to sanction moral indifference: "If even a man after God's own heart like David can fall so disastrously, it cannot be too surprising if we lesser mortals tumble from time to time." The absolutes without the narratives might either generate despair ("Who can live up to the impossibly high standards of Psalm 1?") or produce self-righteous fools ("It's a good thing the Bible has standards, and I have to say I thank God I am not as other people are"). We need the unflinching standards of the absolute polarities to keep us from moral flabbiness, and in this broken world, we need the candid realism of the narratives to keep us from both arrogance and despair. Most of us, I suspect, muddle along with a merely intuitive sense of how these twin biblical heritages ought to shape our lives.

The second factor is how we attach the cross of Christ to all this. The intensity of the struggle against sin easily generates boundless distortions when we do not return, again and again, to God's love for us manifested in the cross. There alone is the hope we need, the cleansing we need, the grace we need. Any pursuit of perfection that is not awash in the grace of God displayed on a little hill outside Jerusalem is bound to trip us up.

34

I'm So Grateful That I'm among the Elect

MANY OF US, I SUSPECT, have played the game where one person says a word and everyone else, without a pause for reflection, responds with what immediately comes to mind.[1]

So, without thinking about it, what springs to your mind when I say "election"? I'm writing this about forty days before November 3, 2020, so if you are an American I suspect the mental referent instantly conjured up by the word "election" is the consequential United States election that takes place this year. Of course, if the people playing the game were a small group of theological students who had just heard an hour's lecture on Romans 9, expectations might well have shifted such that what would spring to mind would lie in the theological arena, not the political. To guarantee the dominance of the theological arena in our little game, we could replace "election" with "predestination," since the former appears to be a subset of the latter, and the latter does not normally call up the world of politics (though doubtless it should!). So what springs to mind when either "election" or "predestination" is introduced into our little game, with the game set in a theological arena? What word associations do these words conjure up? Reformed theology? Divine sovereignty? Theological disputation? Dort? Westminster Confession? Determinism? Mystery? Foreknowledge? Compatibilism? Barth's distinctive view of election? Free will? Grace? The goodness of God?

---

1 This chapter was originally published as D. A. Carson, "I'm so Grateful That I'm among the Elect," *Themelios* 45, no. 3 (2020): 483–85.

How about gratitude?

Forget the game. Just think back to all the occasions when you have thought about or studied election or discussed it with others. Was gratitude the overwhelming response of your heart and mind? Not for a moment should we think that all the other associations are inappropriate. It is right and good to think long and hard about election and all the themes exegetically and theologically associated with it. But why is gratitude so rarely included among them?

I was driven to meditate on this question recently when I was working on the great thanksgiving prayer of Ephesians 1:3–14. "Praise be to the God and Father of our Lord Jesus Christ," Paul begins, "who has blessed us in the heavenly realms with every spiritual blessing in Christ" (1:3). In the following verses, the apostle fleshes out the kinds of things he has in mind when he declares that he praises God for "every spiritual blessing in Christ." The very first thing he mentions is election: "For he chose us in him before the creation of the world to be holy and blameless in his sight. In love he predestined us for adoption to sonship through Jesus Christ, in accordance with his pleasure and will" (1:4–5).

We could usefully reflect on the modifiers. For example, we were chosen "in him" (i.e., in Christ); we were predestined for adoption to sonship "through Jesus Christ." What does it mean to be blessed "in the heavenly realms" in Christ? Surely it is right to reflect on the goal of election, namely, "to be holy and blameless in his sight" (1:4). But what cannot be overlooked is that Paul offers thankful praise to God that he is among the elect. So important is this theme for Paul that he returns to it in verses 11–12, using slightly different words:

> In him we were also chosen [perhaps with the overtone "appointed as God's inheritance"], having been predestined according to the plan of him who works out everything in conformity with the purpose of his will, in order that we, who were the first to put our hope in Christ, might be for the praise of his glory.

In the flow of the prayer, Paul is almost bursting with gratitude.

Those of us who understand that election is frequently presented in the Bible as unconditional understand that one of the proper functions of election is to instill gratitude. We love to sing,

I sought the Lord, and afterward I knew
He moved my heart to seek him, seeking me.
It was not I that found, O Savior true;
No, I was found by thee.[2]

And then, calling up the scene of Peter walking (or not!) on the water,

Thou didst reach forth thy hand, and mine enfold.
I walked, and sank not, on the storm-swept sea.
'Twas not so much that I on thee took hold,
As thou, dear Lord, on me.[3]

At some level or other, we know these things. Nevertheless, I suspect that not a few readers, when they first saw the title, were initially taken aback. "Doubtless we ought to be thankful we are among the elect," you muttered, "but to put it like that hovers very close to arrogance, and is in danger of all the ugliest caricatures of Calvinism. Shouldn't the language be toned down a bit?"

And then I came across a beautiful expression of gratitude for election in the life of a young Christian widow. We'll call her Rachel, and her deceased husband, a faithful and effective pastor, we'll call Robert. Robert died of a disease that ravaged his body and his mind. I have Rachel's permission to share with you parts of her letter. Two or three details have been altered to mask her identity, but the words are all hers, very lightly edited to ensure coherence. At this point in her letter she is talking about singing along, with her children, the songs live streamed from her church:

These songs are moving to me, especially "The Perfect Wisdom of Our God." I picked it for Robert's funeral because of the last verse:

Each strand of sorrow has a place
Within this tapestry of grace.
So through the trials I choose to say,
"Your perfect will in your perfect way."[4]

2   Jean Ingelow, "I Sought the Lord, and Afterward I Knew" (1878).
3   Ingelow, "I Sought the Lord."
4   Keith and Kristen Getty, "The Perfect Wisdom of Our God" (2012). Used by permission.

As Robert was losing his health and his mind, I had about five big reasons why this did not seem remotely perfect. I can remember saying to Robert's co-pastor that I was choking on the words. But at my lowest point I did reluctantly and sulkily choose to sing them. The significant thing wasn't whether or not I was sulky. The significant thing was that I did actually sing them, declaring my faith in God and his big picture—my faith in him. In terms of "moral goodness" (if there is such a thing), I think I'm pretty average. Or maybe I'm being generous to myself: I'm prone to being too carefree and selfish, given to extremes and self-indulgence. But I am often able to show commitment and kindness and integrity. So yeah, average, really, on crude terms. But I do feel *marked out*. I *am* marked out! And I'm convinced that what marks me out is where I choose to put my faith. That's all! I believe myself to be constantly and undeservedly blessed, disproportionately upheld and provided for, unexpectedly finding myself surrounded by joy, peace, hope, love, wonderful people, and uplifting children. My life has been rescued and redeemed over and over again despite my relentless failures and flaws. I have a genuine sense of "why me?" in a good way. "Your perfect will in your perfect way": I know where to place my faith. That's my privilege. That's the gift given me. I have been known to meander and drift and goof up in both trivial and profound ways, but in the end I always come back to the right place, to the right person—the only person. Brother, Friend, Redeemer, Deliverer, King, Lord, Bridegroom, Father, Savior, Creator. I have been able to trust God with my "strands of sorrow." I am under his wings and always will be. That's all! In a way, it's so unfair that I should be able to recognize Jesus for who he is when so many other people who I respect and love don't seem to either want to or be able to. I hear his voice and I just know he's the Good Shepherd. To me, it's a no-brainer. Faith is a gift, but it's a free gift, and there are no exams to pass or morality assessments. Our "strands of sorrow" are only a millimeter long on the rope disappearing off into the horizon where Robert invested his life. He taught and lived and died this "perfect wisdom."

Thank you, Rachel.

35

Spiritual Disciplines

MANY YEARS AGO I WROTE an essay titled "When Is Spirituality Spiritual? Reflections on Some Problems of Definition."[1] I would like to follow up on one aspect of that topic here.[2] The broader framework of the discussion needs to be remembered. "Spiritual" and "spirituality" have become notoriously fuzzy words. In common usage they almost always have positive overtones, but rarely does their meaning range within the sphere of biblical usage. People think of themselves as "spiritual" because they have certain aesthetic sensibilities, or because they feel some kind of mystical connection with nature, or because they espouse some highly privatized version of one of any number of religions (but "religion" tends to be a word with negative connotations while "spirituality" has positive overtones). Under the terms of the new covenant, however, the only "spiritual" person is the person who has the Holy Spirit, poured out on individuals in regeneration. The alternative, in Paul's terminology, is to be "natural"—merely human—and not "spiritual" (1 Cor. 2:14). For the Christian whose vocabulary and concepts on this topic are shaped by Scripture, only the Christian is spiritual. Then, by an obvious extension, those Christians who display Christian virtues are spiritual, since these virtues are the fruit of the Spirit. Those who are "mere infants in Christ" (1 Cor. 3:1), if they truly are in Christ, are spiritual inasmuch as they are indwelled by the Spirit, but their lives may leave much

---

1 D. A. Carson, "When Is Spirituality Spiritual? Reflections on Some Problems of Definition," *Journal of the Evangelical Theological Society* 37 (1994): 381–94.
2 This chapter was originally published as D. A. Carson, "Spiritual Disciplines," *Themelios* 36, no. 3 (2011): 377–79.

to be desired.[3] Nevertheless, the New Testament does not label immature Christians as *un*spiritual as if the category "spiritual" should be reserved only for the most mature, the elite of the elect; that is an error common to much of the Roman Catholic tradition of spirituality, in which the spiritual life and the spiritual traditions are often tied up with believers who want to transcend the ordinary. Such "spiritual" life is often bound up with asceticism and sometimes mysticism, with orders of nuns and monks, and with a variety of techniques that go beyond ordinary Joe or Mary Christian.

Owing to the wide usage of the "spiritual" words, way beyond New Testament usage, the language of "spiritual disciplines" has likewise extended itself into arenas that are bound to make those who love the gospel more than a little nervous. Nowadays spiritual disciplines may include Bible reading, meditation, worship, giving away money, fasting, solitude, fellowship, deeds of service, evangelism, almsgiving, creation care, journaling, missionary work, and more. It may include vows of celibacy, self-flagellation, and chanting mantras. In popular usage, some of these so-called spiritual disciplines are entirely divorced from any specific doctrine whatsoever, Christian or otherwise: they are merely a matter of technique. That is why people sometimes say, "For your doctrine, by all means commit yourselves to evangelical confessionalism. But when it comes to the spiritual disciplines, turn to Catholicism or perhaps Buddhism." What is universally presupposed by the expression "spiritual discipline" is that such disciplines are intended to increase our spirituality. From a Christian perspective, however, it is simply not possible to increase one's spirituality without possessing the Holy Spirit and submitting to his transforming instruction and power. Techniques are never neutral. They are invariably loaded with theological presuppositions, often unrecognized.

How shall we evaluate this popular approach to the spiritual disciplines? How should we think of spiritual disciplines and their connection with spirituality as defined by Scripture? Some introductory reflections:

1. The pursuit of unmediated, mystical knowledge of God is unsanctioned by Scripture and is dangerous in more than one way. It does not

---

3 Cf. D. A. Carson, "The Cross and the Holy Spirit: 1 Corinthians 2:6–16," in *The Cross and Christian Ministry: Leadership Lessons from 1 Corinthians* (Grand Rapids, MI: Baker, 2004), 43–66.

matter whether this pursuit is undertaken within the confines of, say, Buddhism (though informed Buddhists are unlikely to speak of "unmediated mystical knowledge of God"—the last two words are likely to be dropped)[4] or, in the Catholic tradition, by Julian of Norwich. Neither instance recognizes that our access to the knowledge of the living God is mediated exclusively through Christ, whose death and resurrection reconcile us to the living God. To pursue unmediated, mystical knowledge of God is to announce that the person of Christ and his sacrificial work on our behalf are not necessary for the knowledge of God. Sadly, it is easy to delight in mystical experiences, enjoyable and challenging in themselves, without knowing anything of the regenerating power of God, grounded in Christ's cross-work.

2. We ought to ask what warrants including any particular item on a list of spiritual disciplines. For Christians with any sense of the regulative function of Scripture, nothing, surely, can be deemed a spiritual discipline if it is not so much as mentioned in the New Testament. That rather eliminates not only self-flagellation but also creation care. Doubtless the latter, at least, is a good thing to do: it is part of our responsibility as stewards of God's creation. But it is difficult to think of scriptural warrant to view such activity as a spiritual discipline—that is, as a discipline that increases our spirituality. The Bible says quite a lot about prayer and hiding God's word in our hearts but precious little about creation care and chanting mantras.

3. Some of the entries on the list are slightly ambiguous. At one level, the Bible says nothing at all about journaling. On the other hand, if journaling is merely a convenient label for careful self-examination, contrition, thoughtful Bible reading, and honest praying, using the habit of writing a journal to foster all four, it cannot be ruled outside the camp the way self-flagellation must be. The apostle declares celibacy to be an excellent thing, provided one has the gift (both marriage and celibacy are labeled *charismata*, "grace gifts"), and provided it is for the sake of increased ministry (1 Cor. 7). On the other hand, there is nothing that suggests celibacy is an intrinsically holier state, and absolutely nothing under the terms of the new covenant

---

4 Cf. Keith Yandell and Harold Netland, *Buddhism: A Christian Exploration and Appraisal* (Downers Grove, IL: InterVarsity, 2009).

warrants withdrawing into cloisters of celibate monks or nuns who have physically retreated from the world to become more spiritual. Meditation is not an intrinsic good. A huge amount depends on the focus of one's meditation. Is it one imagined dark spot on a sheet of white? Or is it the law of the Lord (Ps. 1:2)?

4. Even those spiritual disciplines that virtually all would acknowledge to be such must not be misunderstood or abused. The very expression is potentially misleading: spiritual discipline, as if there is something intrinsic to self-control, to the imposition of self-discipline, that qualifies one to be more spiritual. Such assumptions and mental associations can lead only to arrogance; worse, they often lead to condescending judgmentalism: others may not be as spiritual as I am since I am disciplined enough to have an excellent prayer time or a superb Bible reading scheme. Yet the truly transformative element is not the discipline itself, but the worthiness of the task undertaken: the value of prayer, the value of reading God's word.

5. It is not helpful to list assorted Christian responsibilities and label them spiritual disciplines. That seems to be the reasoning behind the theology that smuggles in, say, creation care and almsgiving. But by the same logic, if out of Christian kindness you give a back rub to an old lady with a stiff neck and a sore shoulder, then back rubbing becomes a spiritual discipline. By such logic, any Christian obedience is a spiritual discipline, that is, it makes us more spiritual. Using the category of spiritual disciplines in that way has two unfortunate entailments. First, if every instance of obedience is a spiritual discipline, then there is nothing special about the emphatically emphasized, biblically mandated means of grace: prayer, for instance, and serious reading of and meditation on the word of God. Second, such a way of thinking about spiritual disciplines subtly cajoles us into thinking that growth in spirituality is a function of nothing more than conformity to the demands of a lot of rules, of a lot of obedience. Certainly Christian maturity is not manifest where there is not obedience. Yet there is also a great deal of emphasis on growth in love, in trust, in understanding the ways of the living God, in the work of the Spirit in filling and empowering us.

6. For these reasons it seems the part of wisdom to restrict the label "spiritual disciplines" to those Bible-prescribed activities that are explicitly said to increase our sanctification, our conformity to Christ Jesus, our spiritual

maturation. When Jesus in John 17 prays that his Father will sanctify his followers through the truth, he adds, "Your word is truth" (v. 17). Small wonder that believers have long labeled things like the study of the truth of the gospel "means of grace"—a lovely expression less susceptible to misinterpretation than spiritual disciplines.

36

Do the Work of an Evangelist

Do the work of an evangelist.

2 TIMOTHY 4:5

ONE OF THE ODD THINGS about the English language is how many words it has. For example, English has about three times as many words as French. That doesn't mean that the working vocabulary of the average English speaker is larger than the working vocabulary of the average French speaker, of course. Most competent speakers of any language use only a small part of the total vocabulary of the language they are speaking. Nevertheless, the difference in size of the total vocabulary is curious. The primary reason for the difference in vocabulary size between English and French lies in the different ways in which the two languages were formed. In keeping with other romance languages, French has depended on Greek and Latin for much of its word formation (though of course it has "borrowed" plenty of words from other languages). By contrast, English arose out of not only Greek and Latin but also Anglo-Saxon, with side input from Norse and Celtic languages.[1]

The result is that English has many synonyms that have sprung up from separate linguistic heritages. These synonyms rarely share exactly the same semantic range; usage introduces distortions. The subject is *deep*, we say; it is very *profound*. In this context, it is difficult to discern a substantive

---

[1] This chapter was originally published as D. A. Carson, "Do the Work of an Evangelist," *Themelios* 39, no. 1 (2014): 1–4.

semantic difference between deep and profound. On the other hand, we happily affirm that the well in the farmyard is deep; we would not say it is profound. Why not? Simply because we do not use profound in that way. By contrast, a French speaker will have no difficulty averring that both the subject and the well are "profond," and will render both English "deep" and English "profound" by the French *profond*. If a scholar were trying to translate a French document into English, however, and came across the French word "profond," he or she would have to think carefully about whether to choose deep or profound.

This is a rather roundabout way of reflecting on the fact that both translational and theological pitfalls lurk in the underbrush when moving from one language to another. In modern English, we distinguish expiation and propitiation. The former is the sacrificial act by which sin is canceled: the object of the action is the sin. The latter is the sacrificial act by which God is made propitious: the object of the action is God. Given who the God of the Bible is, it is difficult to see how you can have one without the other: the same sacrifice that cancels sin by the sacrifice that God has ordained also turns aside his own judicial wrath. Nevertheless, it is useful to distinguish between the two notions. French has only one word, *expiation*, and it can convey both the cancellation of sin and the setting aside of the wrath of God, depending on the context. Competent French speakers simply do not have a word equivalent to the English "propitiation." That is not to say that French theologians know nothing about the concept of propitiation, of course, for the concept depends on much, much more than the meaning of a single word. But it is to say that they do not have one word that univocally means what English speakers mean by "propitiation." And that in turn means that the history of debate about what the cross achieves differs significantly in French and English scholarship.

Sometimes the fact that English uses two words where the French (and the Greek!) have only one can trip us up and focus our gaze in a slightly misleading direction. For the purposes of this reflection, one of the most telling examples is one so close to us we sometimes fail to see it. English has two words, "gospel" and "evangel," where the Greek has only one, εὐαγγέλιον. *Themelios* is sponsored by an organization called "the Gospel Coalition." What signals would be hoisted if, instead, we called ourselves "the Evangel Coalition"? We may say, "Evangelicals believe the gospel," which does not sound entirely tautologous, but to say it as a first-century Greek speaker must, "Evangelicals believe the evangel," would be passing strange. And then, of course, if we start to reflect on all the related words now used in English— evangelicalism, evangelism, evangelical, evangelist, evangel, evangelization, evangelize, evangelically, evangelicism—we observe that some of them have no Greek counterpart. Interestingly enough, the more or less synonymous "gospel" does not boast the array of cognates that "evangel" does. Most of us would not translate 2 Timothy 4:5, "Do the work of a gospeller" or "Do the work of a gospelist." To make matters more complicated yet, one or two of the Greek cognates of εὐαγγέλιον are sometimes rendered into English in ways that, on the surface, seem less than direct. For instance, one might have expected εὐαγγελίζομαι to be rendered "to evangelize," but in most English Bibles, it is more likely to be rendered, "to preach the gospel" or "to preach the good news" or the like, equivalent to τὸ εὐαγγέλιον κηρύσσω. If this were a different sort of essay, it would be worth exploring why this is the case.

This brings us to the text at the top of this note. Paul tells Timothy, "Do the work of an evangelist" (2 Tim. 4:5). That word "evangelist" (εὐαγγελιστής) is found only three times in the New Testament—once to designate Philip (Acts 21:8), once in a list of ministries (Eph. 4:11), and here. I suspect that most of us read 2 Timothy 4:5, "Do the work of an evangelist," along some such lines as the following. Paul tells Timothy, in effect, that even when he is rightly involved in preaching, teaching, instructing, correcting, even when he is known for keeping his head in all situations and learning to endure hardship, he must not forget to do the work of an evangelist. Certainly it is easy for pastors in busy ministries to be so caught up in church-related service that they have few or no non-Christian friends. They may never share their faith and unpack the gospel to unbelievers from one month to the next. Seeing the danger, Paul commands Timothy to do the work of an evangelist—that is, preach the gospel to outsiders, share the gospel with outsiders, aiming to win converts. Make a priority of evangelism. Herald the gospel to outsiders, whether one-on-one, in small groups, or in larger contexts—this is what evangelism is, and this is what an evangelist does. In the midst of diverse and demanding ministry, do not forget to engage in evangelism.

Doubtless that is excellent counsel—but is this exactly what Paul is saying? Several factors must be raised.

1. For some Christians, "the gospel" (equivalently, "the evangel") is something you preach only to unconverted people. The gospel merely tips people into the kingdom; transformation and sanctification are sustained by discipleship. Once people become Christians, then the work of life transformation begins, often buttressed by various discipleship seminars: "Biblical Leadership," "Learning to Pray," "What to Do with Your Money," "Christian Marriage," and so forth—none of which falls under "gospel," but only under post-gospel discipleship. In recent years, however, many preachers and theologians have convincingly argued that "gospel"/"evangel" is the larger category under which both evangelism and discipleship fall. In the New Testament, gospel is not everything—it is not law, for instance—but it is a very big thing, precisely because it is the unimaginably great news about what God is doing in and through King Jesus, especially in and through his cross and resurrection. A careful reading of Scripture shows how often Christian conduct is grounded in the gospel itself. For instance, the gospel is to be obeyed (e.g., 2 Thess. 1:8); certain behaviors conform to the gospel, while other behaviors do not (1 Tim. 1:10–11). Husbands are to love their wives as Christ loved the church and gave himself up for her (Eph. 5:25)—transparently, this is a gospel appeal. In short, in the New Testament the gospel is preached both to unbelievers and to believers. It calls unbelievers to repentance and faith; it calls believers to ongoing faith and conformity to Jesus.

In other words, gospel ministry includes but is not restricted to what we commonly call evangelistic ministry (note the two words, "gospel" and "evangelistic," making the discussion confusing). Gospel ministry is ministry that is faithful to the gospel, that announces the gospel and applies the gospel and encourages people to believe the gospel and thus live out the gospel. If this is so, then why should "Do the work of a gospeller" mean something more restricted, like "Do that part of gospel work that addresses unbelievers" (which *we* sometimes restrict "gospel ministry" to, calling it "evangelism")?

2. The context of 2 Timothy 4:5 suggests that it is this large view of gospel ministry that is in view. After Paul's passionate command to Timothy to preach the word, spelling out what it means (4:2), he warns that a time will come when people will not want to listen but will prefer teachers "who say what their itching ears want to hear" (4:3). "But you," Paul tells Timothy, "keep your head in all situations, endure hardship, do the work

of an evangelist, discharge all the duties of your ministry" (4:5). This does not sound like a list of discretely defined chunks of ministry, as if Paul were saying, "Study hard for your preaching, visit the elderly, catechize the young, provide good counsel, do the work of an evangelist"—add them all together, and you will be a well-rounded minister. Rather, the list Paul provides focuses not on discrete ministries but on global stances throughout Timothy's ministry: "keep your head in all circumstances" is not a discrete thing to do, something to be added, for instance, to "endure hardship." No, all of the entries on this list are comprehensive. In this context, then, "do the work of an evangelist" simply means "do gospel work"—and that summarizes all of the instructions in the preceding lines. That's what ministers do. They "discharge all the duties of [their] ministry": they do gospel work. Doubtless that includes what we mean by evangelism. In that sense, "do gospel work" includes doing the work of an evangelist. But in this context it is doubtful that Paul is narrowing the field.

3. Of course, a word might become more restrictive in its pragmatic use in a particular context. When Philip is designated "the evangelist" (Acts 21:8), does this mean "evangelist" in the modern sense? Perhaps. Luke might be remembering Philip's ministry to the Ethiopian eunuch, in which he was certainly preaching the gospel to an unbeliever. Interestingly enough, however, this passage designates him as "one of the Seven" (Acts 21:8; cf. 6:1–6). The work of the seven was not Bible teaching and evangelism, though transparently some of them, including Philip, did engage in such word ministry. It is difficult to tell if Luke thinks of him as an evangelist in the modern sense—a specialist in outreach. He may simply have exercised gospel ministry.

The use of εὐαγγελιστής in Ephesians 4:11 is a bit different. There the location of the word in a series of expressions all related to word ministries suggests that what is in view is the kind of gospel ministry that we associate with "evangelism."

4. Though the argument is not worth much, we should note that there is inscriptional evidence of εὐαγγελιστής used in a pagan setting to refer to certain kinds of pagan priests, without any thought that such priests were trying to win converts.

In sum, owing to the way in which two different English word groups— "gospel" and "evangel"—are used to render one Greek word group (εὐαγγέλιον and cognates), it is possible we have sometimes read into our English texts overspecifications that may not be there in the original. In its context in 2 Timothy 4:5, a case can be made that εὐαγγελιστής is a prime example. "Do the work of an evangelist" may well be an exhortation to engage in evangel ministry, in gospel ministry, which includes what we today mean by "evangelism" but should not be restricted to it.

General Index

Scripture Index

TGC THE GOSPEL COALITION

The Gospel Coalition (TGC) supports the church in making disciples of all nations, by providing gospel-centered resources that are trusted and timely, winsome and wise.

Guided by a Council of more than 40 pastors in the Reformed tradition, TGC seeks to advance gospel-centered ministry for the next generation by producing content (including articles, podcasts, videos, courses, and books) and convening leaders (including conferences, virtual events, training, and regional chapters).

In all of this we want to help Christians around the world better grasp the gospel of Jesus Christ and apply it to all of life in the 21st century. We want to offer biblical truth in an era of great confusion. We want to offer gospel-centered hope for the searching.

Join us by visiting TGC.org so you can be equipped to love God with all your heart, soul, mind, and strength, and to love your neighbor as yourself.

TGC.org

Also Available from the Gospel Coalition

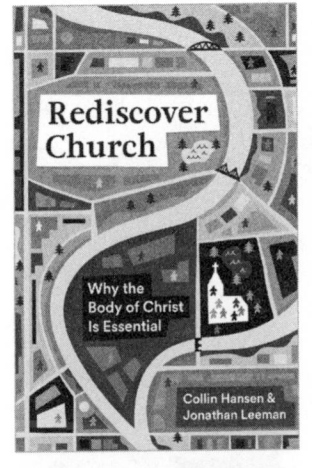

For more information, visit **crossway.org**.